HR Strategy

HR Strategy

Business focused, individually centred

Paul Kearns

AMSTERDAM BOSTON HEIDELBERG LONDON NEW YORK OXFORD
PARIS SAN DIEGO SAN FRANCISCO SINGAPORE SYDNEY TOKYO

Butterworth-Heinemann
An imprint of Elsevier
Linacre House, Jordan Hill, Oxford OX2 8DP
200 Wheeler Road, Burlington MA 01803

First published 2003

British Library Cataloguing in Publication Data
A catalogue record for this book is available from the British Library

Library of Congress Cataloguing in Publication Data
A catalogue record for this book is available from the Library of Congress

ISBN 0 7506 5768 5

For information on all Butterworth-Heinemann publications visit our website at www.bh.com

Composition by Genesis Typesetting Limited, Rochester, Kent
Printed and bound in Great Britain by Biddles Ltd, *www.biddles.co.uk*

Contents

About the author

Paul Kearns is Director of PWL, a specialist, strategic HR consultancy that he founded in 1991. He has a joint honours degree in Economics and Economic History and has been working in HRM since 1978. His roles have included every aspect of HRM from industrial relations and training and development to senior level responsibility for the HR function, in a range of industries.

After extensive research into how organizations measure the effectiveness of their human resource management strategies and practices he has spent the last 10 years developing a whole system approach to HRM.

He has earned a reputation both as a highly respected consultant, a popular conference and seminar presenter and a writer of journal articles. His trademark is a fresh, critical and forthright review of many modern management fads and fashions and, although he is often described as provocative and outspoken, he regards his own approach and methodology as being, first and foremost, based on simple common sense.

Paul can be contacted at:

PWL
PO Box 109
Bristol
BS9 4DH
UK

Phone +44 (0) 117 914 6984
Fax +44 (0) 117 914 6978
Email paulkearns@blueyonder.co.uk

What is a human resource strategy?

A business strategy should give you a competitive advantage.

A human resource strategy turns the way you manage your people *into a competitive advantage.*

An HR strategy is a business strategy.

Introduction

Through the eyes of the HR strategist

The world belongs to the discontented.

Robert Woodruff, former Chairman of Coca-Cola

Real HR strategists are not easily impressed. So don't ever ask one whether they think your business is well run. It would be like asking a top opera singer of the stature of Pavarotti what they thought of your local, amateur, light operatic society. If they were in a good mood and did not want to hurt your feelings, they might suggest that you could be doing a great deal better than you are. However hard they might try to see the virtue in your efforts though, their mental yardstick would be La Scala, not the local village hall.

HR strategists are the truly discontented. So however good you are in the way you manage your people, an HR strategist will see it as amateurish. They will see vast opportunities for improvement. Even if you did everything they asked you to, they would be back in your office the next day with a new list of opportunities to pursue.

This book has taken about a year to write but has probably been over 30 years in the making. It is a response to all the poor 'people' management I have observed and personally experienced – from my own, earliest employment experiences to my more recent life as a consultant working with large, global organizations. These experiences include the failure by all of my former employers to really get the best out of me and the inconsistencies in people management that were so often manifested in the attitudes of senior managers.

Putting these failings right is the aim of this book, but HR strategy is difficult. It takes time. It is a very complex subject. In fact, we are only just beginning to enter the age of true HR strategy.

If you are not convinced by this contention why not ask yourself a few questions? Do you ever get frustrated at work? Of course you do.

Sometimes it is because no one is interested in your ideas. Other times it is just – what? Organizational politics? Lack of direction? A failure of everyone to pull together? A good HR strategy would mean you would not feel like this so often, if at all.

Take another view. How many people do you know who are using their full potential at work? Is it 90 per cent or more like 10 per cent? Are you encouraged, enabled, even allowed to realize your true potential in your job? If not, your organization could improve immensely through developing an HR strategy.

Finally, how many people do you know who find work very fulfilling? Now, this question is very closely allied to the previous ones. The chances are you are in some sort of managerial capacity and you may only be thinking of fellow managers and close colleagues. I would suggest that you need to think about all of the employees in your organization before answering these questions. Then consider this: what impact would there be on customer satisfaction and your bottom line if your organization realized the full potential of every one of its employees? Pie in the sky? Possibly, but the aim of HR strategy is to realize the full value of every employee.

Having answered the questions above you will now have a view on how much more potential there is left to realize in your own organization. So, however well you may be doing as a business, HR strategy is about searching for even greater returns and never accepting the status quo or becoming complacent. If this challenge is not how you view HR strategy, then maybe you need to re-visit your initial interest in the subject.

I view the world through the eyes of an HR strategist. I do not actually see brilliant organizations, however well they are doing; I see organizations that could do much better. I see dysfunction at every turn. I see internal politics and a lack of absolute cooperation. I see ideas and direction poorly communicated. I am totally and utterly intolerant of the status quo and the complacency that goes with it. It is because someone, somewhere wants to do things better that we progress.

If those who like to cling to their comfort zones were left in charge we would still all live in caves. But then those who have the drive and initiative to leave the cave are the minority. The majority only follow when they are sure the new way of living is better than the old. HR strategy will be developed by the minority but its sole aim is to capture the hearts, minds, talents and capabilities of the majority and make the best use of them.

After well over twenty years working in industry and commerce nothing has changed my basic belief system that, generally, employees come to work wanting and trying to do a good job. This does not mean they normally feel inclined to give of their best or go the extra mile. The organization needs to create an environment in which this might happen.

This is my only justification for taking the trouble to produce a book on HR strategy – it is a worthwhile goal. There is almost infinite scope for improving our lives.

Trying to define strategy

I once saw a brilliant episode of *The Simpsons* (never let it be said my references are not impeccable) where all the neighbours played a game involving one team having to guess a word 'drawn' by the other team (similar to 'Pictionary'). One unfortunate guy had to do a representational drawing of the word 'dignity'. You try it. He did not even know where to start and failed miserably. Two seconds later his wife scribbled a simple doodle on the flipchart (not shown to us, the viewers, of course) to which everyone in the room immediately exclaimed, in unison 'That's dignity!'

I feel in exactly the same position now trying to describe strategy. Any pictorial representation would probably include lots of inter-connected arrows but no one would ever guess correctly. So I am going to have to use the whole book to create a reasonably accurate picture of what HR strategy looks like. You will not find it on any one page.

Trying to define strategy often turns out to be a task as elusive and dissatisfying as analysing what makes for good comedy. Somehow, deconstructing the subject into its constituent parts loses something, somewhere, in the process. Actually, there is not much point analysing what makes a comedian funny, all you need to know is whether they made you laugh. HR strategy is a bit like that. You do not need to analyse it to death, all you need to know is whether it is working or not. Any strategy worthy of the name is an inherently holistic, totally integrated concept and has to be viewed as such. Deconstruction does not help.

The essence of HR strategy is in understanding the complex relationship between disparate, often conflicting, variables in a search for a coherent approach to achieving long-term, organizational objectives. What is the connection, for instance, between what you pay your people, their level of motivation, their ability to innovate, customer satisfaction and profit? Only when the right connections are made can any sensible strategy be formulated and because strategy is difficult to define we resort to analogies.

One of the most commonly used analogies in strategic thinking is the jigsaw puzzle. Obviously this gives an impression of the task of a strategist but I think it gives a very limited impression. It suggests there is only one preconceived 'solution', and that is totally antithetical to the whole idea of strategy. Strategy is not about heading for one solution. It is about creating an optimal solution from a whole range of possibilities. It is choosing what sort of jigsaw picture you want first, then seeing which pieces you already have and finally making any other pieces you need. That is enough about jigsaws.

An analogy I prefer is that of the winegrower - not particularly original perhaps, but it captures the essence of what it is to be an HR strategist. Wine itself, just like HR strategy, may look like a generic product but it is one that has almost infinite varieties. Not only are there different types of grape but even producers using the same grape variety will produce very different wines. Yet you need to develop quite an acute sense of taste to be able to spot the difference.

Wine-tasting itself may appear to be a simple practice but we all know that the best wine-tasters take many years to develop a sufficiently wide range of knowledge, and they cannot learn their trade from a book. The only way to become a wine-taster is literally to taste wine. The experience is everything. It allows subtle distinctions to be made and personal preferences to be formed. Similarly, going into an organization and tasting the HR strategy is a multi-sensory experience. You have to listen, look, read; you even have to touch and smell the difference between organizations that are working hard to produce a high value organization and those that are just producing the equivalent of cheap plonk.

Without wishing to labour the point, the other key similarity between wine and HR strategy is the way in which so many other factors have to be taken into consideration. The soil quality, the position of the vineyard, the husbandry involved in tending the vines, climactic conditions. These are not jigsaw pieces; each one can change and the relationship between all of these variables is dynamic. Only when all of the conditions are right will the finished wine be of a high quality. Let us not forget, however, that there are different markets for high quality and cooking wines. The 'quality' and suitability of each wine can only be gauged in relation to its ability to serve its intended purpose.

Enough analogies for one day, except to say that you should enter the world of HR strategy with the mindset of a master wine-taster, not someone who likes playing with jigsaws.

True HR strategy is extremely rare

This is my sixth book. If you have read any of the others, particularly the earliest, you will already know that I like to keep them short and to the point. They are also meant to be very practical, and producing a 'practical strategy' book is incredibly difficult. Strategy is difficult to define, categorize or codify. It has no obvious or clear boundaries or limitations. There are no clearly defined rules. Even if we can spot a brilliant strategy it is another matter entirely to analyse what made it a brilliant strategy. And it is another matter again to try to apply any strategic lessons learned to our own organizations.

One of the reasons that strategic thinking is so difficult is simply the fact that it entails somebody processing enormous amounts of diverse information. It is a very complex, intellectual process. I heard George Mathewson, the present Chairman of the Royal Bank of Scotland (an excellently managed business which seems to be getting it right strategically) speaking at their Group HR Conference on 18 May 2001. He started by saying the one thing he would have liked more of is time to think. True strategists know that thinking time is worth much more than 'doing' time. That is why they stand out from the crowd of business leaders who think inaction is a dirty word. After taking over a much larger bank (Natwest) and having produced some sparkling results, it would appear that he had already used whatever thinking time he had very wisely.

George Mathewson would probably be able to articulate and help us to understand the various elements that make up his strategy (although I am sure he would not dream of doing so, because he would be giving away a clear source of competitive advantage). But that does not mean we would understand the strategy in its totality. We may have no appreciation of the interdependency of the variables at work. There has to be at least one person in the organization that can do this though; hold the vision, the complete strategy, in their head. They not only have to see the big picture but also understand how changes in any one of the variables will have a multi-dimensional impact on many of the other variables. They also need to be able to judge whether and how the overall strategy itself may have to change. That is a very tall order and very few mortals are up to it. That is one reason why it is rare.

There are many layers of complexity in strategic thinking. External factors can make the most forward-thinking strategies look short-sighted (as when Bill Gates of Microsoft completely underestimated the impact of the Internet). Equally, the most outrageous strategies can work very well when a fortuitous set of market circumstances just happens to provide the ideal environment for the strategy to reach fruition (also Bill Gates, when he managed to get IBM to use his operating system).

The brilliant strategist of today can be made to look a fool tomorrow because the one thing that often distinguishes between good and bad strategy is just time or timing. Did many dot.com enterprises fail because they were ahead of their time or were they just fundamentally ill-conceived business models that would not survive in any time? At what stage can we finally decide whether Geoff Bezos of Amazon.com was a prophet or just a brilliant salesman? If Amazon.com lasts long enough, his strategy could prove to have been truly brilliant after all.

How important is HR strategy?

I regard HR strategy as the most important subject in HR, but it is also my favourite subject. Unfortunately though, experience tells me that very few business people, and particularly HR people, have any real understanding of or interest in true HR strategy.

Of course, if you ask any senior HR person whether they have an HR strategy or not they will usually be adamant that they have (a quick survey of attendees at an international HR workshop I ran in April 2002 showed 92 per cent said they had an HR strategy). It does not pay to delve too deeply though because it is soon apparent that what they may call a 'strategy' is certainly not what I would consider to be a coherent and effective HR strategy. That is, one that is directly linked to and integrated with the organization's business strategy (if it has one).

Now, one final comment before we get under way. If you are prepared to admit to yourself either that you do not have an HR strategy or that your present 'strategy' leaves a lot to be desired, what can you do about it? Well you can go to a business school and study what academic texts have to say on the subject. Or you can employ one of the HR practices from the larger management consultancies in the hope that they can do it for you. Or, you can have a go at it yourself.

The point is that anyone who thinks they can get someone else in to do their HR strategy for them has already probably missed the whole point. If you are a parent can you imagine calling someone in to run your family either with you or, worse still, for you? Getting somebody from outside your organization to develop an HR strategy for you is a bit like that, and is not to be recommended. That is why I see a particular need for a book on the subject. This book is not going to do it for you - but it is a serious attempt to give you some guidelines, a framework, insights and a heavy dash of common sense to encourage you and enable you to do it for yourself.

So please do not look in these pages expecting all the answers. They will ultimately only come from within you. Good luck, you will certainly need a dose of that, and happy reading!

Part 1

Being clear what we mean by strategy

Chapter 1

What is a strategy?

The importance of strategic thinking in a business context has been well established for a very long time. More recently, however, studies in chaos and complexity theories have started to challenge the conventional wisdom surrounding strategy: arguing that in totally unpredictable and rather chaotic times the need for, and ability to formulate, a well-defined strategy is now possibly less appropriate and actually may even be impossible.

Add to this the conundrum of the 'chicken and the egg' – what comes first, strategy or structure? – and maybe organizational leaders could be forgiven for not wanting to get too deeply mired. It could be an intellectually challenging but possibly fruitless endeavour.

But surely that is precisely the purpose of strategy? First, to sort out the complex from the complicated, and then to produce a simple plan. If a business can accurately predict the future, it can produce a plan; but a plan is not a strategy.

If Tesco knew exactly what its customers would buy every week it would not need a strategy. A strategy is a guess, a speculation. It is an attempt to deal with the unknown and the unknowable. Tesco does not know what its customers are going to want next year. It plans to provide them with the goods they want but their tastes can change, as with organic or GM-free (genetically modified) foods. A strategy tries to anticipate change as well as plan for the future. It is this uncertainty that is at its core; without risk there is no need for a strategy.

There is also no such thing as a perfect strategy. We will always live in an imperfect world and many organizations make good profits from those imperfections. Customers' knowledge of the market is certainly imperfect and so they may be prepared to pay the inflated prices of your competitors because they do not know that you offer an equally good service at lower prices. Some organizations even like to confuse customers so that they cannot make a straight comparison between different providers (do you really know what the difference is between your mobile phone tariff and all the others available?).

Organizational leaders have to take risks; it is an inherent part of their job, whether they enjoy it or not. But boards of directors and shareholders are very wary of taking unnecessary risks. Strategy is an attempt to minimize risks while running the enterprise. It may be an attempt to exploit market opportunities fully but it should never be a gamble. Gamblers may talk about their strategies and foolproof systems but when the coin is tossed they can do nothing to influence whether it turns up heads or tails. Strategists are subject to the laws of probability like anyone else but they will manage them as much as they are able to. More importantly, they will have contingencies built into their strategy to ensure they make more winning calls than duds.

Chaos theory may intimate that strategy is pointless but chaos, by definition, cannot be managed. I would choose a strategic, structured and systematic approach over chaos anytime. When it comes to getting the best out of people, this is the starting point for our journey along the road towards HR strategy. Maybe the first step on this journey is to see if we can learn something from some of the best strategic thinkers – those engaged in the art of war.

Military strategy, HR strategy and the art of war

> **strategy** *n.* 1. The art of war 2a. The management of an army in a campaign 2b. moving troops into favourable positions – *Concise Oxford Dictionary*

Imagine you are an army general and you have a thousand troops at your disposal and you have just been dropped into the middle of a war zone. It is very early morning, the sun is just coming up over the horizon, it is clear but there is still a dampness in the air from the dew. All you can see in front of you is a ridge about half a mile ahead. You know that on the other side of this ridge is the enemy. You do not know what they look like. You have no idea how many there are. You have no intelligence about their arms, equipment, positions, their battle readiness or the state of their supply lines. One thing you know for certain though is that they are aware of you and if you do not defeat them first they will be doing their utmost to defeat you.

So what do you do?

I put this scenario to a group of VPs-HR and the first reply I received was 'I'd retreat'. (Why does this response from an HR person not surprise me?). I told her that was not an option because they would catch up with you anyway and would have the psychological upper hand in any ensuing battle. Also, doing nothing was not an option for the same reasons; they may attack at any minute and catch you unawares and unprepared. No, the only answer to getting you safely and successfully out of this situation is to devise a strategy. Strategists take the initiative, and this cannot be just any old strategy. The strategy you choose is literally going to decide whether you and your troops live or die. So you had better make sure that your strategy is the best strategy available to you. The 'best' means the best you can come up with in these circumstances, with your existing resources.

We never actually know how many strategic options are available but one thing is for certain, of all the options open to you, one must be *relatively* better than all the others. If a computer were to process all of the available options and assess their relative strengths and weaknesses it would produce one that, overall, should be the first choice.

So would anyone be able to tell whether the 'wrong' strategy was chosen? It may be unfair to ask a Chief Executive whether they got their strategy wrong because none of us could come to that conclusion without the benefit of hindsight. In the mobile telecommunications industry what appeared to be very successful strategies have looked decidedly sick when one considers how much some operators have paid for 3G (third generation) licences for mobile services such as video. However, we can ask whether the strategy chosen was the best of all the available options at the time. Strategy is unforgiving, so think very carefully; think wisely.

When put under pressure to respond to this hypothetical situation you might feel inclined to say that it is not realistic. Generals and their troops do not get dropped into war zones without excellent military intelligence and, even if they did, they would only be able to act 'tactically' rather than strategically. Well, let us not get hung up on semantics at this stage; we can distinguish between tactics and strategy later. Furthermore, there have been numerous occasions when forces have found themselves dropped in the wrong place or been sent into war zones without a great deal of advance intelligence to go on. So give this one your best shot for now. What are the options available?

How about a 'gung ho' strategy, where you give the order to fix bayonets and mount a full-scale attack by charging over the ridge? I don't think we need to spend too long discussing the merits of that approach, do we?

One of my workshop group suggested they would immediately send out a small reconnaissance party to see if they could see what was going on over the ridge. That sounds eminently sensible to me. In fact, you do not need to have any military experience to at least consider this option. Without gathering military intelligence any strategy is likely to be a rather hit-and-miss affair.

Nevertheless, while you have scouts checking out enemy positions you are still vulnerable to any immediate and unexpected attack. So the next consideration might be to prepare some sort of defensive formation; at least to buy some time and repel any immediate threat. This might mean 'digging in'; or training any big guns you might have on the ridge itself; or having your troops in a state of readiness to fire at the first sign of an attack.

How about the existing position of your own troops? Are they all in one tight group or are they spread out over the surrounding area? A tight formation makes you susceptible to heavy casualties from an unseen mortar attack. Are there any natural defences or cover at your disposal, such as rocks, ditches or trees?

What about communications with your own troops? What is their present frame of mind? Are they hungry and tired? Are they well aware of the threats that face them? Are you a general who inspires confidence based on a track record of successful military campaigns behind you?

If you do have to retreat, where will you retreat to? Have you got any idea in which direction you would need to head and what obstacles or terrain you might face?

While all of these variables are being assessed and processed in your brain what parameters are starting to condition your thinking? Can you radio for help or call in the air force, either for reconnaissance or support? Let us assume that in this scenario these options are not available to you. So now your thinking has to work within these constraints.

One big possible limitation, of course, is the state of your own resources both in terms of the people and the equipment and ammunition. At what stage should an assessment be made of your resources? Common sense and logic suggest that this should be a very early consideration, if not the first, and yet we have only just mentioned it as a critical element in your strategic thinking.

Another dimension we have not covered yet is the historical time dimension. If this scenario was set in the early nineteenth century the expectations of the troops would be very different from those in the Second World War and different again from troops sent into conflicts in the present day. Modern armies may well have the world's media watching their every move, and this would influence their behaviour and actions.

A great deal of thinking has to happen if you are to choose the right strategy.

So what constitutes a strategy?

The simple scenario painted above provides just a small insight into the complexities of strategic thinking. While anyone with any reasonable intelligence can understand the separate elements that make up a strategy, it is the *art of joining all the separate elements into one coherent whole* that is the real intellectual challenge: processing lots of different pieces of information; making causal connections between numerous variables such as the formation of the troops and an assessment of casualties in the event of an aerial attack; deciding what the parameters are and which variables you can influence and which you cannot. Also, each variable connects with the others in different ways. Any effect from increasing the amount of ammunition is limited by the number of arms available and the number of soldiers able to bear those arms. Changing the types of arms has to take into account the capabilities and training of the troops.

HR strategy, like military or any other strategy, is also not about individual battles; it is rather the thread that ensures all individual battles are making a contribution to the overall common cause; the winning of the war. More important still is the ability of a clear strategy to offer guidance to each and every officer; even to every single one of their troops. If a war is being fought on 'moral' grounds, for example, then how troops deal with prisoners is bound to influence to what extent any victory could be regarded as a moral victory.

An effective strategy therefore leads to an effective MO (*modus operandi*). The ethos, principles, values and objectives of the organization should all be encapsulated within an HR strategy. But this should not be construed as a straitjacket on organizational behaviour. The general working to the moral strategy will give the enemy as much chance to surrender as possible when that opportunity arises, while following a 'take no prisoners' strategy would have very different consequences.

Pinning strategy down

Having said earlier that most HR 'strategies' are pale imitations of what they could be, it is important that we try to pin down this term 'strategy'. There are numerous books on business strategy but the ancient, seminal texts on strategy were concerned primarily with military strategy, or more specifically, strategies to win wars, such as Sun Tzu's *The Art of War*. Interestingly, such strategies may well talk about finding and holding strategic positions and they may also cover the strategic management of resources such as ammunition and equipment but, first and foremost, they are all inherently *people* strategies. That is, the effectiveness of each one of the troops is determined, primarily, by the strategy not by their own capabilities: the wrong strategy renders them all ineffective.

Machiavelli, whose very name has become synonymous with devious, political machinations, had to advise his masters on just such matters. In *The Prince* he refers to the relative merits, or otherwise, of using mercenary troops when conducting a campaign (*The Prince*, 1995: 12):

> Mercenaries and auxiliaries are useless and dangerous. If a prince bases the defence of his state on mercenaries he will never achieve stability or security . . . The reason for all this is that there is no loyalty or inducement to keep them on the field apart from the little they are paid, and this is not enough to make them want to die for you.

He goes on to say that he 'should have little need to labour this point', probably because it is so obvious that any 'employer' who hires mercenaries is never likely to get the best out of such people compared to regular, loyal, committed workers.

Even today, battle planners have a choice between regular soldiers, reservists, conscripts or mercenaries, and the sort of troops at their disposal are bound to influence, significantly, their ultimate military strategy. Troops that know what they are doing are inevitably going to be more effective than temporary or half-committed troops.

So in war or business can we ever talk about strategy without automatically referring to the people aspects of that strategy? Military leaders would love to be able to conduct a war purely with technology, and no doubt many business leaders would be equally keen to run their businesses at the push of a button, if they could. But until the day technology takes over completely they will have to include the people factor in their strategic thinking.

Strategy and tactics – when is a strategy not a strategy?

Military strategy has been defined as the general scheme of the conduct of a war, while tactics are the planning of the means to achieve strategic objectives. Tactics are a necessary condition of implementing a strategy but they are not sufficient to comprise a strategy. Karl von Clausewitz, the Prussian military theorist, described strategy as the planning of a whole campaign and tactics as the planning of a single battle.

Von Clausewitz also talked of a 'grand strategy' which linked military strategy directly to national strategy. This provides some insight into the scale on which strategies can be developed and the timescales that they can encompass. If every organization had a brilliant people strategy what difference would this make to a nation or society as a whole?

The immediate relevance of this to the HR strategist is that tactics will never make up for poor strategy. A strategic decision to recognize a union and to have a particular relationship with them will immediately tie the hands of every line manager at a tactical level. They will only be able to manage their team within the confines of the industrial relations environment created for them. If they want to get rid of an employee they will have to think long and hard how to get this accepted by the union, regardless of the actual merits of their case. You cannot rectify a bad HR strategy at an operational or tactical level.

Using military language does not necessarily make strategy a more accessible subject, because what is so difficult to pin down is the inherently dynamic nature of strategic thinking and strategy formulation. One key variable can completely throw out all other calculations, as the destruction of the twin towers of the World Trade Center by terrorists on 11 September 2001 illustrated so tragically. A new strategy was immediately required for a new world order.

It is this sense of scale and completeness that for me characterizes strategy. Effective strategies take all the known and guessable variables into consideration. This is a tall order and one which military and business strategists only embark on because they have to. The same cannot be said for HR strategy, but as Machiavelli said:

> One should never allow chaos to develop in order to avoid going to war, because one does not avoid a war but instead puts it off to his disadvantage.
>
> (Machiavelli, *The Prince*, 1995: 3)

Organizations are afraid to address many of the human resource implications of their business strategies. Organizations who have a legacy of poor industrial relations, particularly in the public sector, have never really addressed this fundamental issue as they always wanted to avoid a 'war' where both sides may actually end up losing. Machiavelli was right though; putting off the war disadvantages the organization's performance and therefore the citizens it serves.

A failure to formulate a complete HR strategy inevitably means working at a disadvantage. As we will see later, what most HR people call strategy is, in fact, a collection of tactical plans unconnected in any coherent way. Therefore, the 'war' has been avoided and, as such, no *strategic* advantage can be gained.

What is an HR strategy?

It will take the whole of this book to answer this question fully, but one thing that can be said for certain is HR strategy is not a document produced by the HR department. It is a philosophy owned by the board of directors or it is nothing. Having said that we need a quick working definition of what constitutes an HR strategy before going any further. Here is my best stab at a simple definition:

> *An HR strategy is a conscious and explicit attempt to manage the organization's human resource to gain a competitive advantage.*

So an HR strategy, like any other strategy, is a grand plan but it is much more than a mere plan. It not only has to align with the business strategy; it has to be an integral part of it. Strategic HR considerations may even inform the business strategy, although this is unlikely to happen very often. However, the HR strategy does not look any further ahead than the business. How can an HR strategy decide what sort of people the organization needs in 10 years' time if the business does not know where it wants to be in 10 years' time? What it can do though is try to prepare its employees for any likely eventuality.

Now apart from the more obvious elements that might form part of an HR plan (numbers of employees, types of employees), some of the things that will be implicit in an HR strategy will be a description of the sort of culture the organization wants to develop, its values and the principles it will endeavour to adhere to.

On a more practical level, the HR strategy will have to have a clear idea how the organization should be configured in terms of its structure and processes. However, if we can define HR strategy for a moment in the negative, that is, what is *not* part of HR strategy, then personnel policies and procedures come well after strategy and should be regarded as purely tactical. All strategies have tactics but no amount of tactics will make up a strategy. A strategy will indicate what calibre of human resource is needed, while a pay and reward policy will decide how much to pay them.

All of the elements of an HR strategy identified here will be addressed throughout the rest of the book, but for now we need to look at the only real place to start, which is to ask whether the organization has any sort of business strategy. Why? Because HR strategy has to be aligned with business strategy if it is to help create value and wealth. However, we need to make a short digression here first to discuss this issue.

Wealth and value

You may not immediately see the relevance of this section but I ask you to bear with me. HR strategy should be about wealth generation. It is also about getting the most value out of employees. If employees are not fired up by the idea of wealth generation then the HR strategy will fail to deliver its full potential.

This connection has to be crystal clear. HR strategy should generate value because value leads to a wealthier society. Wealthy societies are in everyone's interest. Regardless of how well it is distributed, it is a cake that we would all like to have a slice of and that slice should be as large as possible. Keeping the size of the cake small is in no one's interest.

So how big is the cake? If you asked any investment analyst to answer the question 'what is the value of this company?' they would immediately show you some hard figures on market capitalization, return on capital employed, revenue growth history or some similar ratios or financial measures. Until relatively recently their objective would be to use 'shareholder value' as the main criterion to gauge 'value'.

These figures may tell us how well a particular company is doing but the same analysts would be hard pressed to use their techniques on a public sector body or a non-commercial organization like a school or state hospital. What exactly is the value of a hospital that saves thousands of lives or a school that educates the next national leader? I think we should all be very interested in the answer to that one. No one would suggest that these are not highly valuable institutions and yet no answers can be gained by trying to use conventional techniques to measure their value to society.

One fundamental contention throughout this book is that value will always, ultimately, manifest itself as a dollar (or euro, or pound) sign. Art experts could argue ad nauseam about the relative merits of Leonardo Da Vinci, Van Gogh, Andy Warhol and even Damien Hirst, but the market value of their works is a pretty good indicator of what the art market 'values'.

I might come to look at a Damien Hirst calf in formaldehyde in a new light when it has the same market value as Van Gogh's sunflowers or Da Vinci's Mona Lisa. I can't say whether this is ever likely to happen; over time, however, most human beings do agree on what real value is, and can tell the difference between a fad, a gimmick and the genuine article.

All of this may be very obvious, so why bother to spell it out? Well, maybe some things are not quite as obvious as they appear on first inspection. For a start, it is all right for me to talk about value and wealth but would the average employee see it the same way? Do they know what we mean when we talk about shareholder value and would they view maximizing shareholder value as a worthwhile aim for them, personally? Or would they immediately think of some remote investor who already has more money than they know what to do with? A fat cat who dabbles in the stock market and is just as likely to sell their shareholding if it suits them? Someone who has no intrinsic interest in the business other than as a figure in his or her portfolio?

How would they regard their own pay packet? As a slip of paper that tells them once a month whether they will have enough to pay their bills? A figure that is never as high as they would like it to be? Maybe the only reason they have joined the union is that it might lead to a better pay increase than not being in the union? They could even be aggrieved because their perception is that the size of their pay packet and the value of the shareholder's shares are directly but inversely related. In other words, the value of the shareholders' stock can only increase if their pay is kept in check.

This may look like a cynic's view of employee perceptions. We all know excellent companies where the employees are committed and do not stay awake at night thinking about shareholders. Yet even if that is true it is not the same as saying that employees truly see value generation as a worthwhile goal; that they are truly inspired by that prospect and are willing to go to extraordinary lengths to achieve maximum value.

Let me try to explain what I mean more clearly. I have always been amazed by people who, after having worked for many years in industry and who have had a successful career, feel the need to do something else in order to 'put something back in' for the benefit of society. This implies that, hitherto, they felt they had only been taking something out. Their business contribution has been rather selfishly driven.

The 'something' that they want to put back in usually means working for a charity, on a community project or something similar, usually for no payment. Of course, I can see exactly what they are getting at. Many of us want to feel we contribute to something that is in the interests of society at large rather than just a narrow, profit and loss account. We also get satisfaction from working with people who share our values of community service. It is much easier to identify with the obvious virtues of, say, setting up a shelter for the homeless than it is with producing nuts and bolts, even though we could all stand back and admit that they both play an important part in society.

In the eyes of the HR strategist though what really matters is that employees are totally engaged with the aims of the organization they work for. In essence, this means that they perceive value in much broader terms, value to the business, value to themselves and value to their fellow human beings. But more importantly, it means that they see all three as mutually inclusive and not conflicting in any way - whether that is making fizzy drinks or life-saving equipment. Either they believe that the product or service they provide is of value to society or they do not. No doubt there are many gradations along the scale from total engagement to total disengagement, but if an employee of a large oil company were to genuinely believe that the company was promoting profit at the expense of environmental concerns then we should not be surprised if that employee's level of engagement is low.

Any HR strategy that manages to raise levels of employee engagement has a much greater chance of maximizing its value, in every sense of the word. The organizations that get the highest levels of employee engagement will have a platform for providing the most value to society. It is likely to be those organizations that manage to align their employees with the goal of value maximization, and completely engage them in the process, that will make the greatest contribution to wealth. The converse of this logic, of course, is that organizations that purport to maximize shareholder value alone are unlikely to develop, enhance and harness the full talents of their people and therefore will never become a high value organization.

What is a high value organization?

Market analysts could no doubt send me a list of many organizations that already have a 'high value'. Yes, but value will always be a relative as well as an absolute concept. About five years ago I happened to be introduced to a reinsurance business based in the City of London. Traditional reinsurance businesses in the City were run along very similar lines until a man called Matthew Harding took over Benfield Reinsurance and started to re-write the reinsurance business rulebook. By making some fundamental changes, like listening to what customers really wanted and ensuring claims were settled promptly, he attracted a great deal of business. His Chief Executive at the time told me that they employed 65 talented people and made a profit of £30 million. A profit per head of £461 000. One of their, erstwhile, nearest rivals employed 120 people and made approximately £1 million profit in the same year (£8333 per employee). Both companies worked in exactly the same market and both generated value, but the comparison is stark.

Perhaps the best way to explain the above story is simply to regard the City as a place where old-fashioned methods left the market wide open for an innovator like Matthew Harding to bring in some simple principles and some dramatic improvements (although his methods were regarded as those of a maverick by some envious peers). In effect, fundamentally changing the method of working enabled a significantly higher amount of value to be created by each employee. It is also worth noting that the employees at Benfield were not imported from another planet. They may have had to adapt to new ways of working but basically they were the same people who could only have generated £8000 per head if working within the confines of one of their competitors.

Yet despite everything I have said above, Benfield would not qualify as a truly high value organization within the definition I am using throughout this book. A high value organization *maximizes* its potential value. Here, getting the competitive business strategy right and, admittedly, the right people, made an incredible difference. But was there an HR strategy at work? An HR strategy at Benfield could have produced even more value. But who would have been looking for an HR strategy when the business was already doing so well?

HR strategy has to be a conscious decision. It does not happen by chance. Matthew Harding may have had a longer-term strategy in mind but it was quite obvious that he could see the enormous potential of simply changing the way he did business first. Sadly, he met a very early and untimely death in a helicopter accident some years later, affording no opportunity to observe how he might have developed his business strategy in the long term and what effect this would have on other entrenched attitudes in the City to the value of employees.

Chapter 2

HR strategy starts with a business strategy

> *What business strategy is all about - what distinguishes it from all other kinds of business planning - is, in a word, competitive advantage. Without competitors there would be no need for a strategy ... Corporate strategy thus implies an attempt to alter a company's strength relative to that of its competitors in the most efficient way.*
>
> Kenichi Ohmae, *The Mind of the Strategist* (McGraw-Hill, 1982)

For me, Ohmae's understanding of strategy is as absolute and complete as any writings I have come across. What is more, he manages to show both the simplicity and complexity of strategy. I have never seen such a simple and clear definition of strategy as this but its implications for HR strategy are even more profound.

It is probably quite obvious to most business leaders that the reason they need a strategy is to beat their competitors. In fact it is their competing strategies, more than their operational efficiencies, that will determine who will win the 'war'. But where does this business strategy come from?

Business strategy starts with vision

We are not going to spend too long looking at what constitutes a business strategy and how it is formulated. Search on Amazon.com using the words 'business strategy' and you will find nearly 2000 titles using those key words. That is already a well-covered subject. What we are concerned with here, primarily, is acknowledging when there is a business strategy in place. This business strategy can then be used as a basis for developing an HR strategy (although later on we will touch on the notion of the HR strategist actually informing and helping to formulate the business strategy itself).

The business planning, or direction setting, hierarchy shown in Figure 2.1 is very simple and can be applied to any organization; commercial or otherwise. Like all 'textbook' approaches though, it is much easier to describe than it is to make it happen. What this model says is that for strategy to work well someone at the top of the organization has to have a clear view, or vision, of what the future holds. If we take banking as an example, it is conceivable that some industry visionaries see a much greater role for the Internet in the future of banking. Others may believe that personal service will never be replaced by a computer interface.

Of course the vision could encompass many optional scenarios, so the mission of the organization has to state in which particular direction the organization is going to head. There may be, for example, a mission to be the premier online provider of personal financial services, or may be the

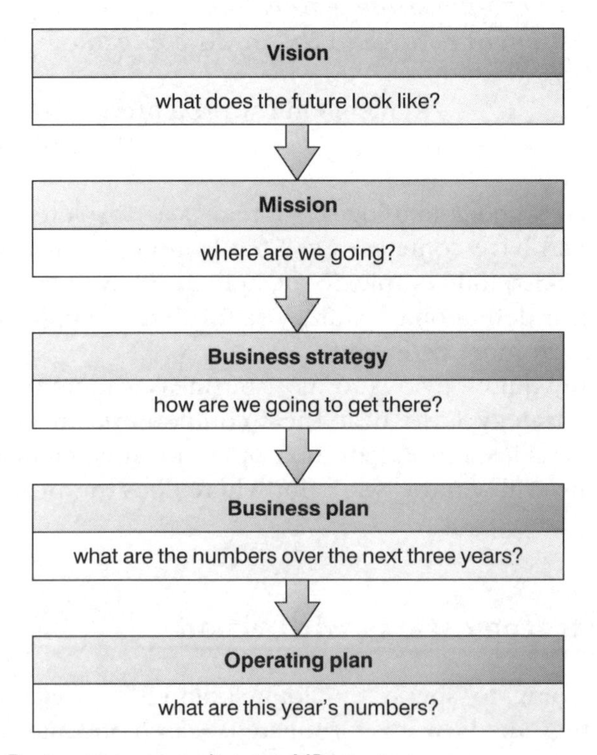

Figure 2.1 Business strategy dictates HR strategy

number two in personal service. This starts to provide much clearer clues as to the type of roles needed and ultimately the sort of people that the bank will have to employ. We are not going to discuss the merits of either of these scenarios but at some stage someone has to put a strategy together to make the vision and mission a reality.

It is this business strategy that HR strategy has to connect with, directly, whilst understanding the overall vision. Also, when it comes to the business and operating plans the HR strategist should already have had a significant influence on the design of the organization. This will lead to the design of roles for individual employees; an idea we will explore in more practical detail in Chapter 13.

Yet if you were to ask a VP-HR why he or she needed a strategy, I wonder if they would give the same answer? Do VPs of HR perceive the importance of HR strategy as being an integral part of a competitive business strategy? Consider this quote from a former VP-HR at American telecoms company Verizon when interviewed for www.HR.com on 18 June 2001:

> I worked with the business presidents and general managers running the lines of business. I said, 'Here's the HR strategy, now let's brainstorm what questions you need answered from a human capital perspective. What are the questions that are keeping you up at night?'

The first thing that should strike any true HR strategist about this quote is that the HR strategy is offered to the board *before* they brainstorm the 'human capital perspective'. Surely that is the wrong way around? Any HR strategist needs to know what all of the key business issues are before they can decide what human resource capability the organization needs.

One can only assume that he must have already had some sort of HR strategy template to work to, regardless of the business strategy at Verizon. Does this tell us something about the mindset of senior HR professionals? One obvious answer as to what this 'template' might be is a belief, in the HR profession at large, that there is such a thing as 'best HR practice'. They must believe that the HR function has something to offer a business, more or less regardless of what the business circumstances are.

If this is the case then such VPs-HR are doing precisely the opposite of what Ohmae is suggesting. Rather than using HR strategy to give the organization a competitive advantage they are copying their competitors. This will never be a successful strategy because even if what your competitors are doing 'works', by the time you have copied them they will have already moved forward and left you behind.

True HR strategy, like any good business strategy, has to involve thinking ahead of your competitors. But then how many business strategies actually do this, never mind HR strategies?

Generic business strategies

The plethora of books and articles on business strategy can be daunting for anyone new to the subject, and a full review of what is available would serve little or no purpose here. Suffice it to say that before we can discuss the existence and merits of an HR strategy there must be a clear business strategy in place. In effect, how could a VP-HR produce a strategy which says 'this is how we need to manage our human resource' if the business does not know in which direction it is heading or what it is trying to achieve?

Ever since Michael Porter wrote his seminal work *Competitive Strategy: Techniques for Analysing Industries and Competitors* (first published in 1980), it has been widely accepted that there are a finite number of generic business strategies. Porter originally referred to cost leadership and product or value differentiation as the two main, generic strategies, with a third being a combination of both. Other writers, such as Michael Treacy in *Harvard Business Review* (Jan–Feb 1993), have added other generic strategies to these main headings, such as 'customer intimacy'.

All of these strategies presume that the people in the organization can deliver what the strategy dictates. Cost focused strategies demand tight cost control systems and people who can cope with a tight cost control environment. Customer focused strategies require customer focused systems (e.g. rapid response times) and people who want to give customers excellent service.

The main, but certainly not sole, purpose of an HR strategy is to ensure that the organization has the right sort of people, doing the right things, to deliver the business strategy. So, in order to establish what part HR strategy plays we will now start to look at different business strategies and ask whether an HR strategy is in place and to what extent the success of that strategy has anything to do with the HR strategy.

The best businesses do not necessarily have the best HR strategies

All business strategies are inherently people strategies in the sense that the actions of the people in the business will be dictated by the business strategy. If McDonald's decides that its new business strategy is to sell products other than burgers and fries, then the people who work in McDonald's will have to learn how to make and serve pizzas or tortillas. The strategic decisions of today inevitably become the operational tasks of tomorrow. However, this does not mean the business has an HR strategy. Many businesses are very successful without any formal HR strategy but *maximizing potential organizational value* will only come from a combination of an effective business strategy and an effective HR strategy.

I will probably make some provocative claims in the course of this book, intentionally or otherwise, but there are two things I am prepared to say with absolute certainty:

- A good business strategy does not guarantee a good HR strategy will follow.
- A good HR strategy will never, ever, make up for a poor business strategy.

I would go even further and suggest that it is difficult to have a good HR strategy where the business strategy is poor. Consider the figures in Table 2.1, published in *The Times* on 19 September 2001, when the world was still coming to terms with the aftermath of September 11th and, in particular, its impact on the airline industry. It may take you a couple of minutes to absorb the enormity of what these figures illustrate.

Here are two businesses working in exactly the same industry, albeit in different market segments, whose relative performance contrasts so sharply. British Airways has an illustrious history and an enormous customer base. Ryanair is a relatively young upstart with no pretensions

Table 2.1 Choose your HR strategy – BA or Ryanair?

	British Airways	*Ryanair*
Staff	62 000	1500
Planes	294	36
Airports served	230	47
Pre-tax profits	£40 m	£77 m
Share price	174p	543p
Market value	£1.88 bn	£1.97 bn

Source: From 'BA's "hard landing"', *The Times*, 19 September 2001

of being anything other than a budget carrier. By any definition of the words 'success' or 'organizational value' though Ryanair seems to be doing everything right at the moment. So the first obvious question here is who has the best business strategy?

Or maybe an even more interesting question is who has *had* the best business strategy. They are where they are because their strategies, or lack of them, got them there. Their relative positions cannot be completely put down to the September 11th disaster. Their relative market values may change considerably but their margins would make you think that BA is the 'pile 'em high sell 'em cheap' airline, not Ryanair.

Now from an HR strategy perspective we can ask whether HR strategy has had anything to do with their relative positions, positively or negatively? Maybe some insights into this can be gleaned from what has subsequently happened at BA.

In a *Financial Times* piece on 2 November 2001 under the heading 'BA navigates a crisis course' we are given an inside view on how BA was coping with trying to save costs through making 7000 employees redundant. In one passage we are told that 'in talks with unions, it has also been forced to reconsider early proposals for pay cuts. It gave ground yesterday on controversial plans to scrap a holiday bonus and a service-dependent annual rise.' Later, we hear from the head of human resources, who remarked that 'when it comes to permanent staff reductions, we try to do it on a voluntary basis'.

This is not the first time BA has had significant redundancies, having shed 5000 jobs in the early 1990s after the Gulf War. It has also had other human resource problems, with a damaging cabin crew strike in 1997. So what can we deduce about BA's HR strategy based on some of these snippets? Maybe one question is why has BA still got such strong unions? The answer to that might be simply that they believe they are stuck with them or they do not have the inclination to want significantly to change the situation.

Perhaps a more strategic question is what has BA done, since the redundancies of the 1990s, to ensure that it is more lean and flexible for the future? How much contingency does it have built-in? Is it ready for any eventuality? The reference to a 'service-dependent annual rise' suggests that some very outdated practices are still in place. Perhaps the most telling quote in the *Financial Times* piece cited above comes from an unnamed union official, who said 'Morale in the airline isn't bad. It's confidence among the public that isn't good'!

It would be difficult to see how the obvious HR challenges facing BA are being addressed. Also, when BA is fighting for its very existence, maybe the employees should actually be much more concerned than the union official suggests and be doing everything they can to help keep the airline afloat.

A couple of months after this article appeared, *Personnel Today* ran a story on 5 February 2002 on how all airlines were dealing with the post-September 11th crisis. It referred to Ryanair's approach, where they had

> tackled the situation head-on, galvanising staff with the same gutsy, go-getting attitude it featured in its customer advertising. 'Let's Fight Back!' ran the slogan, next to a picture of General Kitchener (an interesting choice for an Irish company). But the campaign seemed to do the trick. 'Morale at Ryanair,' says one company source, 'has never been better.'

Ryanair does not have a reputation as the most progressive of employers. Its attitude to its workforce seems to be the same, no-nonsense, no-frills approach it has to its business and its customers. Currently the figures suggest that Ryanair is a much more successful business than BA, and its employees seem to be helping it to thrive in difficult circumstances.

The business strategy/HR strategy matrix

Figure 2.2 is a simple matrix that attempts to plot the relative positions of most of the companies referred to in this book in terms of how effective their business and HR strategies are. I will openly admit that this is based mainly on a very personal and subjective assessment and, as such, it will be seen as highly provocative. There are only a handful of organizations in the top right-hand quadrant. There is no one at all in the top left-hand quadrant because organizations that are poor at business strategy are unlikely to be any good at HR strategy.

Now, take Motorola's relatively low HR position for example; why did they deserve that ranking? One contra-indicator that put them there is simply that they set a target for manufacturing VPs to achieve a given, average number of training days per employee, per year. You might think this is a simplistic and trite indicator. On the contrary, when viewed through the eyes of an HR strategist this one measure is very revealing. First, it is a pure input measure. It says nothing about what employees learn or whether there is any business impact. Organizations that use HR input measures know very little about HR strategy. More tellingly, it either shows what a simplistic view management at Motorola have about training and learning, or that they do not have any better performance measures on learning to set their VPs. Either way, it suggests any HR strategy they might have will be less effective than it could be. Verizon join them because, as we saw earlier, their VP-HR put their HR 'strategy' in place before he asked about the business strategy. If you get your HR strategy the wrong way round, how can it be any good?

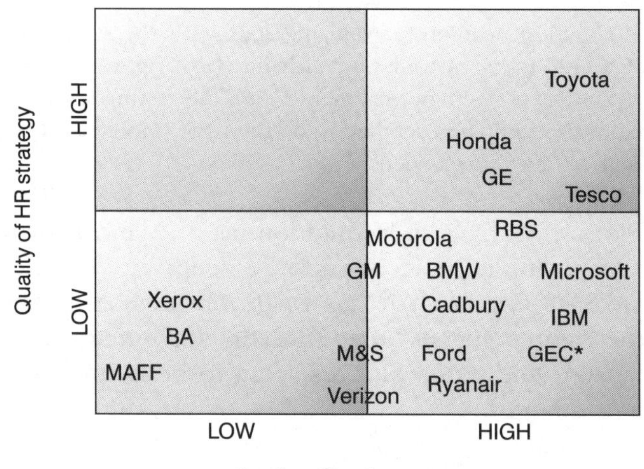

Figure 2.2 The business strategy/HR strategy matrix

Regardless of my own justification for the positionings shown in Figure 2.2, however, how many city analysts would disagree with the view that BA's present business strategy is highly questionable? Moreover, objective observers could be forgiven for thinking that its failure to produce an HR strategy that gets to grips with the real HR issues is making its difficult trading circumstances even worse.

The same city analysts would praise Ryanair for its business results, but would HR observers heap praise on its HR strategy? Its staff obviously deliver what the business needs, but is Ryanair maximizing their value? By definition it must have the right people doing the right things as well, but that does not automatically mean it has a good HR strategy.

Under a heading of 'Ryanair goes on attack over grandiose HR tools' on 6 February 2001, *Personnel Today* quoted Eddie Wilson, Ryanair's head of HR, at a conference on 'Measuring the value of internal communications' in Dublin as saying 'We don't waste time on programmes or initiatives that 80 per cent of people don't know or understand and we don't treat our people like morons.' He also claimed that Ryanair's no-nonsense approach to HR had contributed to increasing the productivity of its workforce and that the workplace culture is strongly influenced by the chief executive Michael O'Leary, adding, 'It's a culture of living and breathing cost control. We take an "à la carte" approach to personnel, not one of best practice.' Ryanair applies its cost control philosophy to everything it does and apparently communicates with its staff through a 24-hour workplace TV channel that was set up for only £20 000.

Business strategies and fortunes change over time

Let's face it, Ryanair is doing well because of its business strategy; it is doing the right things in the right market at the right time. Ryanair's business strategy is a classic cost leadership strategy and it is doing fine at the moment. But nothing stays the same for very long these days. In the present airlines market, characterized by operators with enormous overheads who were previously 'protected' by all sorts of barriers to entry from competitors (e.g. availability of slots at key airports) its cost strategy will remain a major strength for some time.

However, what if a mid-range airline suddenly set up in business that combined tight cost controls with excellent customer service for which passengers paid a small premium? My experience of flying with Ryanair on several occasions is that their staff seem fine, but there is always plenty of room for improvement.

One real test of an HR strategy is to ask how it would cope with a significant change in the company's fortunes. If this scenario ever happened, would Ryanair's cost-conscious staff be able to cope with suddenly needing to focus on better customer service? Their whole attitude might have to change. It is possible Ryanair could find it had exactly the wrong sort of people for a different business strategy.

Business and HR strategy alignment – the Holy Grail

This leads us back into the basic concept that underpins strategic HR thinking – the notion of alignment. Alignment is about getting the right people with the right skills, capabilities and levels of motivation that the organization needs to deliver its strategic business objectives.

Another of the organizations identified in Figure 2.2 is Marks & Spencer plc. M&S, as it is more affectionately known, is a very large retailing business that managed to achieve profits of over £1 billion for the first time in its history just a few years ago. It is currently struggling to achieve half of that figure. So what happened?

M&S had an excellent reputation for good, quality products sold at reasonable prices. It was the retailer to middle class Britain and started to spread its successful formula around the world. The only problem was that in order to drive shareholder value even higher the business was being run with a cost cutting strategy. Staff were taken out of the operation as much as possible. In the meantime M&S ignored all the warnings received from its customer surveys, which indicated, quite clearly, that customers were less and less happy with the service they received. The whole situation came to a head when the ranges of clothes that it bought were being left on the racks by its previously loyal and predictable customers.

No doubt many textbooks will refer to the M&S débâcle, but the most interesting and relevant point for this book is whether anyone has addressed the strategic HR issues that M&S now so obviously faces. Admittedly, many members of the board have come and gone in the past few years and there have been significant changes in the ranges on offer (first the Autograph designer label and more recently George Davis's Per Una range), but the vast majority of M&S employees are the ones who were there before all the business changes. Has anything been done in this area?

M&S were traditionally known for being an employer of choice. I was recently involved in an HR benchmarking exercise and asked the benchmark group organizer whether M&S had ever been asked to join. He remarked that they had been asked several years ago but they had responded that they could not see what benefit they would get from comparing themselves with anyone else.

Part of their new business strategy is to become much more customer focused, and this entails all shopfloor staff engaging more with customers. This is a fundamental break with tradition for M&S. They did not have particularly to engage customers before: the shopping environment, the ranges on offer and M&S's reputation were enough. Now they are targeting different types of customers, more discerning customers, customers who have left M&S in droves to shop with competitors who have steadily been building their own reputations.

This is a good example of where HR practices have become misaligned with what the business is trying to achieve. Part of the problem at M&S was that they did not listen to the feedback from staff about disgruntled customers. Innovation and creative ideas in retailing were not M&S's strong point. They now have thousands of employees who were suited to the old M&S way and there has to be a big question as to whether M&S can change itself fundamentally when a majority of the staff were happy enough with the old methods.

The Holy Grail of HR strategy is to make sure everything that is done under the name of 'HR' is totally aligned with what the business is trying to achieve. Ensuring this happens is actually simple in principle but incredibly difficult in practice.

You will have noticed that I have not mentioned other organizations shown in the matrix in Figure 2.2. As we proceed I will be giving evidence to support their particular position in the grid and we will start to see how rare true HR strategies are. Also, where there is some semblance of an HR strategy, we will see how easy it is for the practice to be misaligned with the business.

Where there is total alignment, where organizations get the business and HR strategies right, the value of the business will speak for itself. So before we go any further we need to be absolutely clear in our minds just how valuable an HR strategy can be, otherwise why bother?

Chapter 3

Why is strategy so important in HR?

How much is a good HR strategy worth?

What would the value of a really effective HR strategy be? How much difference do you think it could make in terms of hard, measurable business results? How about 1 per cent of profit or a 10 per cent increase in market capitalization? These could be very large figures, depending on the size of business.

In Figure 3.1 the whole HR strategy/value proposition is represented. It suggests that all organizations' 'total market value' is below their true 'total potential market value' without an HR strategy. As soon as an HR

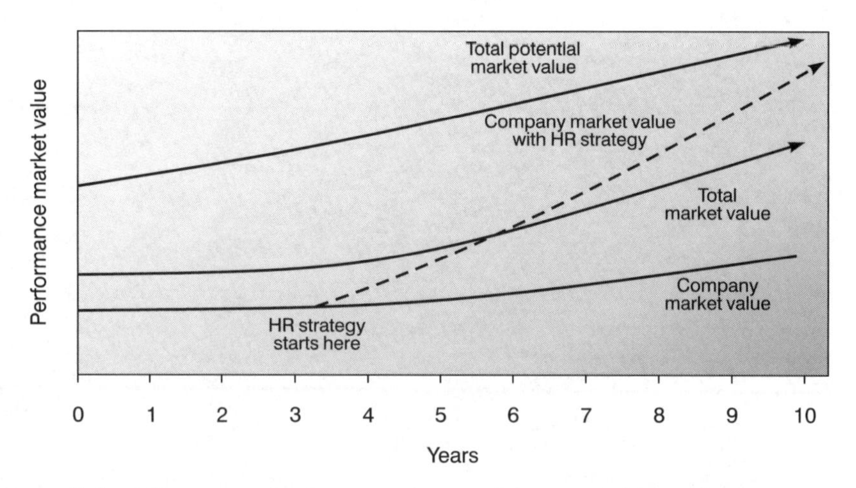

Figure 3.1 HR strategy looks at total potential not relative performance

strategy is introduced by one company it starts to reap the benefits relative to its competitors and also increases the absolute value of the market.

Appendix 1 presents a league table of automotive manufacturers, in order of total market capitalization, showing Toyota at the top, with a value nearly four times that of Ford. However, Toyota's sales volumes are only about two-thirds of those of Ford. That sounds as if they must have managed to secure a really significant competitive advantage.

Each of these companies has access to the same technology and equipment. Their business strategies try to achieve low costs with as much product differentiation as possible. Most of the companies shown have been around since the very early days of car production, so they could all potentially have risen to the top of the league if they had constantly made the right, strategic decisions. Ford and Toyota have both been aggressive in their global expansion, so why the big difference?

This question could be put to different managing directors and they could come up with all sorts of reasons as to why these companies' fortunes have fared so disparately. Whatever financial analysts might make of the figures, they would be hard pressed to make a case that says Toyota manages its finances so much better than Ford. Similarly, could anyone actually say that Toyota is any better at marketing than Ford?

Perhaps if we asked production and operations directors about the discrepancy we might start to get some meaningful answers. Toyota's lean production system is world famous and many manufacturers, both inside and outside the automotive sector, have done their best to emulate it. Probably just as many manufacturers emulated Henry Ford's original mass production systems in the 1930s when that approach brought with it such advantages. So would lean production start to explain the gap?

Ford themselves must have thought so at some stage, because they have tried to do virtually everything Toyota do. They have tried to introduce total quality management (TQM), a philosophy of *kaizen* (continuous improvement), and if you visited a Ford factory you may well find just-in-time deliveries, *kanban* production systems, quality circles and all of the other techniques used so effectively by Toyota. So, despite all of their efforts, why have Ford not been able to keep up with Toyota. Maybe the strategy guru Michael Porter has the answer.

In an interview with Richard Pastore in *CIO* magazine (1 October 1995) he remarked that:

> Sustainable advantage comes from systems of activities that are complementary. Companies with sustainable competitive advantage integrate lots of activities within the business: their marketing, service, designs, customer support. All

> those things are consistent, interconnected and mutually reinforcing. As a result, competitors don't have to match just one thing; they have to match the whole system. And until rivals achieve the whole system, they don't get very many of the benefits.

Maybe this is something all of the other car companies still have to learn: the whole system has to work as one if you are to have any chance of achieving Toyota's levels of efficiency and effectiveness. It is only a short, conceptual step from the need for a whole system approach to realize that only a 'whole system strategy' is going to get you there. It is an even shorter step to then realize that a business strategy that does not incorporate an integrated HR (people) strategy is never going to achieve a complete 'consistent, interconnected and mutually reinforcing' system.

The Toyota way

Toyota is the only business I have ever come across that has both a very long-term business strategy and, simultaneously, an equally long-term HR strategy. Having said that, if I mentioned the term HR strategy to Toyota's founder, Eiji Toyoda, I am not sure it is a term he would have used himself. I am absolutely convinced, however, that he would be able to articulate why he could not have hoped to have achieved the same success without having a workforce that was working for the company every step of the way: a workforce that valued lifetime employment, who could see their best mutual interests would be served by not having a confrontational industrial relations environment, who were willing to come to work thinking of ways to work better, being prepared to learn various tools and techniques to constantly reduce costs. The same workforce might want a reasonable level of pay, terms and conditions but would be willing to ensure that their target number of cars are produced at the end of each and every shift, come what may.

The Toyota strategy is a complete strategy. The system is indivisible and cannot be deconstructed and copied piecemeal. Certainly Ford must have benefited from introducing lean production techniques, but the value they are able to achieve is only a very pale imitation of that achieved by Toyota.

A management development specialist who worked for BMW (UK) attended one of my workshops in 1999 and made no attempt to hide his cynicism when I was extolling the virtues of Toyota as an employer. He seemed to take pleasure in pointing out to me that he knew people who worked in Toyota dealerships who were certainly not so enamoured. I did not try to dispute this; I personally would not want to work for Toyota. Their method of working would not suit me personally, and I am sure they would not be inclined to hire me because their selection system would identify this at the outset. But then, that is not the point at issue here.

Regardless of whether employees *want* to work for a particular company or not, it is whether that company gets the best value out of them that is the key strategic HR question. Toyota's performance figures indicate quite clearly and unequivocally that they must be getting great value out of their employees, even if there are some who do not quite buy into the Toyota way of working. As I said before, there is no such thing as a perfect strategy. Effective HR strategies work better, with more employees, more often than poor strategies or non-existent strategies.

What you will tend to find from speaking to Toyota managers is that they say they follow a clear set of principles – principles that have been enshrined in Toyota's ways of working; that have stood the test of time and still continue to guide their actions and their decisions every day. This is precisely the sort of foundation that is a prerequisite for developing any HR strategy.

What are the lessons for HR strategy?

There are several key lessons here for anyone wanting to develop an HR strategy:

- The business strategy and the HR strategy must be totally integrated.
- The two have to run side by side for many years.
- The highest levels of management must not only understand the holistic, systemic nature of the strategy but give their complete commitment to it.
- The strategy should be founded on simple, durable principles so it will last for a very long time in the face of most foreseeable circumstances.
- Simple principles can be explained to any level of employee and once they understand the principles, and follow them their daily actions can be regarded as directly contributing to business strategy.
- In this way a grand strategy also becomes a strategy for individuals in the organization.

Why business strategy fails without HR strategy

So, we have identified at least one organization that seems to be moving towards the ultimate goal of maximizing value from its people. It is a pity though that such good examples are so hard to come by. This is certainly not because organizations do not try to achieve this same goal. Businesses are always trying to improve if only to keep shareholders off their back. Unfortunately though, despite many initiatives that are designed to bring about significant improvements, few seem actually to deliver.

According to the Cranfield School of Management, research commissioned by KPMG suggested that 70 per cent of balanced scorecard initiatives fail (Lewy and Du Mee, 1998) (see also Chapter 12). This is not much different to the figure given by the authors of *Reengineering the Corporation*, Michael Hammer and James Champy, that 75 per cent of all business process reengineering initiatives failed to deliver what the methodology promised. The history of management fads is littered with similar stories of results not matching expectations. Proprietary and generic 'solutions', developed *outside* organizations, all tend to follow a well-worn, tried-and-tested cycle of failure. They start with hype, followed by a big bang launch and end in disillusionment and recrimination.

Such initiatives never gain the requisite commitment and ownership from the people who have to try to make them work. Sometimes not even the board gives the level of commitment that is necessary for it to succeed. Probably even more of a problem is the fact that outside consultants launch such initiatives and this tends to make the whole process a detached and abstracted exercise. This flies in the face of the fundamental principles of whole system thinking. Only whole system HR strategies are ever likely to deliver significant added value.

Chapter 4

What makes an HR 'strategy' a strategy?

A sheep in wolves' clothing

In my notes for writing this book I have collected many examples of documents with the words 'HR strategy' on them. They may look like strategies to the untrained eye but to the eyes of the true HR strategist they do not even come close. I wish I could tell all the non-HR strategy stories I have but that would be a very negative way to proceed. Nevertheless, it is time to offer a critique of whether such documents really constitute a true HR strategy. Or whether they are sheep in wolves' clothing.

One publicly available, ready source of such documents is UK universities, which publish their HR 'strategies' on their websites (see www.city.ac.uk/hr/SLA/hrstrat.htm for one example). I presume they do this because of a government diktat rather than out of personal choice. This would also partly explain why they are all very similar in structure and content. Yet this is the first sure sign that they are not really strategies. HR strategies cannot be written to a set formula and, if they are, no university gains an advantage. Also, anyone openly sharing an HR strategy is admitting that they believe there is nothing in them that could be of any benefit to competitors.

What does a closer inspection reveal though? The example given above shows a very detailed document that looks as though it is linked to the university's business strategy. It looks and feels a bit like a strategic document but looks can be very deceptive. So what sort of indicators should we seek? Only a keen-eyed HR strategist knows what to look for.

First, is this a strategy for fundamental change? Or is it a mere business plan? What different attitudes do academic staff have to have? I remember meeting an academic in another university who refused to refer to students as 'customers', even though many of them now pay their own fees. Would he have been welcomed as a member of staff in this university? Does this university want to attract the best academics or is it happy enough with second best? Do you feel that it sees itself competing with other universities, both in the UK and worldwide, to gain the right staff, students and a high reputation?

Study the document in as much detail as you wish. For myself, I have been looking at such documents for so long now that I do not need to read every detail to come to my own conclusions about whether this university is really determined to become an institution of academic excellence. Even if it were aiming for excellence, it is highly unlikely that this HR 'strategy' is going to help.

Deconstructing strategy

One way of looking at strategies is to see them as a means for solving very complex problems. Most approaches to problem solving start with looking at effects (e.g. high staff turnover) and then breaking the problem down into its root causes (e.g. poor induction, low wages). This analytic, diagnostic process eventually leads you to a solution. Many things can be deconstructed in this way, but before we go any further it is worth pointing out that you cannot deconstruct strategy. It does not lend itself to this most commonly used technique. Let me use a simple analogy to illustrate this crucial point.

Imagine you are managing a burger chain and you want to cut costs; but you do not want to lose customers. So you decide to run a trial selling burgers with no pickle in them; maybe hoping that most customers will not notice and you will achieve a cost saving that will go straight to the bottom line. You could even track sales of these burgers; with and without pickle, in different stores; to check whether your strategy was working. You would, in effect, be trying to isolate each variable in the profit equation and seeing what effect each one had on the business. If it worked, you may also start looking at reducing the cost of mayonnaise in the same way. You might go for a cheaper brand or just put less mayonnaise on the burger than usual.

What you could *not* do, though, is to take the eggs out of the mayonnaise completely to reduce the cost. If you did that your burgers would just have oil on them. This may look like a silly point to make a point but strategy is like the mayonnaise. It is an amalgam. It cannot be deconstructed to look at the impact of each variable in isolation. Take any constituent part of it away and you do not have a low cost strategy, all of a sudden you have you have no strategy at all. Either all the ingredients are there or what you set out to produce does not exist.

Another way of looking at this is that if you just play around with strategy, tinker with parts of it, you will not get all of the benefits that the total strategy has to offer. In other words, take HR strategy seriously, or don't bother.

Taking HR deadly seriously

We have all heard the old adage that 'people are our most important asset' a thousand times and we also know that, like all motherhood and apple pie statements, it is just as much a platitude as it is a truism. It looks like a statement of the blindingly obvious, but what exactly does it mean?

If what it means is that people like Jack Welch were an invaluable asset to companies like GE then we would have to agree with it. Some employees are indeed the company's most important asset and, as the share price starts to climb, the board starts to realize just how important that asset is.

However, if it is also supposed to mean that every individual employee at GE is regarded as a very important asset then I am not sure that it holds so true. It is one thing to subscribe to a generalized statement such as this and it is another thing entirely to actually *regard and treat* employees as though they are the company's most important asset. What about in organizations where the chief executive gets the business strategy completely wrong? There are probably more examples of this in corporate life than there are textbook versions of how to get the strategy right: one only has to look at the Enron débâcle or the way in which companies like Digital disappeared off the face of the earth. These companies probably had many committed and loyal employees but their poor business strategies resulted in their employees adding no value whatsoever.

So, merely saying that employees are an important asset is, in itself, both misleading and, in many instances, just plainly untrue. Moreover, the actions of many managers show no adherence to this principle anyway. For example, we all know lots of businesses like restaurants and fast food outlets where, presumably, high levels of staff turnover are accepted as the norm. Consequently, managers do not believe that losing this asset on a regular basis is important enough to undermine the company's performance. This is why this phrase is so often ridiculed and regarded as a cliché; most employees know exactly what their bosses think of them – because they experience their behaviour every day.

Maybe that is why a more modern version of the 'people are our most important asset' theme has started to emerge. The new version is the notion that people are the only sustainable source of competitive advantage. When the same technology is available to everyone and capital moves around the globe at the press of button, the only thing that will distinguish the high performing organizations from the also-rans will be the way in which they manage to tap into and realize the full potential of the talents of their people.

Does this sound like a more intelligent and mature interpretation of the old adage? Is it any more true or meaningful?

What about Microsoft as a business? With such a huge market value and obviously employing some very highly educated and highly intelligent people, can it be said that it is managing to use its people as a source of competitive advantage. Is the high value in the business a direct result of a high value HR strategy? What might start to provide the answer to this question – the business strategy or the people strategy?

If you asked anyone what is Microsoft's strength as a business, they would immediately point to their Windows operating system and their Office suite of software. When Bill Gates started developing the original MS-DOS operating system he was prepared to give it away for free, initially, because he knew that whoever developed the platform for PCs would rule the personal computing world. He was absolutely right. Bill Gates is just a very old-fashioned monopolist at heart. Once that key strategic decision was made, and he managed to get the Microsoft system as the industry standard, all he needed were people to help grow the business.

Of course, that is a very simplistic view of what has actually happened over the past twenty years or so but is it very far from the true picture? Look at Bill Gates's failure to spot the ubiquity of the Internet. Once he realized Microsoft had missed the Internet 'bus' his understanding of the strategic importance of becoming the 'industry standard' meant he had to do everything possible to ensure that he achieved this with the Internet as well. These key, strategic decisions drive the actions of everyone in Microsoft.

What Microsoft proves is that making the right strategic business decisions can still create an incredibly high value business regardless of any particular people strategy. So we immediately have to look at the general statement about people being a sustainable source of competitive advantage in terms of specific businesses, in specific markets. The IT industry is still a relatively young and constantly changing market. Maybe HR strategy is not going to be the biggest differentiator here for some time. I am sure Digital would have talked about their HR strategy years ago, but where did it get them?

What about a much more mature market like automotive manufacturing? All the automotive companies would give anything to produce a breakthrough product that leaves the rest of their competition far behind. The reality though is that they are all fighting tooth and nail just to hang onto their current market positions.

In short, therefore, what I am saying is that there will always be opportunities for new products or services that are innovative or manage to achieve a virtual monopoly. In such circumstances getting the best out of your people is of secondary importance, albeit just as desirable as in any organization. On other occasions, however, an effective HR strategy may be one of the only ways to sustain a real competitive advantage.

In order to explore this basic idea further we will look at where different organizations are in terms of their understanding of the connections between HR strategy and business strategy.

The HR maturity scale

I do not know what it must have been like to work in a 'dark satanic mill' at the beginning of the industrial revolution, but I guess it was not much fun. Probably about the same as working in one of the many sweatshops that are still in operation in different parts of the world today. If sweatshops were such a good way to run a business though, they would probably still be the predominant type of business organization. So why are they not?

Sweatshops tend to be the type of production method used only in simple, low value goods, the sort that can only be produced by highly labour-intensive methods in low wage economies. Many textile and shoe businesses still operate this way. As do many of the craft shops selling cheap jewellery that so many of us encounter on our travels. Typically, they will operate outside any legal or regulatory framework.

Obviously you would not choose to buy your prescription drugs or your brake pads for your car from such a supplier because you would not expect any safety or reliability guarantees. Quality systems would be unlikely and the producers of such goods may not be around very long to deal with any returns or defective goods. Those who work in sweatshops probably do so out of necessity and probably do just enough not to upset their boss. This is not an environment in which to discuss the possibilities of maximizing employee value. Consequently we will not be looking at sweatshop HR strategies. That would be a contradiction in terms.

If sweatshops are at the bottom end of the 'strategic HR' scale then presumably large, global businesses are at the other. They employ thousands of people and use sophisticated marketing or production techniques. Here, attracting the right calibre of people and managing that human resource well is more likely to be a key issue. Pharmaceutical businesses would be one good example.

In between these two extremes though must be a whole range of different types of enterprises that employ people, from small family owned businesses to medium-sized public companies, as well as a whole range of public sector and not-for-profit organizations. Where would all of these be on the scale?

The HR maturity scale shown in Figure 4.1 offers a range of positions against which an organization can assess the maturity of its HR thinking and systems. If this strikes you as familiar, then you may recognize that it is along very similar lines to the HR scale explained in *The Bottom Line HR Function*. However, it also owes a great deal to the Software Engineering Institute - Capability Maturity Model for Software (CMM) - from which it has borrowed some key ideas (for further information contact SEI Customer Relations, Software Engineering Institute, Carnegie Mellon University, Pittsburgh, PA 15213-3890).

In essence, maturity is the key concept in both of these models. So, using an IT example, does your organization just buy in new software or IT systems as and when a need arises or do they take a much more forward-looking, long term, holistic, systems thinking approach to the whole issue of IT systems?

Although it is extremely difficult to define precisely what your organization's perspective is on any particular issue, this scale at least offers a framework and a starting point. It should be used as a means for assessing your organization's view of the importance of human resource management and its role in trying to maximize business performance and value. It also represents an organizational journey through a series of clearly identified stages of evolution and development.

At the far right of the scale, Stage 6, is the 'whole system' view that accords with much of Peter Senge's 'Fifth Discipline' (1993) concept of systems thinking. The worst position on this scale, Stage 0, is for those organizations that do not even have a view on how they manage their people. Over time, any organization will have to go through this series of phases or stages in order to mature into an organization that really does get the best value out of its people.

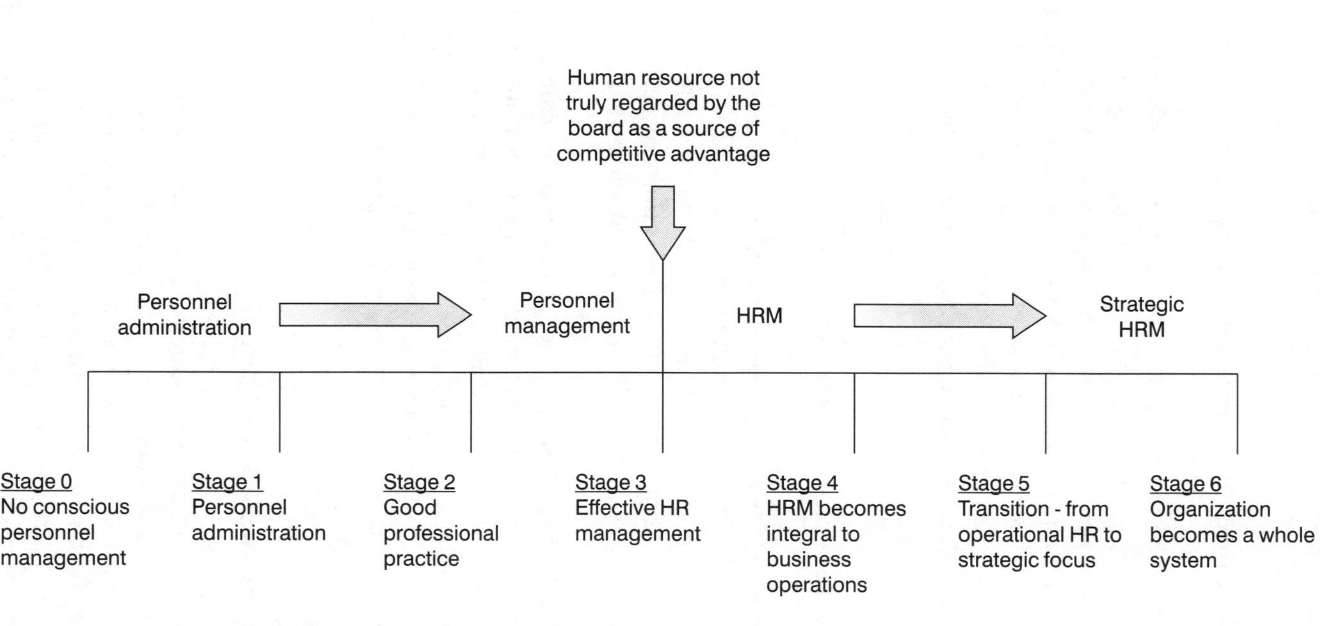

Figure 4.1 Where is your organization on the HR maturity scale?

The stages of the HR maturity scale

Let us look at each stage in a little more detail.

Stage 0 – No conscious personnel management

Stage 0 is a point that is not actually on the scale. There is no sense here at all that any form of human resource management is taking place. For an example of Stage 0 we could envisage a small contract catering company that recruits casual workers for occasional contracts such as a wedding or party. There is no real selection process and the workers get paid in cash at the end of the event and no records are kept. Based on this description, there should be very few organizations left who are still at Stage 0.

Stage 1 – Personnel administration

For the catering company to progress to Stage 1 it starts to keep records of previous recruits and contacts the same people for the next contract. By now everything is being done in accordance with the law and a proper payroll system is in place. The company can tell the tax authorities how many people it has employed and how much they were paid.

Any MD satisfied with Stage 1 perceives people management as just managing 'bodies'. Man management means controlling staff, making sure the job gets done and dealing with any immediate disciplinary matters. This is seen as the sole preserve of their catering managers or supervisors. Such an MD does not know anything about human resource management and would not understand the difference between this and simple man management.

Stage 2 – Good professional practice

To move from having the bare minimum personnel records at Stage 1 to developing a Stage 2 personnel approach the company has to start seeing that there is more than just man management involved if you want to have any chance of getting the best value out of your people. The company starts to realize that good, professional personnel management practices can make a difference. So the personnel records used for payroll purposes are used to record rudimentary performance comments from the supervisor. These are then used during the next recruitment exercise to contact only those previous employees who did a good job.

It is worth noting that there is no mention here of actually having a personnel department to do this work. The supervisors could quite easily carry out this function. So the HR maturity scale is not necessarily saying anything about the need, or otherwise, to employ a team of HRM professionals. However, a professional, personnel practitioner could well introduce other ideas such as a simple psychometric questionnaire to gauge an applicant's suitability for catering work, which could result in a better selection of candidates, a better quality of customer service and less waste through staff turnover.

There is nothing very difficult about getting to Stage 2. It requires simply a belief among the management team that 'personnel management' disciplines bring something to the operation that good man management skills, on their own, do not. Stage 3 though is a significant shift forward in management thinking.

Stage 3 – Effective HR management

Stage 3 is a conscious move towards a systematic and structured approach to HR management. It is an open acknowledgement that there are such things as professional HR practices.

Some benefits will be gained at Stage 2 from the rudimentary systems being put in place but as time moves on the catering company finds that some of its competitors are winning more contracts on price. So the MD wants more effort put into cost controls and efficient ways of working. The MD finds that some supervisors have no understanding of portion control and levels of wastage are unacceptably high, so he or she decides to try to raise the standard of supervision by assessing the supervisors' skills and providing training where necessary. But the MD does not have the time or the skills to do this and so decides to hire an HR professional.

The HR professional quickly establishes that some of the older supervisors will never make the grade in the new, leaner company and advises the MD to bring in some new blood, increase salaries to attract a higher calibre of supervisor and institute a structured training programme for new supervisors. Very quickly the MD sees wastage figures, staff costs and turnover tumble. The company drops its prices accordingly and starts winning more contracts still with a healthy margin. The MD really starts to value what effective human resource management can offer and this helps as the business strategy of moving the company into bigger, longer-term catering contracts starts to take shape.

Some of the longer-serving supervisors who managed to keep their jobs have found the transition quite difficult. Nevertheless they raise their game and start to improve their own people management skills. This is supported by the new formal performance management system, introduced by the HR manager with the blessing of the MD. Every employee, on every contract, now has to have a formal assessment on file. Those who do not reach the required standard are managed out of the business. The whole atmosphere of the business is changing slowly but surely. This is a well-managed business, it does not carry passengers and, crucially, the workforce see that as a positive development. We start to see the beginnings of a performance *culture*.

Before we move on to consider Stage 4 we should stop for a second and ask whether an organization has to move, sequentially, through each of the stages on the maturity scale. There is probably a two-pronged answer to this. In an existing organization at Stage 0 a decision could be taken by a new MD to bring in an HR manager and try to move the organization immediately to Stage 3. While there is nothing to stop them doing so, it raises many questions about how line managers would cope with suddenly having an 'HR expert' advising them how to do their job.

In general terms, if an organization wants to short-circuit the natural, evolutionary, organizational development cycle the chances are there will have to be a firmer and less easy-going approach to HR matters (some would call it brutal or hard-nosed, but that is a bit emotional). I mean issues like replacing supervisors with new blood and allowing less time for the remaining supervisors to cope with the changing demands of their role. One only has to consider other HR matters such as attitudes to employee relations and unionization to realize that there are some very contentious areas that cannot simply be swept aside or leap-frogged so easily.

In new organizations, with all of the human resource management benefits of starting on a greenfield site (which will be specifically covered later), it is much easier for the 'entry level' to be set at a much higher standard in HR terms. Here the management selected and recruited will already probably come from organizations where HR thinking is well developed and they will be working with performance management systems that are regarded as the norm from day one. It is likely that a clear decision about union membership will also have been made already.

Stage 4 – HRM becomes integral to operations

If the move from Stage 2 to Stage 3 represents a significant shift in thinking then the transition to Stage 4 is an even bigger step, both conceptually and practically. The main reason for this is the obstacle between these two stages referred to as 'human resource not truly regarded by the board as a source of competitive advantage'. Only consciously addressing this hurdle enables an organization to get over it. Lip service and rhetoric does not work. Saying 'our people are our greatest asset' or 'are our only source of competitive advantage' counts for nothing. To get to Stage 4 the organization has to put its money where its collective mouth is. So what does it look like in practice?

Budgeting and management information systems change

One simple example is Provident Financial Services in the UK, a business that built 10 per cent extra cost into its staff budgets to allow time for training and coaching on the job. They knew that managers would never find the time for this unless they had it built in. Another indicator, using the catering business as an example, might be that budgeted staff turnover figures for the coming year dictate how much money is available for recruitment and training. Managers that do not manage staff turnover will be struggling to find the funds to shore up levels of turnover that are higher than planned.

These sorts of indicators, of course, on their own do not automatically mean that the organization has reached Stage 4. There needs to be a whole collection of indicators to earn this position (don't forget what I said in the Introduction, that we are learning the complete art of wine-tasting here). Stage 4 sets a very tough standard in terms of HR thinking and action.

Business measurement systems start to produce 'people measures' rather than just financial and operational measures. This could mean that the annual employee opinion survey starts to correlate employee views and attitudes with actual business performance. Managers who get good employee opinion ratings and are performing well in the business start to become the role models.

In fact, the whole organization's management information systems start to be regarded as employee, performance measurement systems. Someone actually measures project lead times and identifies who was running and sitting on the project teams that were the best and the worst. When choices for new project team leaders are made these measures are used as the basis for such decisions. Similarly, in an R&D environment, each phase of the product development process is closely monitored so that those staff that deliver what they have to, on time, can be distinguished from others who seem to delay the process or fail to produce an acceptable output.

Line management sees effective HRM as integral to their role

Another significant shift that has to happen is that line managers no longer simply value HRM expertise; now they cannot do their jobs effectively without it. At Stage 3 they could actually choose whether to include HR considerations in their management decision making. Now they do not have that option. They are not able to restructure their team or develop new roles (or even agree new job titles) unless this fits with the HR strategy. They also have actively to engage in developing and coaching their staff to meet the needs of the business. It is no longer an optional extra. Managers who do not have these coaching skills no longer work for the company.

Stage 5 – Transition: from operational HR to strategic focus

While the organization is developing a much more strategic perspective on HR, and ensuring that line management follows suit, the emphasis still tends to be on existing business objectives and targets. An organization at Stage 4 is very well *managed* but somewhere along this continuum it needs to move away from super-management methods to a state where everyone in the organization is focused not only on delivering performance today but is thinking about their performance tomorrow. The production line manager who manages to reduce wastage or scrap parts to very low levels is already thinking about how to redesign the production process to move onto another level of performance entirely.

Stage 5 might be a slight misnomer because it is a transitional phase. At the far left of this maturity model are organizations that are very tightly controlled. There is no freedom to act and decision making only takes place at the highest levels. In the middle are well-managed organizations, which inevitably includes varying levels of controls and accountability. On the far right is an organization where only the strategic direction is set and everyone in the organization translates that into both their day-to-day operations and their forward thinking.

Organizations have to pass through Stage 5 to get to Stage 6. There has to be a period of management enlightenment. The reins have to be completely loosened. Teamwork is absolutely critical if the extremely high levels of performance that can be achieved are to become a reality (have another look at the league table in Appendix 1 to see how far Toyota have moved away from all of their competitors). While the organization may look like it is structured according to a conventional organization chart, one that shows functional silos and reporting lines, the reality is a much more fluid organization. For example, individual managers do not have to get agreement from their own boss every time they are asked for assistance by another department or project team.

You may have noticed that the indicators of each stage become much more difficult to define clearly and pin down the further along the scale we move from left to right. This is not surprising when we are talking about the difference between a personnel activity such as using a simple psychometric test for selection purposes at one end and a whole new mindset at the other. Mindsets almost defy categorization and specific, detailed description. Nevertheless let us try to establish what Stage 6 might look like.

Stage 6 – The organization becomes a whole system

Can you remember when you stopped being a teenager and became an adult? Or how about when you moved from being a trainee to being a fully experienced professional? These may seem like valid questions but they are very difficult to answer because there was never a single point in time when you were transformed from one state to another. In fact, it is not even a continuum. You were expected to act like an adult maybe to go for a job interview but later the same day you acted like a typical teenager with your friends. Or, despite being professionally qualified, whenever you are faced with a completely new challenge you know only too clearly what it feels like to be the 'trainee' again.

This may not be schizophrenia in the technical sense but we, and the organizations we work for, often manifest schizophrenic tendencies. To make matters worse, sometimes this behaviour is quite conscious and on other occasions we are not conscious at all of the inconsistencies. Let us paint a scenario to explain exactly what I mean in an attempt to provide some real insights into what Stage 6 might *feel* like if you worked in such an organization.

For a start, you cannot use your present frame of reference. Stage 6 organizations are extremely rare, if they exist at all. So you cannot imagine what it might feel like in your own organization because that will not be at Stage 6. Maybe the first fresh perspective is to consider whom you report to. You see, even the word 'report' might be inappropriate. You will still have a nominal boss but you may work with many other individual managers and teams on a regular, or even a completely ad hoc, basis. This will seem quite natural to you.

You will not feel much frustration. You are already contributing a great deal but you are always coming up with new ideas. The reason you are not frustrated, even if your idea is not adopted, is that you have confidence in the organization's system for appraising such new ideas. If the idea did not get through this process it was probably for a good reason. You certainly do not feel that any unnecessary barriers have been put in your way.

I will not try to spell out in every detail what might happen at Stage 6. The rest of the book will put more flesh on these bare bones.

What are the indicators?

A summary of some key indicators for each stage of maturity is shown in Table 4.1.

We could also look at what each of these stages of maturity means in terms of specific areas of HR policy such as employee relations, resourcing, training, development and employee communications. Here we will just follow through what might happen to reward policy as the organization matures.

Stage 0

An unwritten 'policy' exists to pay as little as necessary and there will be few additional benefits. The payroll is managed by the accounts team but overseen by a senior manager, possibly even the managing director. Inconsistencies arise rapidly due to a range of unforeseen circumstances such as:

- good employees threaten to leave unless they get a better package
- while recruiting new employees the company reacts to market rates but existing employees who are not asking for more slip behind
- the extra effort required for specific contracts attracts ad hoc payments by managers under pressure
- favoured employees, for whatever reason, start to move ahead in pay terms.

In such organizations there is obsessive secrecy about salaries; employees leave unnecessarily because the company did not recognize or react to their genuine complaint quickly enough. More importantly, the company's salary bill is not well aligned with the relative performances of its employees.

Table 4.1 Looking at all stages from the HR policy perspective

Maturity level	*Organizational Indicators*
Level 0	No conscious approach to personnel management Accountability rests only with senior managers Little decision making below top level Command and control mindset fosters blame culture Intuitive rather than systematic management style
Level 1	Personnel administration acknowledges that intuitive personnel decisions are not optimized
Level 2	Recruitment and selection procedures from professionally trained staff Appraisal and personal reviews take place but in a perfunctory manner Training and development tends to be courses, programmes, initiatives
Level 3	HRM systems and processes are evident with an operational focus Appraisal becomes a performance management system The value of generic solutions is questioned Evaluation/feedback systems are put in place
Level 4	Performance management system starts to include clear business measures Levels of personal accountability increase significantly and rapidly Under-performance is managed effectively Tailored solutions start to replace generic
Level 5	Individual accountabilities are superseded by team and project accountabilities Performance measurement systems cross departmental boundaries Reporting lines stay clear but flexible Organization is restructured around core processes Organization is structured to maximize customer satisfaction Training and development replaced by concept of learning
Level 6	All activities in the organization have a line of sight to strategic objectives Strategic objectives are owned by all employees A 'not seeking to blame' culture exists The 'initiative' approach to continuous improvement is replaced by a natural, systemic and dynamic obsession with improvement Unionization does not exist because of absolute trust between employer and employee

Stage 1

In a Stage 1 organization pay rates are monitored and so discrepancies and inconsistencies are inevitably highlighted. This tends to generate some moderating actions by management. Employees realize that inconsistencies are less likely to occur so their expectations are managed accordingly. More importantly, the salary bill tends to be better directed to where it should be spent.

Stage 2

At Stage 2 the basic payroll and salary records become a proper job evaluated reward system. This would include grading jobs and deciding on pay bands for different grades. This is a much more systematic way of managing rewards but it is also much more restricting. No one can get a salary increase without going through a mechanistic process of re-evaluating their job and managers do not have much leeway to reward staff who are in the same job, nominally, but are performing much better than their colleagues.

To digress slightly for a moment, it is also worth mentioning here that reward policy and employee relations policy obviously go hand-in-hand. A strong unionized environment tends to lead to rigidly controlled pay scales. Just one more example of the holistic nature of HR strategy.

Stage 3

At Stage 3 the strict adherence to the job evaluation system is toned down by the introduction of the concept of performance management. Simple performance measures start to highlight the high performers and the importance of recognition in the reward equation grows. Now the reward system is made up of a base salary linked to the grading system but topped up by a simple performance element in the total package. Managers start to use the combined system to ensure the rewards are targeted at the right people: the ones who really make a difference.

Stage 4

At Stage 4, after a period when the organization starts to realize just how much difference the good performers make, project teams start to be rewarded, as a team, for delivering on time. This is a difficult stage to get to because some people start to question the validity of the performance targets. Individual accountability is increasing sharply and rapidly and some employees react to this by being defensive and making excuses as to why their performance is dependent on the performance of others.

At Stage 4 the importance of looking at complete processes and the value chain becomes a serious issue. Some organizations fail to address this so never get past Stage 4. Where this is anticipated, as part of the HR strategy, there has already been a process of managing out of the organization those who do not want to accept personal accountability. Strenuous efforts are also made to free up the organization structure with cross-functional performance objectives in place.

Stage 5

Stage 5 is the transition period during which the organization moves from a low or mediocre performer to a high performing organization. It can take a long time as it enters into unknown territory. How will different departments work with each other to achieve common goals and how much will turf wars and egos get in the way of progress? Only very strong and clear leadership will crack heads together when necessary and be brave enough to avoid the inevitable drift back towards a blame culture when things are not going according to plan.

Reward structures and systems are becoming infinitely flexible, with interim management and ad hoc specialists employed when the need arises.

Stage 6

It is very difficult to resist the temptation to describe Stage 6 as some kind of organizational Nirvana. Everyone is working well together and departmental and functional boundaries, even if they are drawn on paper, are almost non-existent in reality. Transparency is the rule of the day. The organization is now really tapping into the intellectual capital of its employees, ideas are exchanged freely, innovation and creativity start to move the organization well ahead of its competitors who are still mired in rigid hierarchies based on functional silos. Those who are generating the highest value ideas are being extremely well rewarded to ensure they do not leave or get poached by the opposition.

We could run through a similar scenario depicting other aspects of HR strategy and you may be reading this thinking that all the big organizations automatically gravitate towards the right-hand side of the scale, but this would be a total misinterpretation of the maturity scale.

Admittedly very few, if any, businesses remain at Stage 0 or even Stage 1, but my experience tells me that very few have truly reached Stage 4. Moreover, I am absolutely clear in my own mind what I am saying here. Despite all of the hype surrounding what good organizations are supposed to be doing, in terms of human resource management, virtually none of them has evolved to a very high level when gauged on the HR maturity scale. Why should this be so? Because the sort of HR strategy that I have tried to describe throughout is itself virtually non-existent.

Call that an HR strategy?

Of course, as I mentioned earlier, if you asked any VP-HR whether they believed they had an HR strategy they would say they had, and most of them would genuinely believe that their HR policies constituted a strategy. It is a bit like asking any parent whether they believe that their children have been brought up well; what answer would you expect them to give?

You may have noticed that I did not suggest asking a CEO whether they had an HR strategy, even though this question should actually be targeted at the CEO more than the head of HR. The reason for this is that if a CEO has not experienced HR strategy then how would they even begin to know what an HR strategy might look like? Yet, if HR strategy is not fundamentally influencing the very fabric and mentality of the organization, then it is not worthy of the title.

Let us look at one particular example of a very large organization, in a very competitive market, trying to manage its human resources for maximum value. In 2000 the Ford automotive company announced that it was thinking of shutting its Dagenham production plant in the UK. Almost simultaneously, it also announced a new policy of encouraging all of its employees to learn at home; with personal computers supplied by the company. Meanwhile, its 'white collar' workers were discussing strike action for the first time in years.

Maybe the timing of the announcements was just very unfortunate. Perhaps it wasn't expected that anybody would be watching closely enough to spot the irony of the situation. Regardless of how these policies came about, the key question an HR strategist would ask is do they all form part of a coherent and HR strategy? We could be forgiven for coming to the conclusion that these statements appear to represent glaring, strategic inconsistencies. This, in turn, would suggest that if

Ford does indeed have a coherent, long-term HR strategy, that is intended to get the best out of its human resource, it has a funny way of showing it.

If this discussion about strategy were just a matter of semantics then it would not matter. The problem here though is that the choice of incorrect terminology suggests woolly thinking. This inevitably leads to woolly HR strategies, and that is not in anyone's interest. Unclear thinking does not provide the solid foundation necessary for developing a consistent and coherent people strategy.

If you want another way to check whether your own organization has something that qualifies as a strategy you might like to consider these two questions. First, does your organization tolerate under-performance? If it does then how can it have a high-performance strategy? Second, do you cap your reward scheme for the majority of employees? If so, what logic is there in this? What is more important, your salary bill or the added value from each of your employees? These may look like simplistic questions but they do unearth some slightly illogical attitudes in HR thinking.

HR strategy must engage the business

One key word that is so important in strategic HR thinking is *engagement.* I will always remember the chief executive who told me that his head of training and development, who had recently left the company, had never 'engaged the business'. This resulted in him delivering all sorts of training programmes, none of which was rooted in addressing real and urgent business needs. The training head started from the premise that the people in the company needed training and development and provided generic programmes to suit some very ill defined needs. So managers got management development programmes, supervisors were put on supervisors' modules.

Of course, whoever decided to employ a Head of Training and Development (yes, the same CEO) must have already decided that the employees needed training. But they would do so on the assumption that the Head of Training would have the means for finding out who exactly needed what type of training. What they do not really want is pre-prepared training solutions looking for a problem. One way of viewing the concept and principle of engagement, in HR strategy terms, is to think of it as the opposite of *generic* initiatives.

Engagement is much more than just listening to what the business really needs. It means actually developing a relationship with line managers and employees at all levels to ensure they, themselves, are engaged in the running of the business and are not just bystanders. Engagement is about checking levels of commitment to common goals and taking whatever steps are necessary to gain the highest levels of motivation.

Engagement requires explicit and conscious actions focused on clear and measurable outcomes. How can employees feel engaged by vague and nebulous company mission statements? Surely alienation and apathy are the signs of an organization that has not engaged its people. Moreover, the board of directors has to be engaged in a constant debate about the alignment of its business strategy with the way it treats its employees.

What can we learn about HR strategy from businesses that fail?

Many HR professionals now like to refer to themselves as business partners, a term used often by Dave Ulrich. He has his own very clear indicator of when HR people are acting as business partners: when he cannot spot them amongst any group of managers discussing business issues. This probably is an indicator of HR working in an organization at Stage 4 but it tells us virtually nothing about whether there is an HR strategy in place.

A better indicator would be to ask that HR person whether they were prepared to accept shared accountability with those managers for the achievement of their objectives. This is a much tougher test, and if HR people fail to take on this challenge it is their organizations that ultimately suffer.

Let us assume for a moment that modern, progressive HR policies do indeed make a difference to organizational performance. Certainly there have been many studies in recent years trying to demonstrate a correlation between business performance and HR practices. Such studies are normally based on the simple premise that, if a common set of HR practices is seen to be present in successful companies, then this must indicate that those very HR practices must have made a direct impact on those businesses' performance.

What such studies do not seem to take account of though is the conclusions that could be drawn from companies that have failed, despite using exactly the same sort of HR methodology. In the earlier comparison between the fortunes of BA and Ryanair (Table 2.1), any objective observer would have suggested that BA uses much more progressive HR methods than Ryanair. In fact, in HR circles in the UK BA was often cited as an organization demonstrating best practice HR.

When the business was doing very well it was easy for the HR team at BA to claim some credit and suggest that their HR practices constituted best practice. But if these practices do have a direct impact on the performance of BA, then can we reasonably conclude that the 'best' HR practices also contributed to the company's downfall when the performance of the business became so poor?

Can HR strategy be negative as much as positive? Or do we merely conclude that BA got its business strategy badly wrong and an effective HR strategy could not do anything about this? Surely, though, a 'correlation' that only applies in the good times is hardly a correlation. So maybe all we can conclude is that HR practices at BA have little or nothing to do with business performance – in other words, their business impact is neutral – they are just looking after administration and other hygiene factors.

A case of an even more rapid decline in a large business is that of Marconi plc (formerly GEC run by Lord Weinstock). Anyone who ever had any dealings with GEC felt the influence of Lord Weinstock's management style straight away. Each business was assessed regularly on very clear, hard, measurable criteria. It was a no-nonsense company, which was probably appropriate for many of its heavy engineering businesses. It was also not particularly well known for being at the forefront of innovation or using the latest, sophisticated management practices. In this environment it was no surprise to find that HR only ever existed as a business support service (Stage 2). That is all GEC wanted from its HR team.

Jeff Randall, the BBC's Business Editor, wrote a valedictory article about Lord Weinstock in the *Sunday Telegraph* (28 July 2002) shortly after his death, remarking that he 'often picked over the numbers well into the wee hours; it was cost control raised to an art form'. He also commented that he 'held fast to simple, old fashioned values. He dismissed too-clever-by-half accounting as a "magic show" and championed the merits of cash'. After 33 years of running GEC Weinstock stood down as chairman in 1996, when the business was worth £11 bn, profits were £1 bn and the share price was £3.63.

During the stewardship of his successor, George Simpson, GEC was 'transformed' into what was to become Marconi plc, which (at the time of writing in February 2003) has a share price of £0.022 with £3 bn of debt. By the time you read this book it is highly unlikely whether Marconi will exist in the same way, if at all. This catastrophe is now the subject of many articles and no doubt will be used in business schools as a 'how-not-to-do-it' case study for many years to come.

Now, in all of the opprobrium levelled at George Simpson and his Finance Director, John Mayo, I do not remember seeing one inch of column space about what Marconi had been doing in terms of HR strategy. Of course, City analysts do not see this as having anything to do with Marconi's downfall, but if that is true, what does it tell us about the value of HR at Marconi? The whole Marconi débâcle does highlight a serious issue in HR strategy, or more accurately, the lack of it.

If you asked the HR team at Marconi whether they had an HR strategy they would most probably say yes. No doubt they would also like to think they made a significant contribution to the business. In fact, Marconi had introduced some very progressive HR practices, particularly in the area of management development. So this is not even a case of singling out a business with an acknowledged poor reputation in HR. In their defence, the HR team might wish to argue that they were using best HR practices, but what value 'best practice' in such circumstances? How could anyone in an HR team contend that they make a contribution when their business is not making an operating profit and its market value has hit rock bottom?

The second, key strategic HR question in this case – was the HR strategy *aligned* with Marconi's business strategy – is probably even more worrying. If the HR strategy was aligned then it must, in its own way, have contributed to Marconi's downfall. And if it was not aligned? Well maybe we do not need to go into that one.

From whatever angle we look at this issue, it looks like a no-win situation for anyone trying to put a case for effective HR strategies. However, I think everything that is happening here can be explained fully, and quite simply. When it comes to HR, Marconi, *like the vast majority of other large organizations,* has only reached Stage 2. They employ professionals in HR to do a professional job. The professionals use the best professional practices they know, but they are not integrated with the business strategy (Stage 4) and therefore they make no significant impact one way or the other. This is a very damning conclusion to come to.

Fortunately I am not alone in reaching this conclusion about 'best practices'. David Creelman, Editor of www.HR.com, is fully abreast of all the latest thinking and practice in HR and is someone for whom I have the greatest respect. He made this comment about best practices in the context of Microsoft and their approach to HR on 12 April 2002:

> Microsoft is an enormously successful business, so if you didn't know any better, you might want to discover its 'best practices'. It always makes me despair when I read a breathless article about what we can learn from Microsoft's recruitment practices or training programmes.
>
> What everyone in business knows about Microsoft – besides that it is enormously successful – is that it is not an innovator, it has a terrible time

delivering new products on time, its products are buggy, it's hated by its customers and it's in trouble with the justice department. If you want to achieve these things by all means ape Microsoft's HR practices.

Microsoft is successful not because of any HR practices, but because it is a monopoly. Software, particularly operating systems, is a natural monopoly. Someone was bound to achieve a monopoly, Microsoft did. It did so through the brilliance and ruthlessness of Bill Gates and his immediate circle and, no doubt, through a certain element of luck.

We shouldn't be following the HR practices of Microsoft any more than we should be adopting the practices of that other great ex-icon of corporate success – Enron. I'd be far more interested in mundane good companies like The Men's Warehouse (discussed by Pfeffer and O'Reilly in *Hidden Value*), Agilent, or The Hudson's Bay Company (which was doing business long before the War of Independence).

Let's be careful about who we choose as our heroes and mentors. Let's understand who has something of true value to teach.

Best practice gets results or it is not best practice

What David Creelman is doing here is much more than 'bashing Microsoft', as one of his readers suggested. He is telling HR people something truly fundamental. The assumption that the best performing businesses must have the best HR practices is erroneous. HR people do need to know where the best HR practices are, and I think – like David – that we are more likely to find these in organizations where the competitive advantage has to come from the people rather than from a monopolistic market dominance.

The term 'best practice' used to be associated with another overblown and overworked phrase – 'world class': copy the practices of world class leaders in your market and then your practices must, by definition, be best practices. It was this kind of thinking that made lean production the goal of virtually every company involved in mass production. But then, you can easily tell when someone is using lean production techniques and you can also see whether it is achieving better results. Unfortunately the same cannot so easily be said about HR practices. Can you tell the difference between a motivated and unmotivated workforce, an empowered or unempowered culture?

Let us redefine what we mean by best practice in HR. The only HR practices that can be called 'best practice' are the ones that help a particular organization, at a particular time, to achieve its strategic objectives. This means 'best practice' can only be judged within its own particular context and has no universal or global applicability. If best practices correlate with best business results, then in Marconi's context their HR practices must be about as far from any notion of best practice as it is possible to be.

To really *earn* the title of HR best practice those who say they are developing HR strategies have to accept that they, too, have a direct responsibility for all the key performance indicators of their business. Whether they be sales volume, profits, return on capital employed (ROCE), return on net assets (RONA), share price/earnings ratio, earnings before interest and tax (EBIT) or even without allowances made for depreciation and amortization (EBITDA). Even more importantly, anyone purporting to help their organization manage and control its people should also be able to spot when a CEO and Finance Director are working with a board that is allowing them to do serious damage.

Where does this leave us? I think it leads us right back to the very beginning. We have to start again from scratch. Re-visit the first principles of strategic HR. We need to question the fundamental theories of human resource management that somehow seem to have become, quite erroneously, the conventional wisdom.

Chapter 5

HR theories need to be revisited

Throughout the earlier chapters I tried to establish how important HR strategy can be. In Chapter 4 we looked at what might actually constitute a real HR strategy and also at some of the practical, policy implications. Now this may seem like getting the chicken and the egg in the wrong order, but before we go any further we need to consider the theoretical underpinnings of any HR strategy. Why is this chapter not the first? Well the logic is this – if we do not know what the potential value of an HR strategy might be, why would anyone want to delve any further into the subject?

Everything has to start with a theory

Theories do not always get successfully translated into practice, but one thing is for certain, if something does not work in theory then it will never work in practice. Sound theories should lead to sound strategies. So, are conventional HR theories robust enough for the job? Is there any coherent theory that binds together all of the strands that could make up a cohesive strategy? Or is the current state of the HR world just a very loose amalgam of disparate ideas?

This, in turn, begs the question of how 'scientific' HR management is. Like most social sciences it is difficult to create the 'laboratory conditions' to test the theories out. So there is an even greater need to make sure the theories are as well founded as they can be. How can we be certain that they work?

Nothing we do in management can be predicted with absolute certainty. Every time we try to solve a problem or improve performance we have to start with a hypothesis. The only way for any professional to prove or disprove their hypothesis is to evaluate the outcomes of their actions. Doctors see patients get better, lawyers win court cases, astrophysicists see their rockets safely into orbit.

This may be stating the obvious but there is one particular difference when it comes to discussing the theoretical basis of HRM. The outcomes are usually neither clear nor easily attributed to the actions we take. Strategies are very complex hypotheses. Did the change to the reward system have any beneficial effect on motivation and performance? Do managers perform better as a result of all the development programmes we send them on? Has the re-structuring exercise really put the right people into the right roles? We are back to trying to isolate the separate effects of eggs and oil in mayonnaise.

Not only must good strategists understand the connections between many variables, they must also know which way the arrow of causation points. So, does improved employee morale lead to improved business performance? Or is it the other way round? Is high morale really just a result of employees knowing that they work for a well-organized business that gets results? Getting the direction of causation wrong can lead to an entirely erroneous strategy.

One theory that is currently in vogue is the employee–customer–profit chain theory. This is a simple theory that satisfied employees lead to satisfied customers and that, in turn, produces a sparkling business performance. The Sears Roebuck case study (Rucci, Kim and Quinn, 1998.) supporting this view is possibly the best known and most often cited by HRM academics and observers. The whole of Sears' business strategy was intertwined with its HR strategy and they would have us believe that a direct and measurable correlation exists between employee satisfaction and business performance. The results in this case study are not only impressive, but appear to prove the theory.

So why might I be sceptical? As an HR professional is it not in my interest to believe the evidence placed in front of my eyes? Well, I might be inclined to believe it if the theory itself made any sense. If there is a simple correlation between employee satisfaction and business performance is that relationship linear and infinite? Can employee satisfaction increase ad infinitum and would business performance possibly match it all the way? That does not seem feasible. Also, we saw quite clearly that there was no simplistic correlation between HR practices and business results in Chapter 2. So there must be other reasons for the Sears results.

There is also the same old chicken and egg question. Does employee satisfaction lead or follow business performance? Are employees more satisfied because of improved conditions or because they get much greater satisfaction out of seeing happier customers? I guess the answer is a bit of both. (Nothing about HR strategy is simple is it?)

My third reservation though is the main one. If it worked for Sears (whatever 'it' means) would 'it' automatically work for any other organization? Would they have to replicate the whole package or would increasing employee satisfaction be enough on its own? Don't forget Michael Porter's analysis (see Chapter 2) that says the whole system has to be replicated.

It is this third reason that actually has the most serious implications for HR theorists. Even if an organization seems to be getting its business and HR strategy to work well, is there any benefit in another organization copying just a piece of the strategy? For example, employee attitude surveys have become very popular with HR teams because they believe in the employee–customer–profit chain theory. This then dictates their actions. If there is a decline in employee satisfaction between one year and the next they deem it necessary to take actions to address it. But that is where the problems really start.

Simplistic theories are dangerous. If employees are not satisfied the obvious thing to try to do would be to make them more satisfied. So does this mean that they should have more money, better terms and conditions, a boss who looks after them, better career prospects or what? After doing all of these things, next year's survey results may indicate good news – an improvement in employee satisfaction, but does that automatically mean that the business is performing better? Having one result without the other seems pointless.

If formulating HR strategy is ever going to be a worthwhile exercise the theories that underpin such strategies are going to have to be much more robust and subjected to more rigorous tests.

Do good HR theories merely tell us what we already know?

Whoever coined the original saying 'it was the final straw that broke the camel's back' knew something, intuitively, about structural stresses and strains. It was probably hundreds of years later before this basic idea was developed into a theoretical basis for structural engineering. All of us understand the world around us much more *intuitively* than we would ever be able to articulate in words. This is particularly true of theories about human nature because we all study the behaviour of our fellow human beings every day. It is the key to our own survival and evolution.

Most normal parents (in the purely statistical sense) do not need psychologists to tell them whether or not it is appropriate for them to discipline their children, or how to discipline them. Whatever methods are used, withholding sweets or rationing TV viewing, if the parent thinks they are acting in the best interests of their child they will follow their instincts quite naturally. We just know that it is the right course of action, even if we cannot provide any clearly thought out, scientific reasoning behind it. A child psychologist may know a great deal more about the theories of disciplining children but they cannot tell us something we already know intuitively, and it does not guarantee that they will automatically make us better parents either.

Similarly with motivation. Classical motivation theories tell us *what* tends to motivate people - but we know that already because, funnily enough, we are all members of the same species! We have all experienced praise and we also see the appreciative look on someone's face when we give them praise or recognition for a good deed. What the theories do not really tell us is *how* to motivate people in organizations to perform at their best.

Peter Senge's work illustrates that if everyone views the organization as a whole system then the system should work more effectively. He does not tell us *how* to get everyone to work together within a whole system. His theories are only likely to work when an organization is in 'systems thinking mode'. So one of the real challenges in HR strategy is to try to achieve this state. However, let us not underestimate for a second the size of this challenge. Systems thinking could be described as a general theory, and they are very difficult to embed.

The best HR theory of the twentieth century?

Brilliant, overarching, general theories are rare. Big theories require big brains and they do not come much bigger than Albert Einstein or Stephen Hawking. How many people though, even with a reasonable level of intelligence, really understand what their theories predicted? General theories such as Einstein's completely undermined many other physicists' theories at the time. Not only did Einstein's theory of relativity displace earlier theories but, post Einstein, most theories about the universe had, in effect, to use his work as their baseline because it had already addressed the fundamentals of how the universe, and everything in it, seemed to obey some immutable laws.

At any single point in time one general theory tends to push every other theory into the shade until a better general theory comes along. Many other scientific fields have their own general theories and if HR is to be taken seriously as a socio-management science then maybe we should ask whether it too could have a theoretical base from which all other aspects of the subject can be drawn. Perhaps there is already a 'general theory', of sorts, that suggests how an organization should be able to get the most value out of its human resources; one that most organizations would happily subscribe to.

As a long-standing critic of the received wisdom in HR, I have often asked the question 'so what was the biggest breakthrough in HR theory in the twentieth century?' Who would be the main candidates? Elton Mayo and the Hawthorne effect? Maslow, Herzberg and the whole school of motivational theorists? Or would we come much more up-to-date and ask whether people like Senge, with his 'systems thinking' theory, had shown us the true way to organizational effectiveness through people?

All of these have been highly influential thinkers. Very few people would argue that their theories do not contain some essential nuggets of universal truths regarding how people should best be managed. However, none of these even attempts to be holistic theories. They look at key perspectives of motivation and learning but they do not, for instance, really address the reward and recognition or employee relations elements that would have to be an integral part of any general theory or effective strategy. There is nothing wrong with any of these theories but they are only any use to HR strategists if they can be made to work.

Don't tear up the old theories – make them work

Anyone writing a book that says tear up all the earlier theories on the subject is asking for trouble, so that is not what is being suggested here. We do not need any new theories of organizational or people management; we already have more than enough competing for our attention. Worse still, the more recent theories (e.g. core competence theory, employee–customer–profit chain theory) not only do not build on what we know works but compound the crime by sending us down the wrong road.

Take the 'core competence' school's view that organizations should concentrate on what they are particularly good at (economists have been referring to this as specialization for many years). This might look like a new view of the world, but Sony were experts at – sorry, had a core competence in – miniaturization long before the phrase was ever coined.

Like many popular theories it tells us the blindingly obvious and can be applied to almost anything. I could say McDonald's has a core competence in producing fast food rather than burgers. When they start adding pizzas or tortilla wraps to their repertoire it proves that they have applied this core competence to develop their product range. An alternative theory might suggest McDonald's are a very aggressive and ambitious company who will always strive to improve their position relative to their competitors. Such a theory will predict that they will start selling similar products to those of their competitors. You can choose which theory you want.

One view I would find hard to accept though is that organizations are run by people who do not have any theories to work to; they do things purely by chance or intuition. Is this the theory of serendipity, or chaos perhaps? You would be hard pressed to come up with the names of many large organizations that operate on this basis. Organizations work on the basis of systems, cause and effect, linked processes. This sort of thing cannot happen by chance. All organizations, implicitly or explicitly, work on the basis that if they do activity X properly then the result Y will follow.

Many organizations have latched onto the basic notion of core competence and it has encouraged them to focus only on the types of business where they already had a market lead. There is nothing wrong with this, *per se*, but theories can spawn other theories and this one helped to spawn what I consider to be the worst HR theory of the twentieth century - management competence theory. This theory says that when the organization knows what its core competencies are the HR team can get to work developing the competencies of the people in the organization to match those organizational competencies. This in turn led to a huge competence industry where competence frameworks were put in place requiring dictionaries of competence definitions and then rewards were meant to be aligned with the development of said competencies.

Although it would be very difficult to get any organization using competence frameworks to admit it, they have been an unmitigated disaster. It would be equally difficult to get any clear evidence that they have added any value whatsoever. Certainly I have not seen any evidence of the value of competence frameworks from the clients I have worked with over the past ten years or so.

Bad HR theories never die, they only fade away

Any theory is only as good as its practical implementation. When the theories do not seem to work well, we refer to 'difficulties in implementation' rather than revisiting their shaky concepts and inherent design flaws.

What about the theory of the learning organization? Senge is only one of many writers who have contributed to the development of this theory. Conceptually it has always had enormous appeal for HR professionals. It sounds like a perfect win–win situation, with personal development and organizational performance being totally intertwined. But what are the chances of any organization becoming a true, learning organization? I am not sure because, after all the hoo-ha 10 years ago, interest in the subject has waned because no one got anywhere with it.

Maybe it was an idea way ahead of its time? Or maybe it was just a bad theory? Now, that brings us to an interesting question. At what point do we stand up and admit that a particular theory was a poorly conceived theory in the first place? Very rarely, if ever, in the field of HR management. In fact I cannot think of a single theory, in more than twenty years in HR, which has been openly dismissed by the majority of professionals as just a bad theory. Some people even still swear by the use of T-groups, a technique that earned itself an awful reputation when some participants were reduced to tears when confronted with their own weaknesses and inadequacies.

This is not that surprising really. We choose to keep such theories alive rather than face the fact that we have ardently pursued something that has promised much and yet achieved little. The personal credibility and professional capital invested in such ventures conspire against any open admission that the theory simply does not work. Add to this the fact that measures of effectiveness are conspicuously absent in most HR functions and it is quite easy to understand how this situation has persisted for so long.

The earlier reference to competence theory is just one illustration of a more general point. The reason why anyone wants to come up with a new theory is that organizations have to latch onto something in a desperate attempt to improve. CEOs cannot offer greater shareholder value through 'business as usual'. Any new strategy has to have a big, new idea in the background.

Competency, like many modern management fads, has wonderful face validity. It sounds like it makes sense and might actually work in practice. However, does it really stand up to any rigorous test?

Testing HR theories

One commonsense test of any new theory is to view it in the negative. So, is the negative of 'competence' called incompetence? In other words, is competence an either/or state or is there a halfway house called semi-competence? How would you like to be flown by a 'semi-competent' pilot or be operated on by a semi-competent surgeon? No, competence has to mean 'qualified', and this is exactly how the dictionary defines competent. Until you are actually qualified to do the job you have to be regarded as incompetent.

This leads to the next question, which is should managers be *allowed* to manage before they are *totally* competent? The purist would answer no but the realist would say there is no such thing as a perfectly competent manager and that every organization is run by managers who are, by the strictest definition, usually incompetent.

Competence theory, like any other management theory, has to recognize the harsh realities of organizational life. Human beings are not hamburgers; you cannot decide whether you want pickle, mayonnaise or lettuce with them. They come as a complete package. It is a bit like asking the captain of the England Rugby Union team, Martin Johnson, to be super-competitive but to control his emotions in the heat of battle. These two aspects of his behaviour are inseparably linked and indivisible. You either want him to charge into a ruck with absolute determination or you want him to stand back objectively and weigh up all the potential implications of his actions. To pull one string you have to release another. If we want ultra determination maybe we have to accept the odd transgression of the rules.

In their groundbreaking book *First, Break All the Rules*, Marcus Buckingham and Curt Coffman (2001: 89) put competencies in their place with a very cautionary note:

> if you do use them, be careful. They lump together, haphazardly, some characteristics that can be taught with others that cannot . . . even though designed with clarity in mind they can wind up confusing everybody. Managers soon find themselves sending people off to training classes to learn such 'competencies' as strategic thinking or attention to detail or innovation. But these aren't competencies. These are talents. They cannot be taught.

I strongly recommend this book to HR strategists.

We all know managers who get results but ride roughshod over their staff. What we want though is the best of both worlds: results focused managers who get the best out of their people. This is expecting a great deal.

You may be asking yourself why are we spending so much time looking at one particular theory. Are there any general principles here that could be used to test the validity of any theory but particularly those used in HR management? If we want to research true best practice in HR strategy we will need to be able to distinguish the good from the bad. How good, for instance, is academic research in unearthing the universal principles or lessons of how best to manage people?

What did the HR academics ever do for us?

I think there are some general lessons that can be learned from the competence débâcle. Competence theory was born in academia. Existing approaches to management development were researched. The result is that management development practitioners now develop (*sic*) managers according to a competence framework. This framework has to be based on agreed competence definitions and assessed against standards. In the worst cases that I have personally encountered, the result is a dictionary of competence definitions with up to 200 competencies identified by management development staff at NatWest bank (before it was taken over by Royal Bank of Scotland). Practically it looks like the cure may turn out to be worse than the disease.

This is where the problems start. Most HR theories emanate from the academic world rather than seasoned practitioners. This has two fundamental flaws. Academics usually research what organizations are doing before they develop their own theories. This tends to lead to adaptations of existing practice rather than going back to first principles. Take the latest views on industrial relations strategy. We now have a preponderance of 'partnership' agreements between management and unions, which are seen as an improvement on the adversarial and confrontational relationships that used to exist historically. But where was the fresh perspective that asked whether unions should exist at all in the twenty-first century?

The second major flaw in much of academic HR research is that many research studies take a macro view or produce meta-analyses from a spectrum of organizations. This tends to assume that what the majority of organizations are doing must constitute best practice. It also tends to make the erroneous assumption that, if the best performing companies are doing it, then there must be some correlation between the activity and the bottom line (an idea we have already revealed to hold very little water in Chapter 2). However, any academic researchers who are prepared to look at HR practices at the micro level and ask much more searching questions about their efficacy will find it extremely difficult to have the same level of confidence that the theories work well.

The third, and possibly worst, flaw is that if you produce a circular argument you are bound to 'prove' what you set out to prove. If better companies, by definition, must be doing better HR, then better HR must lead to better companies. If you follow that argument then the corollary will be that if there is a higher incidence of drunkenness on a Friday night then if you do not let your teenagers out on a Friday they are less likely to become a drunk.

I find it hard to trust such logic but the real danger is that it is on such twisted logic that general theories are often built. So it is with strategy: good strategies are great, bad strategies are a disaster. So a general theory that is popular and is so generally applied has probably done more damage to the cause of effective HR strategy than anything else I can think of over the past twenty years.

Competence frameworks are now being used to underpin performance management systems; career development; pay and rewards; training and development; organization development; recruitment and selection. These may yet prove to be houses of cards. For a theory that cannot provide answers to some very simple questions it is incredible that so many organizations have painted themselves into the same corner with this framework for their HR strategy.

Some of the statements above may seem like very sweeping generalizations. No doubt any HR academics reading this would want to point me towards some research figures that try to disprove everything I have just said. All I would offer in reply is anecdotal evidence. I would ask them to show me one organization that can make a clear line-of-sight link between its competency framework and its strategic objectives. I have tried this test many times and no one has passed it yet. What other evidence do I need?

Ricardo Semler, author of *Maverick* (2001), put an entirely new angle on this when he was speaking at an HR engagement in the UK in 1998 and told the story of a French academic who visited his company in Brazil. The academic was fascinated by Semler's methods but asked him, 'I can see this works in practice but does it work in theory?' You may find this funny or sad. I felt both when a colleague of mine, who was himself an academic-turned-consultant, told me the story of one of his academic peers who said, with precious little irony, 'we academics don't solve problems, we admire them'.

All new theories and ideas can be enticing and that is why they are so popular, but they can only be judged by the results they achieve. If there is no clear evidence that they work in an organizational context it is a clear indication that no one made a connection between the theory and a clear result in the first place. If the competence of your management improves by 10 per cent then the bottom line should improve by at least 10 per cent. Just because you say you are developing your human capital does not mean anything unless that is translated into added value.

Just because you say you need it doesn't mean you can have it

Like many paradoxes in life, it might be hard to understand why organizations go for quick fixes and simplistic solutions when what they obviously need is a long-term strategy. HR strategy is particularly prone to this dilemma. The attitude of many senior managers can be annoying because they put no time or effort into managing their human resources. Yet, when they suddenly realize that change is required, they want their people to behave differently immediately.

If a board of directors suddenly decides they need a new IT or accounting system they go out and get one. If they want to relocate or build a new office they get one designed and move in. If they believe that their employees are not totally committed they try to get something off-the-shelf that will serve that purpose as well. It is this lack of HR vision and planning that means HR strategy often lacks complete commitment and is therefore poorly implemented.

Well-worn analogies may turn into clichés, but the difference between the indiscriminate use of ad hoc HR initiatives and a clearly focused HR strategy is very much like that between the sower who throws seed into the wind and the one who uses a seed drill. Both will achieve some germination but the latter is bound to achieve a greater yield.

One area of HRM most likely to result in a triumph of hope over experience is training and development. Organizations need good leaders so they send their top people on leadership development programmes. When they return there is an assumption that these managers have developed some leadership capability that they did not previously possess. In other words, physically attending the programme is read as an increase in leadership capability. I suppose the same argument would suggest Manchester United supporters must all be better footballers than supporters of Darlington.

Organizations that are really serious about ensuring they have the right quality of leadership have career development *systems* that aim to achieve this over a very long period. Any attendance on a formal, classroom-based leadership programme is only one small element in a continuous process. They never find themselves advertising externally for a managing director. So, while many organizations may have the same wish to grow their own talent, not all of them get the strategic bit right. They might look like they are doing the right things (for example, by sending senior managers to Harvard or Insead) but if it is not part of a continuous, systematic process there is likely to be little real substance to their actions. A key indicator of the difference between HR strategy and mere HR activity. One is made to work, the other is going through the motions.

Take the subject of staff appraisal or personal development plans. I came to the conclusion a long time ago that appraisal systems often seemed to be self-defeating. Good managers generally did not need them and bad managers did not really want them. Good managers always appraised their staff regularly, informally and quite naturally. Bad managers did not, so we had to create a paper-based system to ensure that they sit down with their staff, at least once a year, and go through the motions of appraisal.

The HR Catch-22

It gets worse. The same good managers, who did not need these forms, fill them in properly precisely because they are good, rounded managers. While those reluctant managers, for whom the forms were actually designed, were the very people who were least likely to use them effectively. This struck me as an excellent example of a Catch-22.

My doubts were confirmed to me some years ago when a VP-HR confided that he had just finished piloting a senior management, 360° feedback scheme (another great, ineffective fad?). When I asked how it had gone he said that the good managers loved it and the bad managers hated it. For the good managers it was second nature to listen to their staff and colleagues and accept constructive criticism. Meanwhile the ones who really needed it, who were unapproachable, insecure, afraid to accept any criticism and perpetuated a blame culture, were the same ones who did not learn anything from the exercise or modify their behaviour as a result of it.

HR is very often like that. It is replete with Catch-22 situations. The employees who made use of the new company learning centres years ago were the ones who used to borrow management books from the library anyway. The learning centres never attracted those who were not interested in learning; the very ones who needed to learn new ways of working.

Those avidly using the new HR intranet are the ones who were good anyway at using the old manual system. The people who never miss a day's training are the ones who need it least. The employees who complain about lack of communication are the same ones who never read company magazines or circulars. The list is endless.

If this is a truism, a fundamental of human nature and organizational life, what lessons can we draw from this that can be used to our advantage in strategic HR thinking? Home truths, by definition, are always difficult to accept but, at some stage, we have to acknowledge them and address the issues they raise.

HR practices are only as good as the results they achieve

In spite of what has been said above, no self-respecting VP-HR would choose *not* to have an appraisal scheme of one sort or another. Partly because they would regard this as accepted, good practice but also because, if they do not have an appraisal scheme, what would they replace it with? There has to be some system of reviewing individual performance and training needs. With this mindset in operation it is relatively easy to see why VPs of HR are much more concerned about ensuring an activity takes place than they are with asking too many questions about whether it works or not.

A VP-HR in a UK National Health Service (NHS) Trust hospital once told me, in a very defensive tone, that it was not his fault that the new performance management system was not working properly. He had introduced and developed the system, following what he believed to be best practice, but that is where he saw his responsibility end. It was up to the managers themselves to make the best use of it. If they chose not to, that was their problem. Now we may all understand and have sympathy with his view but it does not alter the fact that, if HR initiatives do not impact on the very target audience for which they were designed, then they become a waste of everyone's time and energy. Regardless of who we try to pin the blame on.

This is the fundamental problem with HR theories, and most of the academics who espouse them. What is the point of developing theories, or the systems to implement them, if the organizational groundwork has not been prepared to ensure the seed takes? One of the primary tasks of an HR strategy is to prepare the ground. In this case, the hospital needed a performance culture before it needed a performance system and no bit of paper was ever going to produce that.

Talking theory as though it is practice

HR practitioners absolutely love discussing their theories. What is not as evident in their psychological makeup is an equally enthusiastic desire to make the theory work. Ask any VP-HR why they have job evaluation or competence based pay systems and they will start explaining the theoretical underpinnings of consistent and felt-fair reward systems. They may go further and start trotting out the latest thinking about how competence frameworks should be linked to an analysis of the organization's core competencies. They suggest that by developing and rewarding competencies they are bound to ensure that people development is totally aligned with organizational development and, ultimately, performance.

This sounds like they are describing what they are doing; they are putting their theories into practice. What is really happening though is they have become stuck in 'theoretical mode'. It is quite easy to demonstrate this. We can ask them what they will do with managers who do not achieve the set competence standards? This immediately raises the question of whether they have set any standards and also whether they are assessing managers against these standards. If they answer that they have such standards and stick to them we can ask what happened to the managers who failed the assessment? Even if they get this far the next question is are they retaining the best performing managers? This sets up another hurdle of having a credible performance measurement system for managers. But the final stumbling block will be for them to demonstrate how all of this competence development is feeding through in terms of business improvement. If they get through all of these questions then it looks as though they have made the theory work in practice.

I was speaking at a conference on training and development measurement in August 2001 where one of the other speakers was a training manager for Xerox. He went into great detail about how they used management competencies, but in the whole of his 45 minute slot not once did he mention the fact that Xerox was $18 bn in the red and in serious danger of filing for bankruptcy. No one in the audience mentioned this either.

Now, even if I had wanted to make myself unpopular by pointing this out, I am convinced he and the rest of the audience would still not have seen why this fact should be seen in any way as a reflection on the performance of the training and development team at Xerox. To this day, many HR people would still hold Xerox up as a shining example of best practice HR, despite its dismal financial performance.

The psychology of changing people

Regardless of what theories we choose to follow, one theory in particular that all HR strategists have to have a view on is whether we can change employee behaviour in the interests of value generation. Even if psychological tools and techniques help us to select the right people for the organization, can they do anything to actually improve employee performance? One of the main aims behind most attempts at HR strategy is the need to bring about organizational change. This is often read as a need to try to change employee attitudes and behaviour.

Yet this would be pointless if the theory of basic, human psychology suggests that we cannot change people in any useful way.

Freud argued that personality was determined by the age of 5. If this is true then what chance do we have of fundamentally or significantly changing someone's personality? By the time someone reaches the age of employment their behaviour patterns are even more well established. If we accept, as a fact of life, that we cannot change employees, in an organizational context, then this presents the HR strategist with a serious question as to how they can add value.

This is obviously a controversial area to stray into, especially for someone who will happily admit to being ignorant in the field of psychology. Nevertheless, anyone trying to develop an HR strategy has to take a clear view on this. Can they change people or can they not? The answer to this question will dictate the entire tenor of any subsequent HR strategy.

As an HR strategist myself I subscribe to the view that changing any adult's intrinsic behaviour is a non-starter. I would not expect a shy and introverted individual to make a great, cold-call salesperson. Instead, I would ask what skills and capabilities that individual has and to what extent they can be utilized to further the organization's strategic aims. Alternatively, and less often, I may ask whether an individual has been poorly developed or whether they have been hiding their light under a bushel. There may well be a dynamic extrovert just waiting to get out of their shell and blossom. I would expect any HR strategy to work on the basis that this is always a possibility: employees all have untapped talent and some of that potential can be released and realized. I would also expect the HR strategy seriously to address the issue of removing all obstacles to releasing that potential.

One quite recent development in HR circles has been the growing interest in Neuro Linguistic Programming (NLP) as a method for addressing the personal 'blockages' that prevent individuals from achieving their personal goals. Whether this really has any applicability in an organizational context is still open to debate. However, the inherent assumption here is that individuals can develop and improve themselves with guidance and support. HR strategists may want to take a view on this to either rule in or rule out the use of such techniques. I have my own views on NLP but the HR strategist in me says I welcome any methods that are safe, legal and will add value.

If you do not believe that people can change then there are really only two generic alternatives. You either aim to select the behaviours you need; and that might include consciously finding people who want to be creative and innovative; or you recruit people who want to be told exactly what they have to do. These are very different strategic HR perspectives. They are at either end of a spectrum and would imply totally different HR management policies and techniques. However, if you want to maximize value I know which one I would recommend.

Individually centred HR strategies

But how generic can HR strategy be? Do we have to manage human resources in a generic fashion or can we have a strategy that enables us to manage each employee individually?

Reward policies are a good example to illustrate the point. Job evaluation is still common in many organizations and this could be described as a generic solution to pay and grading issues, because the system applies to all employees. The focus of job evaluation is the job of the jobholder not the individual employee, *per se*. This tends to mean that all employees with the same job title, let us say production manager, are given the same grading. A more flexible HR strategy could eschew job evaluation in favour of rewarding production managers on a totally individual, performance related basis. This could be called an individually centred HR strategy.

As we will see later, the decision whether to adopt a generic or individually centred HR strategy is critical. Usually no clear, explicit decision is made about choosing the generic or individual options. Things tend to just happen by default. So some training courses are generic, others are bespoke or tailored and some employees also receive coaching or mentoring on a one-to-one basis. Consequently, most HR policies send confusing signals to their employees. Do they value them as individuals or are they tarring everyone with the same brush? Is personal initiative and potential encouraged or stifled by this?

Empowerment was a buzzword of the late 1980s and many organizations professed to subscribe to this notion. They saw it as one possible way to unleash latent talents. Yet there is precious little evidence that organizations have really moved away from their traditional, rigid hierarchies, with multiple layers of management, who command and control staff and allow little room for initiative and personal responsibility. So there is still this inherent conflict between the search for value and the need for control. Unfortunately, clear HR frameworks on which to build such strategies are still wanting. Getting the balance right is very difficult so there is a need to formulate individually centred HR strategies that also generate maximum value.

So the need is clear, but are organizations really ready for what HR strategy has to offer?

Chapter 6

Are organizations ready for strategic HR?

By now it should have become clear that real HR strategy is a tall order. Whatever you may have come across under the guise of HR strategy in the past would probably not match the specification being drawn up here. Therefore I think it is very important to view true HR strategy as being a very new subject. By the same token it must be a very under-developed discipline. Very few people can agree on exactly what it is (although by this stage in the book readers should at least start to get a clear idea of one workable version) and, as a consequence, much of HR practice happens by default. Where it is planned it tends to follow the business rather than lead it. Unfortunately, though, the words 'by default' and 'following' do not sit at all well with the concept of strategic thinking.

Instead of strategy, the reality is that we still see large-scale redundancies when a business finally decides to shut a plant down. The strategist would have sorted out long-term manpower planning and would have constantly re-tuned the size and profile of the workforce to business needs. This failure to plan the workforce sends mixed signals about the board's view on their loyalty and lifetime, secure employment. Such default actions can have damaging effects on employee morale, with employees not knowing whether giving complete commitment to their employer would be recognized, never mind appreciated. But then a true HR strategist, of course, would never give employees a false expectation that they had a job for life in the first place.

To move away from default 'HR strategies' to formulated, explicit strategies is a challenge, and we need to understand the extent of that challenge. Effective strategy is the source of competitive advantage and therefore high added value. The organizations that get it right steal a march on their competitors. The downside of strategy is that if it is the wrong strategy then there is an enormous risk involved. While business leaders are used to making strategic business decisions they normally do so based on a measurable or calculated risk. HR seems to present them with something that is unpredictable and, if it goes wrong, it may present a major, internal operations risk; in the worst case scenario people leave or down tools.

Even if boards get past their initial reluctance to grasp the strategic HR nettles, the next hurdle to overcome is to have a systematic method which will give boards a confidence level that their HR strategy will indeed add value, without exposing them to too much risk. This, in turn, leads to the fundamental question – can boards of directors be trained to understand, formulate and successfully implement HR strategy?

One key element in HR strategy, in fact what distinguishes it from mere 'planning', is the timescale involved. Where organizations have a long-term, strategic planning cycle they can hope to have a similarly long-term, focused HR strategy. However, organizational politics being what they are, it is difficult to get consistency in HR strategy. Often the hidden agendas of ambitious board directors may well not be focused on the declared aims and objectives of the organization and others may well be working to different timescales. The classic CEO's dilemma is whether to maximize cash in the short term at the expense of long-term investment. By the time the damage is apparent the perpetrators may be already sunning themselves on their yacht in the south of France. Which brings us to another key element in HR strategy – the principles by which the organization is run.

Back to first principles?

If you asked any employee, in any organization, whether he or she trusted the people running it to look after their interests, I wonder what the response would be? Do employees place much trust in their employers? I have worked with companies that have been taken over by venture capitalists and the lack of trust from the workforce has been palpable because they know what venture capitalists do. They tend to do everything they can in the short term to boost the company's fortunes so that it will be in the best shape possible to sell on to the highest bidder. Needless to say, this does not engender a nice warm glow in the hearts of any of the employees – especially if they do not own shares in the business.

Now a large number of HR people reading this will have already started taking what they believe to be an ethical stance. They see something ethically wrong with venture capitalists behaving in this way and treating their employees so shoddily. So we have to ask whether there is anything intrinsically immoral about the way some businesses are run. Many who work in the HR profession appear to think so.

On the UK-based website UK-HRD (www.ukhrd.com), a discussion forum for those directly involved in human resource development, I generated some heated debate in November 2001 by suggesting that all training and development should generate a business return. Several contributors took issue with this and it led to fundamental questions being asked about the very purpose of employee training and development. It became apparent to me that many of these people worked in their profession for reasons other than to help their organization make a profit. Some went as far as to suggest that profit was a dirty word. This comment made during the debate is a good example of this type of thinking:

> There is nothing inherently wrong with the word profit. It is what we have allowed it to do to our culture, our way of thinking, such that humans seem to take second place to it.

I was genuinely astonished to read this. As someone who has always accepted that the high standard of living in western economies is due, in great part, to profit-making concerns, I know the profit motive can be beneficial. At the same time, I am not naïve enough to think that capitalism is a perfect system. I am only too aware of its flaws and unwelcome side effects. But that is as far as this book is going to go into the perennial debate about economic systems.

The pros and cons of the profit motive are totally irrelevant in this context. The most serious allegation to be made here is that some organizations, whose entire *raison d'être* is the pursuit of profit, seem to employ HR professionals who have a problem with this goal. This means that any HR practices espoused by such people could be promoting behaviour that is totally at odds with the strategic objectives of the business: political correctness taking over from clear-headed business leadership.

If you want evidence of exactly what I mean, we only need to consider two of the latest, big issues (supposedly) in HR circles – diversity and work–life balance. Many businesses now employ people with the title 'head of diversity' or something similar. What HR strategy produced such a role? One that is focused on the real needs of the business or one that is focused on solving some of society's ills. There is no reason why these should be mutually exclusive objectives but any coherent HR strategy will ensure that if diversity and work–life balance are desirable goals then they are mutually inclusive with the other strategic objectives of the organization. Those who see the profit motive as being at variance with the well being of society will never make good HR strategists.

Take the familiar tirade of some traditionalist union leaders, usually found in those sections of the public sector where privatization is looming. They argue that you cannot trust the private sector with such important services as health care or air traffic control. Yet the same union leaders apparently see no irony in the fact that their members, whose jobs they are trying to protect, are swallowing life-saving pills produced by commercial pharmaceutical companies and fly to their holiday destinations with airlines run purely for profit and the benefit of shareholders.

For all I know, the contributor responsible for the quote on UK-HRD may well have an insightful and even prophetic view of the world, but what relevance does it have for the training manager who works in an unashamedly profit-making concern? The purpose of a plc is to make a profit. Whether training professionals actually like these rules of the game or not, it is not their job to try to change them.

Of course, even profit-making organizations will always have other, secondary objectives but if they lose sight of their primary objective, of generating a surplus, then they will not be around long to satisfy any other objectives.

Having said all of this, if employees have any moral dilemma with what their organization is doing then what chance have those businesses got of engaging those same employees in achieving their strategic goals? The principles that organizations adhere to and the values they espouse should be made absolutely explicit in any HR strategy because, if they are not, the human resource will not be properly aligned with the purpose of the organization.

This slippery word called 'value'

HR strategy is an area where emotions run high. One word that is particularly contentious and seems open to as many different interpretations as there are people using it, is this word 'value'. I might *value* my privacy, it is very important to me. I want to bring my children up to share my own *values* (why would anyone want to bring their children up using someone else's values), which might include treating others with respect and having some consideration for their fellow man. Some personal mementoes are highly *valued* and are irreplaceable. A friend of mine had an old car that had been handed down through the family and she *valued* it enormously for the memories she had of going on holidays as a child. Perhaps the simplest common denominator to all of these definitions is that the *value* of something equates to the importance placed on it. Hence, it implies that *value* is a totally subjective assessment.

If we now consider the market *value* of the old family car it is slightly sad to hear that its ultimate market value was nil and she had to scrap it. It did not represent any happy memories for anyone else. Worse still, some vintage or classic car enthusiasts will spend thousands on an old wreck, bringing it back to pristine condition, only to have to accept that their costs exceed the market value of the vehicle. This leads us into the difficulties often associated with personal values being out of alignment with market values. Believe it or not, this is a fundamental issue for any budding HR strategist.

Does your organization, for example, truly value diversity? By diversity, do we mean equal opportunities for all and an organization whose people really reflect the society that they serve? Is this a philosophical question or one of substance? Is it an ethical question or is it business-critical? The head of diversity may follow an agenda that says there is a need to encourage more women to achieve senior management positions but would this be consistent with trying to achieve the maximum shareholder value? There is no reason why these two objectives should be mutually exclusive but, then again, there is no guarantee that they are mutually inclusive either.

One possible argument that should pull both objectives of diversity together is that if talent is rare then the net to trawl the available talent should be cast as widely as possible. Assuming no difference between men and women, or one ethnic group and another, then it makes absolute sense to reduce any barriers to entry for potential talent. The '*moral' value* and the *value to the business* could possibly be the same value at the end of the day. The business performs better and we achieve a more egalitarian society at a stroke. If this were possible it would be hard to see how anyone could not buy into and share the values of such an organization. But the problems really start when employees do not share their organization's values.

If employees do not share the values of the organization we should not expect them to give of their best. Imagine a Greenpeace supporter working for a large oil company or an ardent pacifist working for an arms manufacturer? These are obviously extreme examples to make a point. A more subtle example would be women seeing their employer as failing to offer genuine career prospects, or parents who feel their employer expects them to put the company before their family commitments. Goldman Sachs, famously or infamously, has developed a reputation for being an extremely demanding employer. Admittedly, many partners became seriously rich when the company went public but some observers may have concluded that they had paid a very high price in terms of their family and social lives.

Maybe it is just a symptom of a society getting wealthier that employees can stand back and take a view of what they think of their organization's values. Many of the hygiene factors in our lives are now well catered for and we can afford the luxury of choosing whom we work for and we may even want to influence the values that our leaders subscribe to.

You may be thinking that this is not as much of an issue as I am suggesting. Perhaps the thousands of people who work for the big tobacco producers merely regard it as a job: they do not try to rationalize their choice of employer or employment. Many other people do not have much choice at all about whom they work for, so they see nothing wrong with any company that is prepared to help them earn a living. This is probably true, but the point here is the degree to which such people are genuinely engaged with the strategic aims and objectives of their chosen organization.

To make the point more starkly, imagine the level of motivation in someone who chooses to work for a hospital or a charity, or even feels happier in a public sector rather than a private concern. Admittedly, being very committed is certainly not the same as being effective but it would be difficult to argue against the idea that commitment is a necessary condition for maximum effectiveness.

In short, the real issue is the lengths to which organizations should go to ensure that all of their employees are as committed as possible to a common cause - the business strategy. No doubt many organizations will not bother or will just assume that anyone working for them is bound to have a certain level of commitment. A more cynical view would be that managing and controlling staff, rather than tapping into their latent potential, is still the name of the game, so commitment is not really the main aim.

Such thinking would see no benefit in developing an HR strategy. HR strategy is about getting the best out of people. Taking the time and trouble to ensure that the values of your employees are aligned with the values espoused by your organization. This has to be a critical and integral part of any effective HR strategy. So how do you actually do this?

Organizational value is the organization's value to society

Profit is a measure of our service to the community.

Sir Peter Parker (Chairman of British Rail 1976–81)

I had had this quotation in mind as a key notion in the writing of this book before Peter Parker died on 28 April 2002. His obituary in *The Times* two days later provided some real insights into the mind of someone who could see the connection between running a profitable organization and yet, simultaneously, providing a much wider range of benefits to society than just pure profit.

Peter Parker's words here may make him look like an apologist for capitalism, but he was much too clever to have uttered something that is as banal as it might at first appear. To illustrate what I think he meant, let us consider McDonald's. If McDonald's makes a profit it is because its customers value the service they get. The profound can look decidedly simplistic on the surface. The service McDonald's customers value when they are in a hurry, with hungry kids screaming in the back of the car, is fast food, not haute cuisine. They may have a range of restaurant options to choose from these days but, in a particular location, at a particular time, they decide McDonald's provides just the service they need. Now, some of these same customers may even harbour a secret wish that McDonald's didn't exist so that their children would not have the option to whine about going there, but, nevertheless, they are prepared to pay for the service they get. The day McDonald's goes bust I will know that they stopped providing part of the community with a service they desired.

You might think that using McDonald's as a positive argument in support of capitalism is a very unfortunate choice. Many would argue their products are a culinary abomination and unhealthy to boot. Yet the very people who may possibly be clogging their arteries by eating too much fast food are contributing, via McDonald's corporate taxes, to the welfare of heart patients in hospitals funded out of that taxation. Wealth is created through the profit-making process and that wealth is distributed for the benefit of society.

We should also consider, of course, the employment perspective. Many young people pass through McDonald's every year as casual or part-time employees and, while their tenure may be extremely short (most fast food chains will live with a labour turnover of well over 100 per cent per annum), they earn money and gain valuable experience.

Moreover, for the short time that they are there they normally seem reasonably well motivated. So, without wishing to labour a point, we can see that McDonald's provides value to society in many ways.

The question in terms of HR strategy though is do they get the best value out of their employees? Are McDonald's employees really engaged? Would they believe that they genuinely provide value to society as well as the company?

In Peter Parker's obituary (*The Times*, 30 April 2002) he was described as being 'fascinated by the intellectual attraction and art of management, both in practical terms and also, in a grander context, as the reconciliation of efficiency with what he saw as the "social imperatives" of the community'. Apparently, when he was appointed Chairman of British Rail he waged a campaign 'to persuade ministers to convert the nationalized industry's irretrievable losses into a public service obligation subsidy. Though this made no material difference, it allowed managers to show a profit if they did well, rather than being doomed to failure by the uneconomic nature of the rail industry.'

It is quite clear that Parker was a business strategist and always took a strategic view. Whether he was an HR or 'people' strategist is another matter entirely. His obituary writer concluded that, following the arrival to power of Margaret Thatcher in 1979, with her radical views on how public sector organizations ought to be run, 'In the end he failed to achieve a convincing swing to more efficient systems and attitudes among the employees.' Parker may not have won the argument. Maybe he did not really understand that he would only get somewhere with his ideas if he had a holistic HR strategy. That would definitely have included getting a new attitude towards and from the unions in the rail industry.

Who knows what he could have achieved? I am not a fan of virtual history or 'what if' scenarios, but nevertheless, at a time when Britain's privatized rail system has recently seen some of the worst train crashes in its history; and the track authority has been taken back into public ownership; one can only wonder how different things might have been if Peter Parker had been more successful in his time in the rail industry. Even more interesting is that with regard to '*attitudes among the employees*' we continue to witness serious disruption on the railways through union action, in what has still to be one of the most entrenched unionized sectors of the UK economy. Perhaps if Peter Parker had had a true HR strategist working with him, and followed some different principles, he would have had much more success. Perhaps the state of the British rail industry would be a great deal more efficient and safer than it is today. Oh, and its rail workers much more satisfied and fulfilled as well.

What principles does an HR strategist need to follow?

The Oxford dictionary definition of a 'principle' is a 'fundamental truth or law, a personal code of conduct'. Another way of looking at this is that the principles that people adhere to influence their behaviour. If we get the right principles it follows that we get the sort of behaviour we need to make the organization perform well. HR strategists, therefore, have to understand principles and instil the right principles in everyone who works for the organization.

Admittedly, principles, almost by definition, are difficult to stick to and no one sticks to their own principles 100%. We would all like to stick to the principle that we should tell the truth but every one of us has told a lie at some time; white or otherwise. Even so, having principles that mean something, and continually trying to work closer to them, provides a very solid foundation on which to develop strategic HR excellence. Let us not underestimate the power of having clear and unshakeable principles for a moment: HR strategists ignore them at their peril. Also, these principles should not change much, if at all, over time.

So what sort of principles might we be referring to? Here are a few that could be regarded as the cornerstones of almost any effective HR strategy.

Honesty

How about starting with the principle of honesty. It might be regarded as particularly naive to declare that a founding principle of an HR strategy should be honesty when the morals and dealings of so many public figures leaves such a great deal to be desired. We could all be forgiven for coming to the conclusion that one of the key traits of those who get to the top is their ability to sail as close as possible to the winds of dishonesty (although the collapse of Enron and other large corporations proves that the dishonest often get their comeuppance). Let us not forget though that, as we discussed in Chapter 2, many businesses are very successful without having an HR strategy. HR strategy is not about replacing existing business strategies, it is about making them work even more successfully. Many employees may have no problem working for a company whose head is of dubious moral virtue, but it is another thing entirely for them to want to go that extra mile for such a person.

Honesty starts from the moment a potential recruit gets information about the company. Of course, the temptation in most recruitment literature is to paint as rosy a picture as possible because the objective is to attract people. Yet, if Goldman Sachs conveyed anything other than the fact that it demands total commitment from its recruits it would possibly attract people ill-suited to its own way of working. One City law firm I know of tells undergraduates, at its recruitment fairs, that they should forget about having a social life if they want to join them. This probably means most of their new graduates are self-selecting; an excellent way to recruit.

But following a principle of honesty goes much, much deeper than this. Real honesty means giving employees a true and complete picture of how the business is doing. It means giving employees the bad as well as the good news. Of course, you would tell people this when they joined so that it would not come as a shock to them. Giving bad news actually builds trust and commitment, which is really the ultimate aim of any HR strategy. Yet many organizations that believe they follow a principle of honesty would not dream of giving all employees access to their monthly management reports and results, never mind letting them know when the business is under-performing.

I have yet to meet an organization that even attempts to be perfectly honest with its workforce. But I can say with equal conviction that I would never expect any organization to admit that they have a policy of dishonesty. What possible advantage could that bring? So, in practice, honesty tends to be one of those matters 'best left unsaid'. Employees can make up their own minds whether their employer is honest or not, their perceptions happen by default. If honesty is not part of a conscious strategy though, then a strategic opportunity is completely missed. Also – if the point has not yet been made well enough – as it is principles that guide behaviour, if employees think their employer is actually quite dishonest that employer should not be surprised if this encourages them to be less than honest in the conduct of their own employment.

Added value

Next on the list is a principle that we would expect to be strictly adhered to in every organization, the principle of value, or added value. Every minute of every day, all employees should be asking themselves 'Is what I am doing adding value?' Yes – and if you believe that you will believe anything.

Just as an aside, have you noticed that every time a 'principle' is at stake it seems as though we are being totally naive? Of course employees (all of us) do not think this way all the time. We are just as likely to be thinking about the football game last night, whether our children are all right or where we want to go for our holiday this year. No principle is adhered to 100 per cent: we only have to look at honesty to realize that. Principles are guides. When it matters – in a management meeting; working on a project team; being given a specific job by our boss – that is the time to ask 'is this adding value?'

Moreover, if I know that this is a principle enshrined in the company's policies I should be able to turn around to my boss and ask, without the slightest fear of retribution, how the activity I have been asked to get involved in is adding value. If they cannot explain how it will add value, then I should be confident in refusing to do it.

Now do you see how serious HR strategy is? It really does work its way into the very fabric of the organization when it is done properly. An HR strategy without clear, meaningful principles, that are lived in the workplace, is no strategy at all.

In Chapter 12 we will explore exactly what we mean by added value because it is an incredibly powerful and yet very practical concept.

Individually centred

While we were looking at added value one element of that principle is the implicit notion of individual responsibility. We have already set our course towards the goal of individually centred HR strategies. This means that each individual should be responsible for asking whether they, personally, are adding value. One alternative to an individually centred strategy would be a manager centred strategy, where all responsibility resides with the manager. This would tend to be an organization that tries to perpetuate a command and control-type culture. Where employees are told what to do rather than engaging them in the workings of the business and consciously asking for their input.

Often, when I mention the notion of individually centred HR strategies I add that, in effect, this means that the organization is aware of and alive to the needs and potential of each and every employee. This, on the face of it, sounds ridiculous to anyone who works for a global, multinational organization. The reaction I get is how on earth can a company with, say, over 100 000 employees, spread all over the world, possibly hope to treat all of its workforce as individuals? The simple answer is that if the fundamental principles are the same, and there is a common understanding of what they mean, then all that has to happen is the principles have to be supported and reinforced at every turn. Global enterprises can adhere to global principles, even if local practices vary.

So, if an employee on a project in China wants to question a decision made in America because he or she believes it will reduce value (and of course they have the capability and training to question this), then their resolve, their commitment, even their obstinacy, in essence, their own individuality, should be something the board respects and values. But as we saw earlier with 'value', they will only regard this stubborn behaviour as valuable if it is ultimately in the best interests of the business. Of course, organizations that put a higher value on internal politics and the ego of the manager who made the original decision will not have any time for such shameless individualism.

Surely one key aspect of effective leadership is not only to identify a set of core principles but to make sure that the organization lives and breathes them, especially when the chips are down or someone is challenging high level decisions.

If this is a worthwhile principle though how do existing HR practices match up to it? Lean, flexible organizations need to tap into the potential of each individual. Yet if we look at traditional HR approaches, with standard menus of training courses, rigid job evaluation and pay systems and a view that everyone has to have the same set of competencies, it appears that HR practices are based on a principle of 'consistency' rather than individualism and individual accountability. We will challenge existing HR orthodoxy in more detail later.

Measurement and accountability

Perhaps the biggest barrier to organizational effectiveness is a reluctance to impose personal accountability. This is a principle that has been studiously avoided in the past. If employees are not prepared or willing to accept full responsibility for their own actions they will always be looking for an excuse or someone to blame when things are not going well. So to introduce the principle of personal accountability quite a bit of groundwork has to be done first.

Our first principle of honesty is important because who would accept accountability for improving customer service if they cannot trust the information they are getting about complaints, product recalls and the like?

Our second principle of added value is even more important though. Dealing with customer complaints promptly will not improve customer satisfaction much if the production or technical services teams do not produce quality goods or repair them quickly. The principle of added value means none of the different departments is adding value if the customer takes their business elsewhere. Each department has to accept no sale means no value. This means they themselves, individually, have added no value, regardless of the reasons why this might happen. Apportioning blame in the value chain is pointless if the net result is zero value.

The key to achieving the highest levels of accountability in everyone, therefore, is by getting them all to accept responsibility for the complete value chain (measured in revenue, costs, quality of service and output) rather than just for their own particular link. This means, in effect, that everyone is being measured by whether organizational objectives are being met and whether any profit is made, rather than looking at narrow, departmental objectives. Added value, measurement and personal accountability are the three, interlinked facets of any HR strategy.

So not only is the principle of measurement about measuring added value it is a principle that automatically means cross-functional teams have to cooperate. They cannot hide behind their own specific measures. Accepting the added value measurement principle is an open acknowledgement that the silo organization, based on functional hierarchies, is dead.

All of these principles have to be enshrined in the HR strategy.

Part 2

Getting ready for HR strategy

Chapter 7

An introduction to true HR strategy

What makes a good strategist?

> *The greatest help in setting a strategy is a hefty slice of cynicism and the openness of mind to re-examine cherished beliefs.*
>
> John Harvey-Jones, *Making it Happen* (Collins, 1988)

A strategist does not possess superhuman powers. A strategist is at the mercy of the vicissitudes of life just as much as any other mere mortal. The essence of a good strategist though is in their ability to cope with these vagaries by anticipating them and producing a plan that gives them a much higher probability of defying the odds, especially when compared to those who just take life as it comes. A strategist has to take a risk, but does not have to gamble. An inveterate gambler may have their own system for playing at the roulette table but they can no more influence where the ball drops than they can change the weather.

In fact the weather provides a very simple illustration of the distinction between a strategist and someone who just copes with whatever they have to cope with. Weather forecasters have a whole armoury of techniques and technology to help them predict weather patterns. However, the further into the future they forecast, the more room for error and inaccuracy. At some point into the future, say more than three months, the forecast will, in effect, have as high a level of probability as a guess by an ordinary citizen based on their own experience of weather patterns.

One technique that meteorologists are not so famous for is something called 'hindcasting' – that is, of course, the opposite of forecasting. For example, if a ship sinks during severe weather conditions hindcasting can look at what weather conditions were like at the time, draw inferences as to how the ship got into trouble and also learn some lessons to avoid it happening again.

All of this provides very useful information, but one thing meteorologists cannot do, regardless of their forecasting or hindcasting skills, is actually change the weather. They can only prepare or plan for anticipated weather. A strategist, however, tries to make things happen the way the strategist has planned, or wants them to happen. Strategists are definitely not victims, passive bystanders or impotent observers.

A similar perspective to forecasting/hindcasting is that of the futurologist/virtual historian. I wonder, for example, what future historians will make of our beliefs and actions today? Projecting such views might provide one way of gauging, more objectively, whether we are currently on the right track. Let me see if I can explain what I mean. One hundred years from now, when someone is writing the history of Human Resource Management, they will try to illustrate different trends in HR thinking over the previous two centuries (i.e. the twentieth and twenty-first). I wonder what assessment they will make of the twentieth and very early twenty-first centuries?

My guess is that they will see the first half of the twentieth century as an era when we stumbled around in what was a very new field of study. All of the seminal studies on motivation and methods of production were carried out, but HRM did not even exist as a management discipline. In the second half of the twentieth century, however, there was a move towards explicit HR management methods (e.g. systematic recruitment and selection techniques), but two distinct and separate strands were observable. There was a series of attempts to bring scientific management methods into the world of HRM, such as psychometrics and other forms of formal people assessment, performance management and competence analysis. At the same time, there was a belief that the fundamental design of organizations should change towards treating people as genuine human capital to be developed. So we had many references to concepts such as empowerment, the learning organization and knowledge management.

While the historian may be kind and say our intentions were laudable I think their critical assessment, admittedly with the benefit of hindsight and the complete sweep of HR history, will be that this was very much the early days of trying out these new concepts. Our current attempts at learning and competence frameworks will no doubt be rightly condemned as the pathetic joke that they are. There will be little lasting evidence from this time that any of these new ideas were seriously put into practice or bore any fruit. No, the historian will be able to show that it was only after the first quarter of the twenty-first century that real headway was being made, with new organizations taking shape and achieving significant step change and competitive advantage.

Only then did we move into what became known as the era of 'human capital management'. We had learnt from all the early attempts to empower employees by ensuring they were only empowered when they had been properly selected and developed to make the most of their new-found status. We were only able to do that by changing rigid hierarchies and developing new management mindsets. It was realized in the 2020s that tight controls were in fact a contra-indicator of organizational effectiveness, rather than a positive sign.

On the specific subject of HR strategy the historian will be absolutely clear in their conclusions. There was a great deal of talk about HR strategy but remarkably little substance. The historian may even reach the conclusion that HR strategy, as they will then know it in the twenty-second century, did not exist in the year 2000. This was due mainly to the fact that no one had managed to put a real value on human capital.

Assessing human capital

The HR historian of today can see that as far back as the late 1960s and early 1970s several academics tried to develop methods to put a measurable value on human assets. The general approach though was to apply conventional accounting principles to a subject for which they were never designed, and 'human asset accounting' had a very short life. In effect, they were treating people as just another type of bean to be counted.

From a historical perspective it is easy to view these early attempts at measuring human capital as clumsy. Fortunately, the ideas never really gained a serious foothold in management thinking because they failed to answer the question 'what are our people worth to us?' with any clarity or conviction and did not produce anything of any practical use. But the questions never went away.

Nearly forty years later, measuring people is again becoming a big issue. The same question has been asked with more urgency, particularly over the past five years or so, because there has been an enormous amount of interest generated in the whole notion of human and intellectual capital and the potential that can be derived from effective knowledge management. One of the simplest reasons for this was a growing realization by Wall Street that the market value of an organization is often much greater than its book value or the sum of its tangible assets.

This has led observers to ask what accounts for the difference. This is particularly true of computer software and services businesses where there are precious few tangible assets and the success of the company is almost entirely dependent on the knowledge base and expertise that resides in the heads of the company's employees.

This huge difference between book and market values is usually put down to a catch-all category called 'intangibles'. These would usually include the value of the 'brand' and 'goodwill' but increasingly some are reaching the conclusion that a significant part of this intangible value must be due to 'human capital', that is, the quality of the people in the organization and the extent to which the organization capitalizes on their talents. Fortunately this is rarely, if ever, referred to as exploitation these days.

You may follow the logic here and believe there is some validity in these views. For me, I am genuinely amazed how this line of thinking on human capital has earned so much currency when it is so obviously flawed. Probably the biggest flaw is the basic notion of 'intangibles'.

There's no such thing as an 'intangible'

The word 'intangible' means something that cannot be touched. It is because they have no solidity or exact shape that it is impossible to measure or size intangibles. Based on this definition, it might appear at first sight that 'intellect' is a prime candidate for the intangibles list because it is certainly not amenable to any precise measurement. Yet its potential for value creation is enormous and so self-evident. Hence the conundrum.

Maybe, though, this is not as much of a conundrum as we are led to believe. Following the dictum that 'if you cannot measure it you cannot manage it' the reason for trying to measure intellectual or human capital is so that it can be managed. But do we really need to measure 'intellectual capital' *per se*? Is it not the *results* of the intellectual capital that will tell us whether the intellectual capital is being used productively and effectively?

Consider, for a moment, a pop star writing and performing their own material. Their intellect, artistry and even performing skills may all be extremely difficult to define and measure, except of course in terms of their album sales or concert receipts. Choose your favourite artist and try to discuss their relative merits compared with the chosen favourite of a friend or colleague. As a long-time fan of Leonard Cohen (a choice which usually meets with both incredulity and hilarity in equal parts), I could construct a very convincing case for the quality of his poetry but I guess his album sales have never been in the same league as Michael Jackson. So who has the greatest artistic value? Well, to their record companies this is surely an irrelevant question. It is simply who sells the most – that is all the record company is interested in.

Now, let us move the debate on to try to compare the human capital of all the large pharmaceutical companies around the world. In R&D terms which one has the greatest amount of intellectual capital? GSK, AstraZeneca or Pfizer? Some might argue that you could get a handle on this by counting PhDs or the number of articles published per head of the R&D team. Wall Street would be interested in how many drugs they get through the Federal Drugs Agency but would only gauge them on how well they were selling in the market. Who could take issue with this? It would be a very brave financial analyst who would suggest buying GSK shares on the strength of the number of PhDs in the business without checking their track record at producing successful drugs.

So there is no point measuring anything that does not actually lead to value. Moreover, you can only say that the organization has been realizing the true potential of its human capital when the value actually comes through; when their value is tangible in the hard cash that results from sales or efficiencies. We could say that the only real *intangibles* are those things that have not had their value realized. They are worthless. You cannot touch them because they do not exist. While, on the other hand, you can only refer to the talents of your people when those talents are producing something tangible and real, with a dollar, pound, euro or whatever sign in front of it.

So, what relevance does this thinking have for HR strategy? Well the main strategic issue is whether any of the pharmaceutical companies actually gain a competitive advantage from the way in which they manage their R&D teams? In terms of value generation, do any of them get more drugs to market per unit of spend on R&D than their rivals? To answer this question clearly there has to be a common measure used. The only measure that means anything, that is common to all of them, is the language of market value. That is what HR strategy should be focusing on, and all that a competitive advantage HR strategy can do is increase the probability of any pharmaceutical company getting its R&D team to produce more valuable drugs, more quickly than the rest of their competitors, who will then be managing their own R&D human resources *relatively disadvantageously*.

Should any pharmaceutical company take the view, however, that their R&D capability is an inherently unmeasurable, untouchable 'intangible' this will lead to an HR strategy that is constructed on a very shaky foundation. In practice, this would mean they would have to accept that they would have no measures to gauge the efficacy of their recruitment, selection, succession planning, career development, training, coaching, reward, recognition and employee relations policies. No one will know whether they are adding any value. This means the probability of them actually adding any value will be negligible. If you do not know what success looks like, you will rarely find it.

The lesson for the HR strategist is clear. Accept the concept of intangibles and you will produce an intangible strategy. Embrace the reality that value means nothing until that value is realized and the HR strategy inevitably becomes very tightly focused on tangible results. If you ever want to see, very quickly, whether an HR strategy has any value whatsoever, just ask those who devised it whether it is founded on the premise of 'intangibles' and you will find your answer.

Beware of share prices reflecting human capital

Another flaw in the market/book value view of human capital is the very obvious point that share price determines market capitalization or market value. Share prices in many industries are volatile, to say the least, and can swing in either direction for the flimsiest of reasons (an analyst recommends 'sell') on a daily basis. At time of writing the FTSE 100 is currently at its lowest point for six years. Does this mean the human capital in these organizations is also at its lowest point? This never struck me as a particularly good indicator of the organic value of a business. Organic value comes largely from the quality of the people and how they are organized. Share prices, which can be subject to wide fluctuations on a daily basis, can hardly be said to truly reflect the value of human beings.

Taking a much longer-term view, and in more mature markets, then relative share price may be at least one indicator of a company's ability to get the most value out of its people. In Appendix 1 Toyota can be seen to be beating its competitors hands down in terms of market capitalization. If this were just a snapshot, however, I would not refer to it. Every time I revisit current valuations of automotive companies Toyota seem to be way ahead based on the value of the company. It would be possible to argue that its sound track record and history of improvement and effective management give market analysts a very high level of confidence that this business is going to stay ahead. The financial analysts themselves may know nothing about HR strategy or human capital but the figures they see tell them this is a well-run business. However, I would argue that an HR strategy analyst could point to several key elements of Toyota's business strategy that show a very clear link between the way they run the business and how they manage their people to create very high value.

The way Toyota manages the business and its people are indivisible. If Toyota's business model failed then its HR strategy would also fail. But while its model is succeeding it gains an extra competitive advantage through its HR strategy.

It is also worth mentioning Honda here and asking whether they are beginning to reap the benefits of their HR strategy? They have moved up the league table over recent years. Here is an extract from an article entitled 'The Human Touch' by Gary S. Vasilash in the August 2002 issue of *Automotive Design and Production*. It is about the presentations made at a University of Michigan Automotive Management Briefing Seminar on world class manufacturing (WCM):

> The opening presentation on the second day . . . was made by Larry Jutte, vice president, Honda of America Manufacturing. He runs the company's engine plant in Anna, Ohio.
>
> Jutte said, 'The idea of flexibility with high efficiency is instilled at the very core of our operations – meaning, the culture we are creating with our associates. And that is really one of the bold things about Honda – associates are given the responsibility and autonomy to change anything in their work area or production process. As a result, flexibility at Honda is fluid. I'm not talking just about an equipment process, but synchronization of equipment and associates to achieve high efficiency. Mathematicians might call it 'chaos theory,' in that there are what appear to be irregular or erratic fluctuations in behaviour, but also a seeming order resulting from the process. To outsiders or newcomers to Honda, our way of doing things can appear to be utterly chaotic – a waste of energy. Except that it works.

Does Honda really have a 'chaotic' HR strategy? I will leave you to draw your own conclusions.

So share price, which is already viewed by financial analysts as a rather unpredictable indicator of underlying business performance, has to be treated with particular caution in the field of HR strategy. Share price will only ever be one indicator in a whole range of business indices and good strategists ensure they get as complete a picture as possible before they arrive at any firm conclusions. Over the longer term though, the relative market values of two different businesses will surely reveal the difference between not only their business strategy but their HR strategy as well.

Accounting principles only work for accounts, not people

I am not even sure the present debate on human capital assessment is starting at the right point. If assessing human capital is seen as a business measurement question who better to answer it than those who are supposed to be experts in measurement: that is, accountants and actuaries. The only problem with this is that it is not actually an accounting or actuarial problem that has to be solved. For example, attempts to put human capital as an item on the balance sheet assume that this is the ultimate objective. Presumably this is so that analysts can make an informed choice between different companies, having incorporated a view on their relative strengths in terms of human capital management.

Surely human capital is already on the balance sheet even if it is not explicitly listed. A strategic HR 'analyst' will know when an organization is using its human resource well. The analyst does not need accounting practices to give them any further insights. The Enron scandal should help to demonstrate that even well-established accounting conventions can be subverted in order to create a false picture.

An even more simple accusation that can levelled at the accounting/actuarial approach to human capital is that their 'technology', such as double entry book-keeping, has been around, virtually unchanged, for hundreds of years. Yet they are now trying to shoehorn their methods into an area for which they were definitely never intended. Add to this the inclination of all propagandists to believe their own hype, and we start to see the sort of spurious correlations and conclusions that can be produced from a flawed hypothesis.

Let us look at this issue in more detail by considering one proprietary approach on the market – the Watson Wyatt Human Capital Index[R] (HCI), which suggests that good HR management practices will lead to a successful business.

In May 2002 I spoke at a conference on HR measurement in London (IQPC Conference, 'HR measurement: Building HR metrics into strategic decision making to boost your bottom line', 27–28 May 2002) and followed on from a partner in Watson Wyatt, who was described as the 'author of Human Capital Index Research', explaining their HCI. Looking very clearly through my HR strategist's eyes, I was waiting for him to explain the theoretical basis for this model. The key question is one of causation. Do good HR practices produce good business results or do good businesses spend more time and money on HR practices? Which way does the arrow of causation point?

Either view could be described as a basic belief system. Your answers to these questions will determine how you approach the whole question of maximizing value through your people. In Watson Wyatt's case the answer given by their speaker was that the basic premise of their model was founded in the employee–customer–profit chain theory that we explored in Chapter 5. Their chosen arrow of causation points from good HR practices to good business. Using this hypothesis, their actuaries performed regression analyses to show a correlation between effective HR practices (we will call this HR 'strategy' for now) and successful businesses.

A visit to the Watson Wyatt website (www.watsonwyatt.com) on 24 September 2001 found that in their survey of more than 400 US- and Canada-based companies they say 'we conducted a series of sophisticated statistical analyses and found that there was a clear relationship between the effectiveness of a company's human capital and shareholder value creation. This relationship we found is so clear that a significant improvement in thirty key HR practices is associated with a 30 per cent increase in market value.' However, in Europe in their 'HCI – European Survey Report 2000' they admit that their confidence in their system is not absolute when they remark that their North American HCI 'demonstrates a very strong correlation between effective people practices and shareholder value but on its own it *does not prove a causal link* [my emphasis]. Over time, we believe that continued measurement will ultimately prove that superior human capital management leads to superior financial performance.'

There seems little logic here. It does not matter over how long a period you collect data. The length of time will have no influence on the direction of the arrow of causation. For instance, does private education lead to higher academic results? Measuring A level grades in private schools for a hundred years will not prove that private schools provide a better education. It may be that those who can afford private education tend to have better academic attainment levels themselves and these are inherited by their offspring. So, if all the HCI proves is that good businesses have modern HR practices, then the arrow of causation will keep pointing in that direction, regardless of how long Watson Wyatt keep collecting data.

Business writer Tom Lester, writing in *Personnel Today* (5 March 2002) in an article entitled 'Is HR measuring up?', covering recent attempts at measuring human capital, remarked that Watson Wyatt's 'IC ratio is susceptible to market fluctuation'. He shares my concern that share price is not a true measure of how well human capital is being managed.

According to the same article, another organization trying to prove a similar correlation, PIMS, 'contends that 15 per cent of a company's profit performance is driven by HR strategy' and singles out ten HR factors (listed here from pimsonline.com):

Management participation
Open management style
Take some risks but not too many
Top managers spend 20% of time with customers
About 20% outsiders in top management
The importance of management training
Incentivizing top managers
Succession planning
Good appraisal system
Getting employee feedback

Even if PIMS have identified some helpful practices, it is a bit like telling us that what makes Brazil World Cup champions is the fact that they play the best football. We all know that, but that does not help any other country trying to win the World Cup. What they need to know is exactly what makes Brazil play the best football; their skills, team spirit, management or what? Only then would others have a chance of emulating them.

A similar point was voiced by another contributor to the *Personnel Today* article, Laurence Handy, professor of international business at Tilburg University, in the Netherlands, who was quoted as saying benchmarking on the basis of this model may prove nothing more than that successful companies can afford good management.

It is still very early days in this debate. Whether the human capital measurers will prove to have some of the answers or not only history will tell. My guess is that they will be just another group in a long line of management alchemists who have never actually delivered on their promise of producing gold.

Certainly the BA example given in Table 2.1 (Chapter 2) shows that companies that have been known for their 'best HR practices' have often come to grief. In such cases either Watson Wyatt would have to blame a company's downfall on its HR practices or just accept that the HR practices were peripheral activities. Either way, it would not support the theory behind the HCI.

This is not intended to be a diatribe against the Watson Wyatt HCI, which is just one manifestation of a belief system that suggests there is such a thing as HR best practice. If you subscribe to this belief system, your organization will employ such practice in the belief that it will help you to be successful. If the HCI model or your beliefs are based on a fallacious premise, however, as I am suggesting here, it is a very shaky foundation for an HR strategy.

To produce a solid foundation for HR strategy we need to throw out accounting conventions that were not designed for the purpose and start from a fresh perspective.

It's time to challenge accounting conventions

It is high time a serious challenge was mounted against accounting conventions. Take, for example, a basic accounting concept such as 'overheads'. Anyone working in business comes to accept the concept of overheads because the entire accounts are predicated on this basic building block. While we can all understand the concept in terms of buildings and fixed assets, it has always seemed to me to be less applicable to people. Yet many employee costs are shown as overheads simply because accountants do not know what else to do with them. They also put the company's investment in training and development under overheads, not because they are a true overhead (training and development expenditure is infinitely variable) but because accounting conventions do not have a natural home for such expenditure items.

One of the biggest problems with the term 'overhead' is that it has negative connotations: no one will ever argue for an increase in overheads. If human capital is to mean anything at all then it should be seen as an under-utilized investment, not an overhead. If it is treated as an overhead it will always be constrained for no good reason.

Progressive leaders may genuinely want to believe that the way in which human capital is acquired, developed and maximized really produces value but they have no way of demonstrating this. Therefore one task for the HR strategist is to start developing better methodologies to do just that and not try to patch over the shortcomings of accounting convention. Of course, the business measures we use will definitely involve profit and loss accounts, balance sheets and share prices but bean counting is not going to provide the answers that we are seeking. What we need to do is re-phrase and re-frame the original question on human capital.

Re-phrasing the human capital question

While the wrong questions are being asked about human capital (i.e. how do we show it on the balance sheet), it will lead to the wrong HR strategies. So maybe one way forward is to re-phrase the question. The main question in human capital is not how do we measure it, it is *how do we ensure we get the best value out of it*? Measurement may be a means but it is not the end. If there is a conscious effort to release all of the organization's human potential, and this is expressed in terms of what impact this will have on the bottom line, then we should reach a stage where the bottom line actually improves in the way we want it to. We can then say that we have a level of confidence that we are managing human capital. This is a very simple but very different approach to having to define what human capital is and then trying to measure it.

More important still, I know how to develop an HR strategy that is focused on a tangible bottom line. I do not know how to develop an HR strategy that is focused on an intangible called 'intellectual capital'.

HR strategy is only imperative when people are the only source of competitive advantage

Martin Taylor, who used to be the Chief Executive of Barclays Bank, famously said that a 5-year-old could understand the basic principles of running a business. I presume by this he meant things like getting customers to pay more for your products than it costs you to make them. The best business leaders keep their thinking that sharp, that clear. Unfortunately the principles of HR strategy are too complex to be explained to a 5-year-old, which is probably why they also elude many chief executives.

As we discussed earlier in Chapter 2, in principle, there are only so many options open for a chief executive to improve the business. They either bring out new products, sell their products to a wider market or reduce their costs. Even acquisition or technology-led strategies can only basically achieve the same ends. So these are the strategies they normally pursue and they expect their management to deliver the strategy. So, for example, we see Kellogg's bringing out Nutri Grain bars to start a whole new market in breakfast replacement products.

This might necessitate some internal changes, maybe a new marketing director or head of R&D, but it may never be seen as requiring a fundamental shift in the way the organization and its people operate. It is just another production line or marketing campaign at the end of the day. Even if it was accepted that there would have to be some significant people changes, such as setting up new departments and teams, any plans to achieve this would be just that, plans, not an HR *strategy*.

A true HR strategy would have already been developing organizational capability. Not only the present head of R&D but new talent would have been attracted and retained for exactly this purpose. Key players from competitors may have been poached as part of this strategy. But much more than this, historical product lead times would have been measured and become the focus of a determined effort to search for significant improvement. This, in turn, would be providing information to the business on how well prepared they are to bring out new products, on time, to the right specification and quality.

But not every business is that competitive. As we are all only too well aware businesses that are doing well can so easily become complacent. HR strategy is always a challenge and maybe it is the sort of challenge they can do without. I have often heard VPs of HR complaining about the fact that they have been tasked with bringing about organizational change when there is no business imperative to change. They almost wish for a crisis to give them the requisite impetus for change.

In fact, one of the simplest reasons why HR strategy is so rare is because it is not always required. If, for example, Kellogg's can bring new products to market without any significant changes in the way they work, why should they bother trying to develop an HR strategy? I could argue that this will help them keep ahead of a major competitor (say Nestlé), but if there is no business imperative this may not carry much weight.

HR strategy is much more likely to happen when it has to happen. If we think of markets where this is more likely then we can immediately think of the hospitality industry. Hotels, bars and restaurants face fierce competition and the threat of ever-tightening margins. They are also highly, human resource intensive. This is a perfect breeding ground for effective and innovative HR strategies. Equally, the public sector, which also tends to be human resource intensive, has the added HR issue of not being able to pay the best rates of pay. Here, there is the dual pressure of trying to attract, motivate and retain people to provide important services yet with many constraints placed on them.

One factor that militates against HR strategy in the manufacturing sector is the possibility of simply moving the production facility to a low wage economy. On 27 May 2002 it was reported in *The Financial Times* that Mazda cars would 'lift the proportion of non-Japanese purchasing from 17 per cent to 25 per cent of the total' because they could 'take advantage of low-cost sourcing in Southeast Asia and China' where labour costs are 'one-thirtieth of those in Japan'. Whether they have put in place the sort of supply-chain management systems to cope with this strategy is another matter, and whether an HR strategy has been developed to ensure that this will happen smoothly is another matter again.

I do not know what strategic issues were considered when Mazda decided to seek low-cost sourcing outside Japan. There may well have been no strategic HR thinking taking place at all. This could quite simply be a very obvious, cost-cutting, business decision. In its wake will inevitably follow some HR decisions, the most obvious of which will be to manage redundancies among the workers whose work has been sourced elsewhere. These decisions, themselves, will have to be handled professionally, sensitively and diplomatically, especially if unions are involved. However, all of these subsequent HR decisions will be operational and tactical. The only really strategic HR decision that could have been taken, but was not, would have been to set the entire workforce the challenge of being able to compete on price with their Chinese and Southeast Asian competitors. Maybe Mazda management regarded this as an impossible task and saw no merit in pursuing it.

An even more sobering thought that stems from the sort of decision that Mazda and many other organizations are making is that HR strategy now has to be constructed in a global context. The automotive manufacturers left in the relatively high wage economies of America and Europe will have to develop HR strategies that somehow deliver low prices despite high wage rates; otherwise their business will move overseas. It is inevitable, in a world of increasingly free trade, that production will move wherever the best economic conditions apply. An HR strategist would argue that the best economic conditions may be those where the workers are best educated.

There's no point in following 'good' HR practices regardless of business strategy

We explored in Chapter 2 a prevailing view that good HR practices lead to improved organizational performance. One example of just such a supposed 'HR practice', taken from Watson Wyatt's HCI under the heading 'Resource Management', is the 'use of knowledge workers' cited as 'the most significant contributor to value, reflecting a 2.3 per cent increase in market value for a significant improvement'. Even though I do not buy Watson Wyatt's model I really hope that knowledge workers do make a significant difference. If they did not I might as well hang up my HR boots and do something else.

Workers who possess greater knowledge are more likely to bring with them greater value; just as computer programmers, who happen to have expertise in the most sought-after programming languages, will always command a premium. They tend to be working in organizations that are trying to achieve greater value from the use of the latest technology, hence the connection between high paid knowledge workers and high value businesses. But the employment of such people follows the business's strategy, it does not lead it. There is no point attracting talent if the organization is not geared up to use it – more evidence that the arrow of causation points in the opposite direction to that assumed by those who have a vested interest in saying good 'HR practices' lead to good business.

The reason I have put 'HR practices' here in quotation marks is because I am not sure to what degree it actually constitutes human resource management practice. In what sense is the expertise to be gained from professional HR practices coming to bear on the decision to employ knowledge workers? Let us look in more detail at what constitutes real HR practice and what might merely be the inevitable consequence of a straightforward business decision about which direction the organization should take.

If we stay with the HCI notion of knowledge workers, one of the best examples where high value knowledge workers are to be found is in the R&D department. The designers of the next blockbuster drug could be the saviour of a pharmaceutical business. So what does an HR strategist working for a pharmaceutical producer learn from the Watson Wyatt analysis of HCI? All it tells them is that 'most organizations can benefit from using more knowledge workers to add value to their business'. Taken at its most simplistic, face value the HR department could see this as a green light for recruiting more research scientists. I doubt even Watson Wyatt, or anyone else who subscribes to their view, would suggest for one minute that this just means getting into the numbers game.

Somebody could decide to set up a team of research scientists to do completely blue skies research, with no boundaries or constraints imposed on them at all. For all any of us knows this might lead to the development of the next blockbuster drug. But then again, it might not. Serendipity, chance, luck and fortuitous circumstances can all result in the sort of breakthroughs that organizations can only dream of. The discovery of Viagra by the pharmaceutical giant Pfizer shows just how big a money-spinner such breakthroughs can turn out to be. But the word serendipity is as near as you will ever get to an antonym for strategy. Furthermore, if a serendipitous approach does 'work' it is virtually impossible to go back and understand how exactly the breakthrough was achieved. Organizations cannot learn anything from serendipity for the future and an HR strategy that is not a learning strategy would be very short-lived indeed. Does Pfizer, for example, have another Viagra coming through the system at the moment, having already learned some lessons the first time round?

In practical terms this means that Pfizer would need to know what turned a chance find, while producing one drug, into such a blockbuster commercial success. The right skills for Pfizer research scientists may include breaking with traditional protocols, thinking the unthinkable and challenging existing systems. In fact, if they were able to do this and find that it is a much more successful way of discovering and developing new drugs then the conventional skills of many of their own scientists, and those of their competitors, could be virtually value-less, or, in market terms, worthless. An extremely sobering thought for any pharmaceutical business that does not want to change fundamentally.

So, it is the *strategic* business decision to develop drugs in a particular way, or to use a particular technology platform, or to diversify into a particular area, or to go for organic growth, rather than the pursuit of mergers and acquisitions that will lead to decisions having to be taken about how many knowledge workers are required and what sort of knowledge they need to have. It is also self-evident that brilliantly talented employees come with no guarantee that they will ever achieve their full potential. How many talented researchers at Pfizer have already missed similar breakthroughs because their boss wanted them to work on something else?

We only need to look at the sporting world to see how the most expensive player transfers do not always lead to success in the league. There are many other factors that have an influence on whether an individual's effectiveness can be translated into team and organizational effectiveness. Let us just look at this issue of personal and organizational effectiveness in detail and what the HR strategist needs to know. Even if you get the right person with the right skills in the right job, and that is a tall order in itself, it is still not the end of the story.

HR strategists do not confuse individual and organizational effectiveness

For anyone who has spent many years trying to train and develop employees, at all levels, this fact of life is probably one of the most important lessons they can learn. It is also one of the most difficult to accept. Even if the individual you are trying to train is highly motivated, capable and in a position to make use of what they have learned, there are often many other factors that can come into play, which militate against that piece of training having an impact at organizational level. This means I could be a brilliant trainer (i.e. professional, effective, committed, even inspirational) and yet my efforts are worth nothing if some other organizational constraint nullifies the effect (e.g. the research scientists are not allowed to use their newly learned skills or they have to stick to existing, standard operating procedures).

Take as an example the training of police officers. Basic police training will cover cautioning suspects, how to make an arrest, taking witness statements and collecting evidence. Yet all of this is of little or no value to society if the criminal is not prosecuted or fails to be convicted when sent to trial. Even the most professional officers, who follow the letter of the law and are assiduous in their methods, may see their best efforts come to nought because of a legal technicality or the poor performance of a prosecuting counsel. Society only gets the true value of its investment in the policing and justice system when all parts of the system work well together. Consequently, human resource management has to focus not only on the development of the individual but also, simultaneously, ensure that the other factors, which are the prerequisites for converting their individual efforts into value, are managed as well. It is for this very simple reason that unless HRM is strategic it is unlikely to be of any great value.

In theory, there should be very little difference between someone's individual efforts and their added value. In reality there is often a world of difference. The best example I can give from personal experience was when I had to introduce a job evaluation scheme as Head of HR in a division of a large manufacturing group. I hasten to add that this was a diktat from our group HR office rather than something I had instigated, I could see no value in the exercise at all. Nevertheless, I followed the procedures and during the process my own job, and that of my fellow managers, had to be evaluated. At this stage I noticed that despite having equal, management team status with the Head of Finance, in terms of job evaluation scores his job was regarded as of a much higher score than my own. Yet, if I asked serious questions about the relative 'values' of his role and mine, I was able to put quite a convincing case that said producing financial and management accounting information did not, in itself, actually add any value. (This was certainly the case when it was so obvious production managers were not using the information that was given to them.) On the other hand, selecting good people and training and developing them (to do something with management information, for example) did. Obviously my arguments were not convincing enough. The Head of Finance got a higher scored job because the 'best practice', proprietary job evaluation system said that finance heads were worth more than HR heads.

This may sound like a case of sour grapes, but I know that any job is only worth what the jobholder makes of it. There is no reason why a head of finance could not help to transform an organization by setting up creative management information systems; showing the connections between the performance of the best people in the organization and the bottom line. There is also no reason why a head of HR could not do exactly the same thing. 'Best practice' job evaluation systems usually have a built-in, basic assumption that employees in the same job category are performing satisfactorily. This misses the whole point that different jobholders, but with the same title, can bring vastly different amounts of value to their organization and an intelligent HR strategy has to recognize this.

HR people do not develop the best HR strategies

The chances are that this book will be read primarily by HR professionals, or those who have a need to develop an effective HR function. There may be a presupposition that if effective HR strategies are to be developed then these are the people most likely to develop them. As an HR professional myself, I would like this to be the case, but my experience tells me brilliant HR strategies are few and far between and, where they do exist, this has very little to do with HR professionals leading the way.

This brings us back to a point raised in Chapter 2 when we considered the VP-HR of Verizon's approach to HR strategy. He devised the HR strategy (*sic*) then asked the rest of the senior team what kept them awake at night. Only someone who had a 'best practice' mentality would do this. They believe that best practice HR exists on a separate plane; that the same best practices can be applied in any organizational circumstances. There is an assumed link between these so-called best practices and business performance. Just as my group VP-HR must have thought, I suppose, that grading jobs according to a proprietary job evaluation scheme would inevitably have been worthwhile, in some sort of slightly indistinct, intangible way. Therein lies a serious problem.

One might reasonably expect that good HR strategies are most likely to emanate from those professionals who call themselves 'human resource managers' (see Paul Kearns's book *The Bottom Line HR Function* (2002) for a more in-depth exploration of HR managers' capabilities). Unfortunately, while they may be competent at human resource *management* this does not qualify them as HR strategists. The best practice mindset is common amongst HR managers but HR strategists eschew any notion of best practice. HR strategists see each and every organization as a totally separate puzzle to be solved. They acknowledge the huge number of variables and influences that conspire to make an organization either effective or ineffective. They also recognize that there are always many strategic options available from which to choose; not just a few common practices to follow. In short, the mindset of the strategist is at least one step removed from that of the conventional, practising HR manager. A typical response to this from the HR world is that I am merely making a distinction between HR managers and VPs of HR. As I pointed out above though, the job title has very little to do with the role and the value added by the jobholder.

What makes this particular aspect of the subject of HR strategy even more problematic, and more invidious, is that if you ask a VP-HR whether they are strategic and have an HR strategy they will normally say yes. Their perception is that their HR policies and plans constitute an HR strategy. Ask the same people whether they have a seat on the main board and the answer is no. If HR strategy formulation is not taking place in the boardroom then there is no HR strategy.

So how often is HR represented at board level? Surveys show that few large corporations have someone specifically representing HR at board level. In a survey published by Andersen's Human Capital Practice in September 2001 they found only 17 VPs of HR on the boards of FTSE-100 companies (those same companies whose share price we noted earlier are at a six year low). We then have to ask how many, of this relatively small band are likely to be true HR strategists? More importantly, CEOs needing the competitive advantage that is to be gained from HR strategy need to know where to find good HR strategists. But if the present population of HR people are not doing it, who will?

HR department, function or system?

The HR department is not an island. Its relationship with management, and directly with the employees themselves, is a key determinant of its effectiveness. If they wait for problems to arise they might quickly put out the fire but will always realize that prevention is a better policy. However, any procedures or systems instigated by HR are always going to be at the mercy of the managers who have to use them. So procedures such as appraisal never quite live up to the expectations they seem to offer on paper.

As an HR professional I see all of this as just part and parcel of trying to run an HR department or function. It was only when I found myself dipping a toe in the world of academe, as a visiting lecturer on an MBA HR module at Cranfield University, that I realized HR academics make a distinction between 'HR – the department' as opposed to 'HR – the function' and even something less easily defined, 'HR – the system'. At first this struck me as a typical, academic fascination with semantics but it certainly made me re-visit my own perceptions about my own role as an HR professional and where I fitted into the 'system'.

Let us look at this using a simple example in an organization that is trying to improve relations between employees and management. The HR department angle may well be that an employee relations specialist is employed, whose role is to manage meetings with union representatives, monitor adherence to working agreements and advise managers on any issues that may interfere with creating a constructive and harmonious working environment. Regardless of the ability of this employee relations specialist, at best they will keep a lid on what could become a volatile situation, and at worst, if their relationship management skills are wanting, they can actually jeopardize rather than enhance the operation.

Looking at this issue from an HR-function perspective, other angles would have to be covered. So, health and safety issues would come within the HR function remit because of the risk that any management lapses in health and safety might jeopardize employee relations or be used by union representatives to 'support' any claims for improved working conditions. Even simple matters such as payroll are part of the 'HR function', even if they do not report to the head of the HR department, because this is another possible source of unhelpful grievances if employees are not paid correctly and on time. So the functional perspective is a much more, all-embracing view of HR than discrete specialisms.

You may have noticed though that the way in which I have described this HR function implies that it is still undertaken mainly by members of the HR department. For an HR *system* to be in place all managers would have to be alive to the fact that lapses in health and safety have serious employee relations implications, never mind potential litigation risks. Even senior managers, who may be walking around a plant, would have to be aware of this. If they were to spot any breaches they would have to mention it to someone, and then the 'system' would take over. (Although, of course, a perfect HR system would ensure that no breaches occurred in the first place – but then there is no such thing as a perfect system, HR or otherwise.) Either way, the matter would be resolved. Employees would then see this as a positive resolution, a clear indication that the system was working, rather than a potential source of a future complaint.

You can see why making a distinction between the HR system and the usual manifestations of HR in the form of a department or function is particularly difficult, especially as this is only one small example. If we looked at how an HR system influences employee communications, reward, recognition and retention we could see how it is a prerequisite before we could expect employees to perform to the best of their ability. Moreover, the HR system will ensure that constant feedback on how the organization is doing reinforces many positive messages.

This may now look like we have come full circle and the previous paragraph is just re-stating what HR people would call good HR practices of employee communication and policies on such matters as employee retention. The key point though is that such policies, on their own; without having been integrated into the fabric of the way the organization thinks, behaves and operates; have very little value. Only HR strategy will weave the fabric into a consistent and pre-determined pattern.

Strategy not mere policies

Let us return to the example above relating to employee relations. A key strategic question is 'When was the employee relations strategy formulated?' This same question could be asked about any aspect of the HR strategy such as communications and retention strategies. The second, but equally important question is does the employee relations strategy form a coherent part of a total HR strategy? If, for example, the VP-HR convinced the board that a partnership agreement with the unions was the way forward that may sound like a strategy. However, it is more likely to be a mere policy statement.

The test would be to ask how does the partnership strategy fit, coherently, with the performance management strategy? Possibly one would find that performance management is being resisted in union negotiations. Maybe the intended performance management strategy, itself, was an answer to the strategic business need significantly to reduce costs. So now the partnership policy seems already to be out of kilter with the clear demands of the business strategy or, at least, struggling to deliver it. The art of HR strategy is to reconcile all of these, potentially conflicting, issues and ensure that any solution is aligned with the business strategy.

It might still appear that any real difference between an HR strategy and a series of disjointed policies is more a question of nuance than it is of substance or import. Actually it is quite easy to demonstrate that there is a world of difference. All you have to do is ask a few key questions:

1. What indicators do you have to signal that the HR strategy is/is not working?
2. Who reports on HR strategy progress at board level?
3. If the HR strategy does not work, which strategic business objectives will not be achieved?
4. If the HR strategy is working well where will value be created and how much value will be added?

If the answer to question 1 is an HR function indicator (e.g. staff retention, internal promotions etc.) then the chances are you only have

HR policies. If further evidence is required, then the answer to question 2 will help. If no one is specifically reporting on HR strategy, on a regular basis, it is probably because there is no strategy or, at least, no one at board level sees it as integral to business performance, which amounts to the same thing.

Questions 3 and 4 may look almost identical, or maybe the positive and negative images of the same photograph. In fact they are very different questions and only a good HR strategist would really spot the difference. Question 3 is short term (e.g. how much will we undershoot sales projections because we have not got enough people in place?) and indicates that the HR strategy is focused on existing business plans and this is a minimum requirement for any HR strategy. Question 4 is longer term and is really asking what else might happen, outside of the business plan, if the HR strategy really starts to generate value (e.g. how much quicker can we get future drugs to market if we learn better ways of doing it?). Question 3 is an incremental improvement question, while question 4 is a step change question; it is a question about how HR strategy is supposed to transform the organization. More tellingly, the answer to question 4 should not be a guess but a clear-headed expectation of exactly what will happen and when.

It is also worth looking at Appendix 3 now for a further list of strategic HR questions. If these questions do not give you much more confidence in distinguishing between strategy and mere policies, then maybe you need to re-read the earlier sections of this book.

Viewing the negative

Before we move on, I think now may be an opportune time to relate a short anecdote of what a complete absence of HR strategy looks like. In the early 1990s I met an HR manager in a UK computer chip designer and manufacturer. Admittedly, this was right in the white heat of the computer revolution and by any definition of the term 'knowledge worker' their chip designers were probably right at the top of the tree in so far as they were all extremely highly qualified PhD 'boffins'. So I asked the head of HR what it must be like to try to manage such people, especially when they were so key to the organization's future success. The answer I received was a rather odd mixture I would describe as nonplussed resignation. 'We don't manage them. We just let them do their thing. We even let them choose when they come to work – some of them like to work in the middle of the night and as they are essentially very creative people we tend to let them work whenever their creative juices are flowing.'

Now, I do not know how any other chip companies manage their chip designers and maybe the world has moved on a long way since then, but one I thing I know for certain, if HR let people 'do their thing' they are not using any sort of HR strategy. It is also worth noting that this particular chip company no longer exists.

Chapter 8

Who will develop the HR strategy?

Conventional thinking in HR circles has taken the view that the purpose of HR strategy is to support business strategy. Here, a case has been made for HR strategy as being a source of true added value in its own right. This added value will only come from HR strategy when it has genuinely created a competitive business advantage. Its importance, if it is done effectively, is relatively easy to see. Now we come to the question of who, exactly, is going to make HR strategy a reality?

Basically, there appear to be two broad options if an explicit, conscious HR strategy is to be formulated. Either the CEO understands HR strategy and integrates strategic thinking into his or her own business strategy, or the job is likely to be left to the VP-HR. Although it has to be said that a CEO who does not understand the potential of HR strategy will, at some stage, have to be 'educated'; it would be a nonsense to suggest that an effective HR strategy was in place but the CEO did not understand it or was not driving it.

Do CEOs make good HR strategists?

Stephen Hawking (author of *A Short History of Time*) once said that the most convincing argument against the likelihood of time travel being a possibility is that no one has arrived from a different time to tell us (yes, I had to think long and hard about that one before I fully understood his point). In a similar way, if many CEOs had already cracked the code of HR strategy then people like me would not be writing books on how to do it. Admittedly, HR strategies may be not be as unlikely as time travel but they are still extremely rare. Moreover, we can only assume from the absence of books on HR strategy *by* CEOs that either they have not produced any brilliant HR strategies or, alternatively, they have not identified a role for HR strategy that is distinct from the main thrust of their business strategy. This in turn suggests that possibly they do not see the need for it or do not have the ability to do it.

Jack Welch, formerly of GE, will allude, like many successful business leaders who write their memoirs, to the ways in which they have learned to harness the talents of their employees. He has become famous for many aspects of his business career; not least of which is his strategy of all GE businesses having to be number 1 or number 2 in their chosen markets. But one aspect that looks like the cornerstone of an HR strategy is what he calls the 'vitality curve' (Welch, 2001). Very simply, this is a means for assessing the performance of managers every year and then weeding out the bottom 10 per cent (see Chapter 12 for more a detailed discussion of the practicalities of this). Whether this constitutes anything like an HR strategy though is debatable.

Business leaders are much more intuitive than business schools would have us believe – but the word intuitive may be doing them a disservice. It is more likely their 'intuition' is in fact a blend of distilled experience, complex thought processes, options appraisal and reactions to forces they cannot influence as well as sheer gut instinct. It would be difficult to analyse what 'intuitive' really amounts to but that does not mean we should underestimate how powerful it is. The problem is HR strategy is best done consciously – not intuitively. It requires, therefore, people who have the time and inclination to put in the required amount of conscious effort.

One might assume that this will be HR people – but I doubt it. If HR strategy has not been widely used then it is because HR people have not had the experience or an opportunity to develop the necessary skills. More pertinently, the vast majority of them came into what was, primarily, a purely administrative function. If they were attracted to this as a profession it is fair to assume they did not come into HR to get involved in what must be one of the most problematic areas in business management. Following this logic, my prescription is for a new, hybrid breed of senior HR people who will probably come from operational roles but will require a new skill set. Alternatively, and probably in equal numbers, there are some HR people who have the ability to take on this role but they too will need to develop more strategic, business-related skills.

The sort of personal traits and skill sets required will include:

- being business savvy with high personal credibility
- having an in-depth knowledge of the state of the latest HR thinking
- having expertise in organization design
- being politically astute
- possessing a strategic mindset
- having highly persuasive and influential skills
- having a strong character and being prepared to countenance risk to the same degree as any board director.

This is a tall order and there is no existing reservoir of people with a strategic HR mindset, and the range of skills to go with it, that can be readily tapped. A secondary issue will be freeing up and re-positioning such people to allow them the time and opportunity to actually develop HR strategies.

Developing HR people to take risky, strategic decisions

If there has been a paucity of real HR strategies it might be worth exploring in more detail why this should be the case.

One reason senior HR people do not make strategic decisions is simply that they do not make the big decisions. At best they only implement someone else's decisions; at worst they come up with excuses why they cannot make a decision (e.g. we have to develop a partnership relationship with the union because we cannot remove the union). Conventional HR people tend to be highly risk-averse, they generally work out how to avoid risk rather than confront it. They have spent their lives advising other senior managers of the potentially disastrous consequences of failed industrial relations, inconsistency in pay and reward schemes, possible litigation from disgruntled employees or of what might happen if employees decide to leave in droves. If any of this could be called an HR strategy it would only be a risk-avoidance strategy.

Admittedly, HR is not just about avoiding bad news. The very positive side of HR usually involves trying to bring about organizational change for the better. This plus side covers an extremely wide spectrum of 'HR interventions' including the use of employee surveys, competence frameworks, learning initiatives and change programmes, to name but a few. The HR strategist will know, however, that unless all of these interventions form a complete whole there is little likelihood of them achieving any lasting change. This has not stopped most organizations, however, indulging in such activities in the vain hope that they might make a difference. But that is not the most serious issue.

We could debate at length whether any of these activities produces any results or not, but that debate would prove to be inconclusive and rather sterile simply because it would be virtually impossible to get any two senior HR people to agree on what constitutes a 'result'. It is this failure to reach a consensus on how to measure results in HR that has completely undermined any notion of HR 'professionalism' over the past twenty years or so.

Most professional bodies, worthy of the name, have a governing body that can be the arbiter of the standards and quality of those who work in the profession and, fortunately, it is still extremely rare for anyone to be struck off. Nevertheless, we have all witnessed the medical profession dealing with malpractising doctors and the governing bodies of the legal profession calling bent lawyers to account and disbarring them. Being professionally qualified, in itself, is no guarantee of integrity. In HR, however, there are thousands of people practising without being on any 'register'; moreover there is no 'General HR Council' to set standards and distinguish clearly between what constitutes best practice and malpractice. Consequently current HR 'strategies' can include all sorts of practices and there is no authority to act as their judge.

It's not the HR practice it's the environment, stupid

So what sort of practices might I be referring to? Well there are many questionable practices to choose from. We have already debated the merits or otherwise of competency frameworks (see Chapter 5), so how about something like psychometric assessment tools? Do these represent best practice or malpractice? When such instruments were first introduced into the mainstream business arena they were hailed as a scientific way to select and recruit the most suitable candidates for a particular role. So the first question is, do they work? Second, do they work for you?

These are two totally different questions. The first simply asks whether, in a controlled environment (i.e. the same candidates, the same job vacancy etc.), psychometric assessment will help you to pick out the most suitable candidate from the group of applicants. The only way you will be able to suggest that these techniques have worked is when the individual chosen performs well, or well enough, in their new post. This evidence, however, will never tell you that you picked the *best* candidate in the circumstances; it tells you nothing about what you missed by failing to choose one of the other candidates. If you collect this evidence regularly though, across a range of roles, and compare it to situations where psychometrics were not used, then maybe you will start to see a trend suggesting that psychometrics helps you to get it right more often than not. Many HR tools are about increasing probability not certainty.

Regardless of the theory, and the claims made by psychometric analysts, anyone who has used psychometrics regularly will know that, at best, it is a very inexact science. In general terms, the more track record that you have to go on for a particular candidate and the more senior the position then the less importance should be attached to psychometric results. Senior roles are, by definition, quite complex roles to fill. Their span of control influences other people and their position may be situated at a crucial, organizational intersection (the product developer interfaces with research, production and marketing, for example).

Here, the issue is not whether the person selected can do the job in splendid isolation, but whether they are capable of fulfilling the role in reality. Their *fit* with the organization's culture and values is of paramount importance, as is their working relationship with those who directly report to them as well as their colleagues from other departments. They only have to fail in one of their working relationships (e.g. arguments with production about how to make the new products are never resolved) and this may mean that this person has failed the organization in their role.

No doubt the psychometric specialist would defend their tools by saying they can only serve the purpose for which they were designed. They are not a magic bullet. This is true, of course, but where does the responsibility lie for making sure every part of the equation is put in place to reach a satisfactory solution? Only the HR strategist will have such a broad brief and be in a position to cut across inter-departmental squabbles and, where necessary, remove those who are getting in the way of creating organizational value. After all it is only organizational value (in this case the new product is successfully produced and launched) that will give a clear indication of when things are working or not working according to plan. Anyone who suggests their 'bit' of the plan is working fine is missing the point.

Not knowing what works leaves the door open for the 'crazies'

Psychometrics was just one example, for illustrative purposes, of what is a general point. Any HR tool or technique, activity, initiative or intervention cannot be judged on its own merits. It can only be judged on the organizational result to which it contributes. If there is no value added then the activity in question, by definition, has added no value. Blaming someone else for failing to use the techniques correctly may be a lesson for the future but does nothing to improve existing value.

This is a very difficult lesson to learn for anyone who is making a living out of any of the amazing variety of fads and new ideas that come onto the market every year. I have my own personal opinions as to the likelihood of any of these panaceas actually working or not, in any sense of the word. However, I am on much safer ground if I challenge them to demonstrate their results before I draw any conclusions about their efficacy. The only provisos I would add are that any HR practice should be safe and legal (and ethical, I suppose, but I do not want to add another chapter just to define what constitutes 'ethical'). Other than that, as long as the intervention can clearly be seen to be adding value then I have no objection to any new idea, however outlandish some of them may appear.

Many training and development practitioners use all sorts of motivational exercises these days. One of the wackiest is fire walking across hot coals. So is this best practice, just harmless fun, or malpractice? Are the purveyors of such methods insightful or just crazy? Applying the simple results test will elicit some 'success' stories, including some from those who have taken part in the programme. It may even have been a life-changing experience (of course, this could be negative as well as positive).

Yet, if you ask for specific instances where the programme produced a real, added value result many of the stories will fail to produce the evidence. But even if, on occasions, you do hear how a manager produced some real results after the programme, this is usually more to do with serendipity than planned improvement. Moreover, if you push the providers of these programmes to indicate how they might add value, a priori, *before* the programme starts, they will have no clear line-of-sight planned for how any participant is expected to produce greater results after the programme. These programmes are not aligned with the business strategy in any way. Some may even argue that this is precisely the aim of such a programme, it is intended to generate creativity and innovative ways of doing things. They would even suggest that there is something very constricting about having pre-planned, pre-ordained improvements in mind before you try to develop managers.

This is a very clever sales pitch and sadly there are still many wannabe emperors around who are proud to show off their new clothes. None of them, of course, are HR strategists though. They are working to the probability theory that says give an infinite number of monkeys an infinite number of word processors and one of them will produce the complete works of Shakespeare. I am sure that is true but none of us employs an infinite number of people and we do not have infinite resources to throw at them. Therefore we have to make choices about priorities and methodologies.

When is a profession not a profession?

The biggest problem with serendipity as a means for managing human resources is that it can be used to legitimize almost any HR practice. If you do not know, in advance, what is expected to happen then absolutely *any* intervention has the same chance of succeeding (or failing, of course). It is a good job that the members of the medical profession do not run themselves on this basis otherwise everybody would be on regular supplements and medications, regardless of our own real needs, in the vague belief that some of us were bound to benefit.

This is a very serious and damning criticism of some HR 'professionals' and what masquerades as good HR practice. The maintenance of professional, quality standards is entirely dependent on outlawing practices that follow no code. Without publicly challenging the intent and efficacy of some of these practices they gain tacit approval and any 'profession' that legitimizes all of the practices of its members, through tacit approval, is no profession at all. What this really means is that such practices are not taken seriously. If they work, great. If they do not, who cares? Not really a basis on which to develop HR strategies that are taken seriously.

This is not meant to be the start of a witch-hunt. Many HR professionals and consultants offering their services have integrity and produce meaningful and lasting solutions to problems that are often intractable. The issue here is how will anyone know that they are using practices that have any chance of success. The only sound principle to follow is *caveat emptor* (let the buyer beware). The quality of the HR strategies developed by organizations will be only as good as the questions they asked. Vague and nebulous questions (e.g. how well do we work in teams?) usually result in vague and nebulous solutions (e.g. 'teambuilding'). Unfortunately, senior managers are not very good at articulating their most difficult HR issues. So they are often willing purchasers of pre-prepared solutions that look like they might help but they will not have clearly defined their problems first.

Diagnosing HR cause and effect is notoriously difficult but a clear and focused questioning technique should be capable of producing the correct solution. The key question should always be 'how will this add value?' That, in itself, leads on to the next question of what actually constitutes 'value'? Value is a word that appears to have numerous meanings for many stakeholders, all with differing viewpoints and perceptions. HR people know all about organizational 'values' and regard that as somehow soft and cultural. To a line manager added 'value' is hard and only comes from doing more with less, increasing revenue or reducing costs. While the customer only perceives value in the 'value for money' sense. The trick for the HR strategist is to make a connection between all three.

The 'intangible' has to be made tangible

So does a command and control culture, and the values that go along with that, normally result in excellent levels of customer service at the right price? My honest answer is that I do not know. However, there seems to be an automatic assumption behind most change management programmes that flexible, no blame cultures lend themselves to improved customer service. This may be true (I hope it is), but unless it is absolutely clear to everyone concerned how 'change management' is going to add value then where is the motivation for bringing about the necessary change going to come from?

'Change agents' often try to articulate what behaviours will be evident in a no-blame culture. They talk about stimulating innovation, sharing knowledge and improving responsiveness but rarely, if ever, do they use hard figures to back up their theory. The added value question asks where will the hard results start to show up in such an organization? In higher output, lower costs or customer feedback on quality and service? It also, immediately, begs the question of 'what measures do we have in place to gauge this shift'? Funnily enough, the required measures are often not already collected – which leads to the obvious but slightly embarrassing question of what prompted the need for change in the first place?

Not all change is for the better and change without progress is pointless. Questions on anticipated, measurable outcomes should ensure that change actually adds the sort of value everybody is seeking.

Chapter 9

HR strategy and change management

That perennial topic of debate – change

> *There is nothing more difficult to handle, more doubtful of success, and more dangerous to carry through, than initiating changes in a state's constitution. Because the innovator makes enemies of all those who prospered under the old order; and only lukewarm support is forthcoming from those who would prosper under the new. Their support is lukewarm partly from fear of their adversaries, who have the existing laws on their side, and partly because men are generally incredulous, never really trusting new things unless they have tested them by experience.*
>
> Machiavelli, *The Prince* (1995: 6)

What is the most talked about subject in organizational management and yet with very little evidence of any significant progress? The answer is simple – change. The word says it all and yet tells us nothing. The organization has to change – but change to what, how, when? What will happen if change does not take place?

If the term was altered to 'progress management' that would be an entirely different proposition. If you manage progress you should know whether you have moved forward at all. Even if you do *manage* change, you still have to decide whether or not it was for the better.

Machiavelli still gets a very bad press for someone who seemed to possess a profound understanding of some of the universal, enduring, fundamental truths about human nature. Not only was he especially good at identifying the least admirable qualities of human behaviour but, to compound the crime, he knew how to use this understanding to his masters' best advantage. On change management and innovation his words ring as true today, in most organizations I know, as they probably did when he wrote them 500 years ago. I cannot improve on Machiavelli's words, but I would like to re-emphasize that anyone embarking on a programme of changing the way people work in organizations faces some enormous challenges. Only a strategist, therefore, will have any chance of achieving any significant, lasting change. The text following the quotation above goes on to advise that 'all armed prophets have conquered and unarmed prophets have come to grief'. This, of course, does not mean to say that the HR strategist bent on change will have literally to take up arms – only metaphorically.

Change management and HR strategy are almost synonymous. Without the need for change there is no need to produce an HR strategy. Business as usual just requires an operating plan and more of the same. If the main purpose of HR strategy is to create a competitive advantage through people it implies that you have to change the way you manage those people. That does not necessarily mean, however, that the people themselves have to change. It may well just mean changing the people, in the sense of bringing in new people.

Ask anyone running a 'change management' programme what their business objectives are and you might, if you are lucky, receive a reasonably clear answer. Banks have to change because new banks offer better customer service. Retailers have to change because consumer tastes and shopping patterns have changed. Pharmaceutical businesses have to change because of a tighter regulatory environment. Oil companies have to change because of the environmentalist lobby.

These are all valid reasons why organizations believe they have to change the way they operate. There is an assumption hidden in there though that suggests this change is dependent on changing the people, in both senses of the word. However, ask exactly how the people in the organization need to change and the answer you get this time is likely to be much more nebulous and broad brush: 'They need to be more customer focused'; 'we need people with a "can do" attitude'; 'we need a knowledge sharing culture' or even 'managers should not just be task driven'. There may well be validity and an element of truth in all of these statements but any observer would have to admit that the words used are very non-specific and the statements are broad generalizations. It would be difficult to say exactly *who* was not very customer focused and, most important of all, none of them suggests what the solution to these problems might be.

But perhaps I should modify that last statement. These broadbrush statements from senior management are indeed the suggested answer to a very indeterminate problem. If sales are down one conclusion that could be drawn from this, valid or not, is that the organization is not focused on giving customers what they really want. It is then only a short, logical leap to suggest that everyone in the organization should become much more focused on understanding the real needs of potential customers.

This is why change is both open to so much debate and yet produces such little positive progress. Problems that are not clearly defined result in misdiagnosis. Also the solutions sought are generic change programmes because that avoids anyone actually taking clear responsibility for change. Furthermore the change management programme itself has no buy-in or commitment from any employees because they do not know exactly why or how they should change.

The myth of 'change management'

Any student of economic history (myself included) will readily acknowledge that societies have always been through fundamental change. No doubt cave dwellers thought twice about building a simple hut and many others waited to see if they survived before they joined them. There is nothing new in change and the ability of people to adapt to change. The only real difference is that today the rate of change is probably faster.

At a Chartered Institute of Personnel and Development (CIPD) conference in June 2002 in London I listened to a speaker from the Tomorrow Project talking about 'What can we do to shape a better future of work?' but with a subtext that said this was as much to do with the 'future quality of life' as well as work. His introduction referred to dealing with the challenges of the 'new economy. This 'new economy' seemed to be referring to the IT and telecoms markets. They are indeed still young markets in comparison to many more mature industries but in what way are they 'new'? They are actually very similar to any other industry in the sense that they provide employment opportunities. They may require new skills, but if that means they form a 'new' economy then we must have had new economies on many occasions before. This struck me as very similar to the multitude of commentators around on the subject of 'globalization'. They are both 'big ideas' that sound so relevant but when you try to find the reality behind the universal statement there is actually very little of substance with which you can begin to work. This is not an uncommon failing.

In an article in the *Financial Times* (27 May 2002), under the heading 'The workplace revolution that never happened', Stephen Overell explodes many of the modern-day myths about work and the workforce. Samples included reference to the much vaunted idea from writers such as Charles Handy that full-time employment was on the wane in the west and this would lead to a rise in self-employment and portfolio careers. Yet the UK government's latest Labour Force Survey (2002) shows 2.5 million people (8.8 per cent of the working population) are full-time self-employed compared with a figure of 2.6 million (10 per cent) a decade ago. Similarly the forecast rise in temporary workers has not really lived up to expectations, having increased only from 5.3 per cent in 1984 to 6.5 per cent in 2002.

One particularly interesting statistic is the amount of movement in the job market, or should I say the lack of it. Many HR commentators have been warning of the importance of retention strategies yet it appears that most employees do not move around much more than they did a generation ago. In 1975 the average length of service was six years and one month. By 1995 this was five years and six months. A modest change, admittedly, but not really on the scale that the most doom-mongering forecasters had predicted.

Maybe there are a few key lessons that any aspiring HR strategist should learn from this:

- make sure of your facts before you start developing an HR strategy based on forecast trends
- avoid following the latest big idea on the conference circuit
- make sure your own HR strategy concentrates on your own organization's circumstances rather than what might happen in the wider labour market.

Can people change?

So change is problematic at the macro level. What about at the micro, individual level? The people I have known well for over thirty years do not seem to have changed in any significant way at all. They get older and wiser but, as a rule, their personality seems very constant. I can think of a few exceptions, but then usually there are exceptional circumstances in play, such as those who had a very sheltered or cosseted childhood. One or two also decided they wanted a complete life change when they decided their chosen career was no longer right for them.

Now, you may have just read the paragraph above and said to yourself that my views are personal to me with no solid foundation in any academic or empirical research. And of course you would be right if you did think this. Whether we are trained psychologists or not, we all tend to have our own views as to whether people can change. But never underestimate the fact that my own view of the world influences how I deal with the people I meet. If my perception is that people do not change then I will not attempt to change them. Moreover, whether my own perception is right or wrong, you would have great difficulty in changing a view that I have formed, shaped and had reinforced many times over the past forty years or so. Let us also not forget that everyone has their own perception on the subject of people and change and most of those views will probably be as unshakeable as mine, or yours.

There will always be arguments on this subject by virtue of the fact that we all have our own, personal, unshakeable beliefs. Treading on other people's belief systems is a sure-fire way to start an argument. I remember having one such argument some years ago with a senior management colleague on this very subject. He had his own favourite anecdote to support his view that people can and do change. He related a story about a manager who used to work for him who had a serious drink problem. The manager's work was suffering as a result and after many sympathetic, but failed, attempts to get him to change his drinking habits this colleague finally gave him an ultimatum. He had to choose between drink and his job. Apparently this did the trick, and the manager actually became teetotal and resumed his pre-boozing performance level.

I was as unconvinced at the end of this tale as I was at the start. For me, this was not a tale of personality or behaviour change; it was a description of somebody who, for a variety of reasons, had developed a drinking problem that was out of character. What this colleague had managed to do was to shake the manager out of this and help him revert to his normal mode of behaviour. As you can guess, my colleague and I both satisfied ourselves that we had won the argument and then allowed our conversation to degenerate into a semantic discussion on the meaning of the words 'change', 'personality' and 'behaviour'.

Debates on issues such as these can easily become tedious, so it is a good idea to get agreement on something. I find that no CEO could argue with the model in Figure 9.1. This model is often used in employee attitude surveys and it suggests very clearly what dangers lurk beneath the surface of a seemingly compliant workforce. Terrorists are those employees who feel they have been so badly treated by their organization that they are capable of doing damage. Mercenaries are all right as long as they are on your side but they may join the opposition tomorrow. Hostages, on the other hand, may not actually create havoc but they certainly feel trapped; not a particularly positive aspect. The common aim should be to create an environment for apostles.

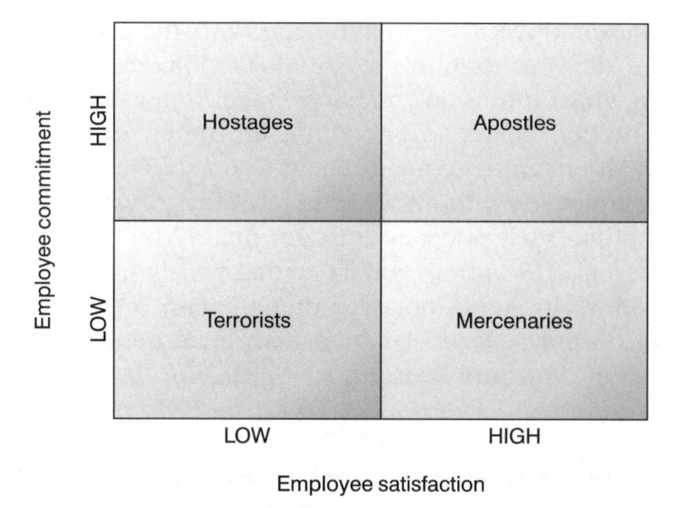

Figure 9.1 Are your employees hostages or terrorists?

Whether we can create the environment so that our people feel positive about whom they work for is the challenge for the HR strategist. However, even attempting to change behaviour is a rocky road with many potholes.

One thing absolutely guaranteed to get you on the wrong side of your employees is to suggest to them that their behaviour needs to change. Most of us are reasonably comfortable with who we are. We are aware of our strengths as well as our weaknesses and we have probably spent many years perfecting our own way of getting through the world within these constraints. Not only are we very reluctant to change behaviour patterns, especially those that have been sculpted out of hard won experience, but we probably could not change much even if we wanted to.

I would go even further by suggesting that 'can we change behaviour' is the wrong question. We do not need to change behaviour *per se*. The aim of a good HR strategy is to ensure the organization has the right people doing the right things to deliver business strategy. If you are running a restaurant chain do you try to train staff to be nice to the customer or do you employ people who naturally enjoy working with the public? You want the natural behaviour of those who have a natural warmth, an eagerness to please and give good service. You do not intentionally recruit awkward, unfriendly and aggressive staff.

This is fine when you are in a position to work on a greenfield site or open a new branch of your restaurant chain. What do you do though with existing employees who have been with the company for some time? Maybe the organization they originally joined has fundamentally changed? So what options do you have? One is to find those who already have the new behaviours you need, create the environment in which they can use them and encourage them to do so. The second option is to replace employees without these behavioural preferences with new recruits who do. What other options are there? The third option is the only non-strategic HR option: you try to make a silk purse out of a sow's ear. This is not really an option, even though many organizations pursue the line that putting staff on change management training courses is the answer to all of their problems.

Adapting existing behaviours to organizational needs

I sat in on just such a training session being rolled out to 20 000 employees in a large retail organization. This was after it had carried out a root and branch review and re-branding exercise in the face of fierce competition. The programme was about developing a different relationship with their customers. As I waited for the event to start I asked some of the staff who had turned up what they expected from this programme. The first person I spoke to was a fork lift truck driver who worked in the despatch bay. He did not know what the programme was about and when I explained he said that in his job he never met customers.

The majority of participants were shopfloor assistants, however, and from a brief chat it was clear that they represented an entire range of levels of interest and motivation. Some had been with the company for over twenty years; they had been with the business through the good times and the questions from one or two of them during the training session displayed a very negative attitude. On the other hand, there were some with equally long service who were naturally warm characters and were willing to give the new ideas 'a go'; they had a very positive attitude.

This is probably close to the reality of 'change' programmes in many organizations: the universal 'sheep dipping' of staff. They may not all have ticks and fleas but it might have the desired effect on some of them, even if that effect is indistinct and difficult to pin down. It has to be said of whoever dreams up programmes like this though that it is an admission that they have failed to develop any sort of coherent strategy. The strategist would know that some of these employees are no longer suitable for the new world order and take action accordingly. They may reorganize so that only staff who really like the interface with the customer have to work there. No HR strategist would treat 20 000 employees as a homogeneous group, even if they were aiming to create a common culture.

Is HR strategy culture-dependent?

When I spoke at a large European HR conference in Lisbon in 2002 (the 34th global HRM conference, 22–24 April 2002, run by Management Centre Europe) I was very interested in the feedback I received from the 500 or so delegates. Although it was meant to be a truly global conference, in terms of the composition of the audience, the majority of them were from European countries and the Middle East. One remark that came up several times was that the speakers at the conference were too UK and US focused; delegates wanted more speakers and case studies from other parts of the world. This may reflect a genuine need for greater cultural relevance or could simply be a matter of national pride, although it is probably a combination of both. Nevertheless, it highlights an extremely important question in HR strategy: is HR strategy dependent on the culture in which it has to work? This is particularly important today in an era of increasing globalization.

As someone whose own formative background in HR was predominantly based on UK experience I would be the first to admit that there are many factors present in the UK that have shaped the way HR has evolved over the past twenty-five years. This would include the 'Thatcherite' revolution that fundamentally changed the power of unions, a cultural shift towards self-dependence and a more recent development of an emphasis on performance measurement and management in all walks of life. This provides a platform for HR strategists working in the UK to introduce ideas that may not be possible elsewhere.

In the US it is no surprise that diversity is now such a big issue when one considers their context from a historical perspective. Also the whole American ethos of self-reliance and rewarding those who perform tends to put reward mechanisms at the front of many HR initiatives and places no restrictions on those who are really ambitious to succeed. This is still very different to the UK and again it tends to put a different flavour on HR strategy.

No doubt we could travel around the world and find all sorts of local differences and cultural nuances just as we might find different styles, flavours and personal preferences for wine, but would the main constituents be similar? Are there similar, basic ingredients to be found in all HR strategies? Should local tailoring of HR strategy be fundamental or just about a different flavour or presentation?

Not long after the Lisbon conference I was running a workshop on HR benchmarking in Athens to an entirely Greek group (albeit working mainly for multinationals). The average age was relatively young, probably late twenties, and I asked whether anyone had a title of 'Personnel' or did they all now subscribe to the HR label? With only one exception, a woman who was probably older than the rest of the group, they all said that they used the term HR. The single dissenting voice pointed out that the word Personnel had been in use in Greece for some years before that. As the workshop wore on and we discussed the maturity of HR thinking in Greek organizations (see the maturity scale in Chapter 4), it was apparent that whatever the group called themselves there was a wide difference in approaches to HR. The level of maturity seemed to be influenced by whether the organization was part of a much larger, international corporation and how well their HR practices had travelled.

I only quote this one anecdote in support of my view that the fundamentals of HR strategy are not culturally dependent. The fundamentals of HR strategy are the recognition of a need for a clear business strategy and then the production of competitive advantage through the way people are managed. These fundamentals do not change and neither do the principles of measuring the effectiveness of HR strategy – either it is measured in terms of added value or it is worthless.

At a more operational level though, the Greeks at my workshop discussed a particular issue during the lunch break – the importance of the siesta in Greek society. Would this 'people' issue be of strategic importance to Greek companies? Would any multinational corporation thinking of setting up an operation in Greece spend much time considering this one? I doubt it, but it would have to be considered and maybe even sensitively managed locally when the HR strategy was about to be implemented.

Part 3

Developing and implementing HR strategy

Chapter 10

First steps towards HR strategy

Parts 1 and 2 have prepared the groundwork for developing and implementing HR strategy. This final third of the book is about actually doing it. This proportional split between preparation and implementation is entirely intentional.

'Doing' HR strategy is two-thirds preparation and one-third implementation. However, the whole thing includes every step from establishing the principles and concepts right through to reorganizing roles. Take away the planning and preparation phase and there is no HR strategy. Plus, we must not forget that the 'planning' bit has more to do with articulating an HR philosophy that encapsulates the organization's values, than it has to do with specifying which strategic business objectives are to be achieved. An HR strategy that does not reside firmly in the mindsets of all the main board directors will be a failed HR strategy, regardless of the clarity of existing organizational objectives.

Notwithstanding all of this, Part 3 will look at the practical tools and techniques that can be used to ensure HR strategy transforms the organization. Conceptually, HR strategy is difficult enough; practically it can be a complete nightmare. This is why it is more common to read books on the conceptual aspects of the subject than it is on implementation. It also helps to explain why discussion of HR strategy implementation is invariably undertaken after the event, with the benefit of hindsight. Here we are going to suggest how to do it in the future. So where exactly do you start?

HR strategy starts with a destination and a direction

My apologies for answering my own question with a negative, but you should *not* start to try to develop an HR strategy by organizing an 'awayday'. I recall being asked by a group of workshop participants in the Middle East what I meant by this word 'awayday' and I found it incredibly difficult to define; the more I tried, the more stupid it sounded. I described it as a day where a management team go away together to take a fresh perspective and develop new ideas and ways of thinking. I could see by the looks on their faces that this definition described a rather pointless exercise. New ideas to do what? Why do you have to go away?

Strategy, to many people, implies blue skies, unfettered, boundary-less thinking. They think it has to involve a group of managers brainstorming ideas, usually with a 'facilitator'. But why? At the very beginning of this book I suggested that the ultra-complexity of strategic thinking means few people have the talent to do it properly. The best strategies are those that are held completely in one person's mind. Adrian Furnham, Professor of Psychology at University College London and an outspoken critic of modern management fads, said in *The Sunday Times* on 29 September 2002 that 'Without doubt the greatest mythology about meetings is that they are useful for generating innovative ideas . . . Study after study has shown that brainstorming meetings produce fewer quality ideas than individuals working on their own.'

Of course, I know what management teams tend to mean when they say they are planning to have an awayday, but the actual purpose of these events always seems unclear. But then maybe that is the point. Whatever the actual derivation of the term, in the UK the 'awayday' was originally a type of train ticket, launched as part of a marketing campaign by British Rail. The concept was that the destination didn't matter too much, the point was just to get 'away' for the day. Anywhere. Away from where you are. It was intended to be a day out, a bit of fun and there was also a subliminal message that it was an opportunity for family bonding.

This is the reality of most management awaydays I have witnessed: a fun day with an indistinct effort to aid team spirit. The participants have no particular destination in mind or even a route map. Sometimes these events are intended to give managers time, especially thinking time, that increasingly scarce commodity that George Mathewson of the Royal Bank of Scotland guarded so jealously. It is a curiously seductive concept. If that is their purpose, then I suppose it sounds just the sort of thing some management teams could do with.

What bothers me, however, is the very idea of going 'away' to develop HR strategy. It is so artificial. When everyone is away from the workface it is easy to forget all the barriers, obstacles and frustrations that are part and parcel of our daily working lives. Without these constraints it is relatively easy to achieve a temporary 'high', a feelgood factor that will always make such events popular. Also, because the fun and the 'high' are seen as crucial elements, the facilitators chosen have to be 'inspirational' or 'motivational' speakers. As any effective trainer knows only too well though, getting good 'happy sheet' scores is relatively easy if the participants have had a good lunch and a few laughs. Unfortunately, the reason no one takes such scores seriously is that they know the likely business impact will be as substantial and durable as a stick of candyfloss.

On a personal level it might well be more interesting for the participants to travel hopefully than to arrive, but organizations that want to develop HR strategies should at least have a clear idea of what their intended destination is. Otherwise what starts out as an awayday soon becomes more akin to that other tourist treat, the mystery tour.

No, the only place to start to develop HR strategy should be to get out the business strategy. This should at least provide a destination and hint at directions. However this not only assumes there is a business strategy but that it is in a suitable format, and as HR strategy is such a new subject this may be too big an assumption to make. Therefore the first step now becomes one of working with the business strategists to ensure their strategy is already designed to act as a platform for an HR strategy.

HR strategy has to add value in its own right

Usually a business strategy will have been developed without a specific, explicit element of HR strategy having already been built into it. This will be due to two main reasons. One is that no one will have had the necessary expertise to do this. More importantly though, no one will have articulated to the board what value an HR strategy might add. HR strategists have to use a language that the rest of the board already understands to convince them of the potential value of spending the time and trouble to develop an HR strategy. Some immediate, practical suggestions can be found in Appendices 1 and 4, but it would be a good idea not to rush into this. To flesh this out, we are going to take a strategic HR look at the mobile telecoms industry, based on an amalgam of my own experiences working with several companies in this sector. It is worth mentioning immediately though how difficult it is to capture the total, strategic picture in a few paragraphs.

So what does the business strategy of a mobile telecoms company look like? Therein lies the first problem. There will be no single document that spells out exactly what the current strategy is. At its simplest level the business strategy of such companies has been one of global acquisitions, so that they have a presence in every major market and develop an international brand. More recently most mobile companies have wanted to acquire 3G licences to enable them to offer the latest range of mobile services.

However, two key factors have forced them to rethink their strategies. First, most of their markets have been maturing and opportunities for revenue growth have become increasingly limited. Second, the 3G revolution has stalled. Add to this a falling share price and all of a sudden the boards of these businesses have moved into cost control mode in an attempt to boost their bottom line and flagging fortunes.

You will, of course, realize that this is my own interpretation of the changing business strategies in the telecoms industry. Much of this is surmise, and for all I know I am giving these businesses more credit than they are due in terms of having a clear business strategy. Many key business decisions often appear to be made in a very reactive, ad hoc fashion. Nevertheless, if any of these businesses want to develop an HR strategy, then at least their present business 'strategy' is something to work with.

As in most companies achieving exponential growth very quickly, in telecoms cost control has not been a consideration uppermost in anyone's mind. Getting their networks up and running, gaining market share and ensuring they had the capacity to handle as many new customers as possible was the main aim. As a consequence very few restrictions were placed on operational managers, who seemed to have an insatiable demand for extra staff. So, as things quietened down it was inevitable that simply re-assessing actual manpower requirements was likely to offer cost-saving opportunities. Better manpower planning would have to be a key, operational element of any HR strategy that could be directly aligned with the company's latest business strategy.

In reality, to take an example from one particular company, two things actually happened. The first was pressure from the board on operating companies to reduce their headcount. The general view was that there was sufficient 'fat' in the system that they could afford to lose quite a few people without missing them. There was no intention to be too scientific about it as long as the cost savings were realized. However, there was certainly an acknowledgement that after the first round of job losses further restructuring and rationalization would inevitably lead to future job changes.

In the meantime the HR team were trying to introduce a more scientific and sophisticated way of reducing headcount. This involved benchmarking manpower levels between each of the disparate operating companies. This was meant to help in making much more informed decisions about what types of job could be lost and from where. When I had finished my own assignment with the company they had established benchmarking data, which had been sanctioned by the board, but further redundancies occurred within operating companies without any reference to this data. So the more sophisticated approach did not actually influence the manpower decisions in the final analysis.

As with all strategic case studies we could go into much more detail. However, from what we have seen here we can learn some lessons that may have universal applicability in strategic HR implementation.

Business measures help to articulate strategy clearly

In Chapter 2 on business planning we looked at a simple strategic model that related business strategy to HR strategy, from vision to operating plan. In our telecoms business example here, part of the company's vision was focused on the future of 3G. An HR strategist could immediately ask what implications this vision might have for HR thinking. The board of directors might genuinely believe that the whole notion of what a '3G future' looks like is clear. The VP-HR might also come to some initial conclusions about what it means for the people who work in the business, in terms of new roles and reporting structures. But visions do not provide a solid platform on which to develop HR strategy because they are too indeterminate; they set a general course not a basis for detailed action.

The first real lesson in developing HR strategy is that the vision and subsequent business strategy have to be articulated in concrete terms if a concrete HR strategy is to be produced. In the instance we have looked at here the future size and range of 3G services needs to be articulated in clear numbers: how many subscribers, using what range of services, generating what levels of revenue at what cost? This is not a five-minute job, and before exploring where this will lead us we need to check whether the company has a good management information system.

What always amazes me when I start looking at linking strategy to business measures is how quickly organizations jump from indefinable visions to hard measures - and how far out the predictions can be. 3G is an excellent example of this. More important from the HR strategist's viewpoint though is how rare it is for anyone to think through, in detail, what the future vision actually means in terms of the behaviours, attitudes and performance of the people in the organization.

I know absolutely nothing about the technicalities of installing a 3G mobile telecommunications network but that does not prevent me, as an HR strategist, from asking informed and hopefully intelligent questions about whether 3G requires 3G engineers and network managers. I can also ask about how much more complex running a 3G network might be and whether this will place any greater burdens on the organization in terms of manpower requirements and the skills of managers. You will notice that all of these questions remain hypothetical until such time as I know exactly *which* managers have to have which skills and knowledge.

In practice, this means asking the financial management team to show me the figures which say a particular manager will have to manage *x* number of 3G services in their part of the network. I also need to know what revenue is to be generated and what cost constraints they will have to work within. This is where any attempt at conventional approaches to HR management start to break down very quickly.

Accountants, however, can have more data than they know what to do with but precious little information that can point HR strategists in the right direction. Worse still, financial information is just that, information on revenues, cash flows and outputs; it is not designed to tell us exactly who has to do what. To get that information we need to speak to the head of network operations, who will be doing their best to ensure their managers manage whatever is thrown at them.

By now you may have noticed that the whole process is already becoming unwieldy and unworkable. You may also have noticed that this is not yet HR strategy. This is just an attempt to ensure that the people in the organization can deliver operational requirements.

The particular organization I mentioned earlier, however, had a poor history of operational managers managing their own human resources effectively; the sudden and severe corrections in headcount are ample evidence of this. This would suggest that exactly the same situation would be likely to arise when a 3G network had to be put into operation. Revenue targets dictate that the network has to be up and running, regardless of the costs incurred, even though everyone would like to see costs much more tightly controlled. But the really key point here is that this is not just about the introduction of 3G, *it should signal a fundamental shift in the way the business is managed because the market may be fundamentally shifting*.

To support this point let us look at a UBS Warburg telecoms analyst's view of the situation in which one mobile operator, Vodafone, finds itself. According to *The Times* on 13 September 2002 'Shares in Vodafone fell . . . after the company's house broker heavily downgraded its rating on the stock, citing the threat of greater competition.' The analyst was concerned that '. . . the group will in future have to spend far more to ensure customer loyalty . . . as quality subscriber growth slows . . . the logical outcome is to intensify competition for each others' customers.'

By quality subscriber the analyst means those who stay with their provider and use their phones enough for the company to make a profit out of them. This analyst is highlighting some serious business issues for the medium to long term that would best be addressed by a strategic response. How is Vodafone going to produce its own ways for managing tougher competition and increasing pressure on cost controls?

In the same article there is mention of Verizon – 'Vodafone's American affiliate' – who were trying to be released from an obligation to pay $8.7 billion for a 3G licence they no longer want. You may remember from Chapter 2 my mentioning that the HR director of Verizon said he had produced their HR strategy and then asked the leaders of the business what was keeping them awake at night. There are some issues here that will keep them awake for some time to come. Whether their HR strategy is helping at all is another matter.

So one possible strategic HR focus may be to raise the level of operational, managerial ability. This can be worked on in tandem with the existing business strategy. The cost conscious culture needed for the long term can start to be developed now. The business measures required to start this process would be comparative information showing the difference between managers who manage costs well and those who do not. This would form a baseline and also help to set a target. Once the immediate and medium term needs of the business are being addressed the HR strategist can explore what other, added value opportunities may be available.

Where are the opportunities for added value through HR strategy?

Staying within our example, there is very little to distinguish between one mobile phone operator and another. One differentiator used to be their relative network coverage but this particular playing field is almost completely level now. The quality of the phone lines seems indistinguishable and billing is a reasonably straightforward affair. So as an HR strategist in the telecoms business you have to ask yourself the fundamental question of how your HR strategy is likely to achieve a competitive advantage in such a homogeneous marketplace? Let us look at the generic options first, as Michael Porter would; and these are genuinely generic in the sense that the same questions could be posed in any organization, commercial or not-for-profit.

Cost advantage

We have already looked at one aspect of cost control with operational managers and no doubt we could look at this issue within every function or department. However, if cost control is to become a strategic objective, that is, a way of *thinking* as well as a way of operating, then the HR strategist has first to get this agreed as a strategic objective by the board. We are not talking here about a one-off, ad hoc initiative but a fundamental culture change in a business where subscriber numbers and average revenue per user (ARPU) currently put any concerted attempt at a cost control mentality on the back burner.

This will not be a mere statement that cost control is important. The board has to see that the long-term interests of the business will be best served by a strategy that will become increasingly important as the means for differentiation disappear. So what may appear to be operational is truly strategic. The distinction may seem quite subtle but the potential impact is huge. Imagine the mobile phone market in ten years' time and think of the advantage gained by the company which is operating at only 50 per cent of the costs incurred by its competitors. If some of these savings are passed onto customers in tariff reductions this may give this operator a huge share of the market. This would, of course, be music to the ears of the UBS Warburg analyst and all of their fellow commentators in the city.

Output or throughput

The second generic option would be to focus on increasing the amount of calls or services being handled by the network. This would require measures on network capacity and capability. In this particular industry the technological legacy of a growth-by-acquisition strategy may mean a multitude of technologies and a wide range of network configurations.

As with the issue of cost control, there could be a drive to get more capacity out of each country's network and this may lead to all sorts of HR initiatives. However, a strategic, business decision to produce a globally configured network (i.e. common technological platforms in each country) may generate enormous economies of scale but would be a potentially huge investment. If it ever became a reality then the practical HR implications of who would run it and what organization structure would need to be put in place to support it would be manifold; ultimately resulting in many detailed decisions on selection, roles, rewards and training.

As with the cost control question though there is an operational perspective and a strategic HR perspective. Regardless of the many cost and technological issues associated with a globally configured network the human and cultural barriers to such a strategic decision could only be addressed through a powerful HR strategy. Each country may currently be operating as a discrete business, with its own history and own level of success and, it would also be fair to say, with nationalistic fervour. Only the most optimistic or naive business leader would give any attempt at producing a truly integrated global operation a snowball's chance in hell of succeeding.

We cannot go into every detail of what an appropriate HR strategy might look like but a strategic move would inevitably mean putting top people in place who had a 'global' rather than a national perspective. This helps to give a much clearer indication of the fundamental gulf between HR strategy and operational personnel administration. It also highlights that the essence of most truly strategic HR decisions is how they offer significant added value but also, inherently, involve a degree of risk and uncertainty.

Price or revenue

Shifting our gaze away from directly trying to impact on cost and operational efficiencies we now need to consider ways in which revenue or prices can be increased. In the world of mobile operators this is a particularly taxing question. What does the future hold in terms of pricing and revenue streams? In a maturing market is there going to be greater pressure to reduce prices? Will customers really want video and other facilities on their phones and how much are they prepared to pay for them? Who knows what the future holds?

Premium pricing or price protection has to be determined, to a great extent, on the strength of your brand and the level of customer satisfaction provided. In a market where such differentiation is very difficult this may not be fertile ground for adding value through HR strategy. Strategy is as much to do with excluding options as it is choosing options.

Quality of service

When you make a call or send a text message on your mobile phone you normally expect there to be no problems even if, on occasions, you still lose the signal. When your monthly bill arrives, as long as there are no enormous, unexpected call charges you probably sanction payment without a second thought. Viewed from this perspective it may be difficult to envisage how much room for improvement there may be in terms of the quality of service on offer. Nevertheless this leads us into another interesting area of HR strategy.

First, does the business have a philosophy of never-ending, continuous improvement? There may never have been any discussion about whether such a philosophy was appropriate given the company's stage in its evolution and development. Initiatives such as total quality management (TQM) tended to be popular with mature businesses where opportunities for growth were limited. It may be that in an industry that is still in its infancy there are too many other obvious opportunities for bottom line improvements that mean no one would be particularly interested in a systematic discipline such as TQM.

Yet this is precisely the sort of area in which the really great organizations start to leave the also-rans well and truly behind. Admittedly, introducing any particular policy will require resources, time and effort. In a very fast moving business this is always in short supply. The HR strategist needs to convince the business of two things therefore, and in this order:

- that a continuous improvement policy will reap significant added value on the bottom line, expressed in financial terms;
- if it starts at a time when all your competitors are still operationally focused, then in three years' time, when the market is much more mature, you will have gained a head start in extracting value out of a business where margins are starting to become thin.

Running a business and having a total quality drive are not mutually exclusive activities. If, in the minds of the board, they *are* then some re-education of board directors is required. They would not be the first to be mistaken in the belief that continuous improvement is an initiative that is somehow a distraction from their core business operation.

I would emphasize here that this is the section of the book that concentrates on practicalities. Any budding HR strategist should be able to produce a presentation for the board around the four added value options identified above. Business leaders, by and large, are employed to extract as much value from the enterprise as they can. Consequently the starting point for any discussion on HR strategy has to follow the same framework and offer other options for value maximization.

What does this organization's existing HR 'strategy' look like?

The mobile phone operator I referred to earlier had already produced an HR 'strategy'. It was probably virtually identical to most other 'HR strategies' I have seen over the years. This is precisely why it did not qualify as a strategy. It offered no competitive advantage. But it also suffered from many of the failings common to virtually every other HR 'strategy' I have ever seen.

Some VPs-HR I have met over the years believe that their main contribution to board discussions is to help clarify and articulate the values of the organization. Does the organization want to be seen as a caring employer or a hard-nosed business for hard-headed business people, for example? A true HR strategist would regard this as putting the cart before the horse. The organization exists first and foremost to produce shareholder value not societal values. As we discussed in Chapter 1 though, the two should, at some stage, become interdependent and mutually reinforcing if maximum value to society is to be achieved.

In the case of the mobile phone operator here I was never quite sure what the values of the organization were. It was still gelling as an international business with all of the national pride, ego and rivalry issues that go with the territory. The board running the business had done a great job in establishing the company as a world player. Whether they were the right people to take it through to its next stages of evolution was not so obvious. The drive and ambition that got it where it was seemed less suited to the consolidation phase that it was entering. The eyes on the big picture maybe were not the ideal eyes for the detail work now required. Their sales and marketing skills had been used to great effect. The emphasis would have to shift considerably to the less exciting aspects of the operational end of the business.

It says something about this business that as soon as times got hard not a great deal of thought went into the possible impact of redundancies on employee morale. In fact I had no sense of a particular culture in this organization. Perhaps that was because it was still relatively young or just because it was growing by acquisition rather than organically.

If we compare this with IBM in the 1980s their employees used to describe working for IBM like being part of a global family. Each part of the IBM organization, wherever it was in the world, held to similar values and IBM employees had an affinity with each other (that does not mean they loved each other necessarily, although the joke within IBM was that it stood for I've Been Married) in the same way we all feel an immediate affinity for our own countrymen when we are travelling abroad. I will make no comment here on the potential value of this culture at IBM or whether it was used to good effect. I am merely stating that some organizations generate that feeling of *ésprit de corps*, a 'togetherness' that binds an organization very closely. Similarly, the Virgin group, under Richard Branson's entrepreneurial, yet fun-loving leadership, has created its own distinctive culture that any Virgin employee would be able to identify with.

I asked several employees at the mobile phone operator what it was like to work there and generally they responded very favourably. They were relatively satisfied employees but it was not the acclamation of those who feel part of a close knit family. Did they have any sense that this company was really concerned about their interests? Was there any common behaviour in terms of conformity, innovation, acceptance of change, for example? More importantly, was this business getting more value out of these people than any of its competitors might? These matters were never raised, and when any attempt was made to raise them it was unfocused, disintegrated and incoherent. Look, for example, at this 'strategic initiative' in their 'HR strategy', to "Improve employee involvement and communications". This is a typically nebulous, unmeasured and strategically disconnected aim. The objective of this initiative was to get the organization ranked in the top 10 for employee satisfaction. This is the sort of objective that appears in the vast majority of HR strategies. Every big company wants to be seen as 'the employer of choice'. It has become a very tired cliché even though the basic idea obviously has some merit in it.

As I tried to demonstrate in Chapter 1, this is exactly why this is not an HR strategy. There is no sense in which it has been developed to produce a competitive advantage. A more damning criticism, of course, is that, whatever it may say in such documents, when push comes to shove, employees' jobs are axed without a second thought. What signal or message does that send to the remaining employees about whether this company is one they might prefer to work for?

Pulling strategic, organizational objectives and organizational culture and values together is a very difficult balancing act: more an art than a science. The clearest indicator that this is not happening is in the way organizational objectives are defined and measured. In this particular HR strategy document there was not a single reference to any strategic, business measure. No reference to output, no reference to revenue and the only cost savings referred to were those resulting from headcount reductions and HR department efficiency. This was certainly not an HR strategy to help transform an organization or move it very far forward.

HR strategy has to *engage* all employees with the task of achieving the organization's strategic objectives. Engagement may require some communication initiatives at some stage but true *engagement* starts to happen in the minds of those running the business or it never really happens at all. As I write this I guess that in this particular company the employees in Germany, for instance, may be focused on their particular business objectives but they are unlikely to be engaged in achieving the long term aims of this global player; simply because nothing has been done to set this as an objective or make it happen. (See Appendix 2 to check whether your organization engages its staff.)

The clearest indication that this HR strategy was not uppermost in the minds of the board, however, is that the HR strategy was formulated well after any strategic, business plans were discussed and agreed. So now we need to move on to the next key step in HR strategy and consider whether it can actually influence business strategy in the same way that strategic marketing and financial considerations do.

HR strategy influencing business strategy

Financial strategy is bound to be a key influencer. Share price, revenues and debt are all going to dictate the potential size of the business and the speed with which it can grow. In the telecoms business the burden of the high price of 3G licences and the debt required to fund them inevitably increased the pressure on revenue generation and cost control enormously.

Similarly, marketing has had a significant, strategic influence on this business. It has set out to create a global brand. It could equally have decided to let each of its different operating countries maintain their own brand image, in much the same way as some airlines now have alliances under an umbrella such as the Star or OneWorld alliances without actually undermining their own individual brand. Going for a single, recognized brand has profound implications because customers who travel abroad will expect a seamless service. Therefore, the internal organization structure and processes will have to be designed accordingly.

It is quite obvious that the financial and marketing directors have seen these issues debated at board level. What is not so clear is whether the strategic HR implications have been appreciated. Maybe this is because there is always an implicit assumption that getting the right people in the right jobs will not be an insurmountable problem. That could be true but could this organization, for example, establish a global billing operation, based in one country, and achieve significant economies of scale? Or would its present, ad hoc, individualistic culture be a serious hurdle?

Let us consider these three, different, strategic perspectives in terms of the order of their complexity and intractability. The natural order might be that financial strategy comes first, then marketing, then HR. Financial and marketing matters are reasonably well bounded by clear measures and their priority is reasonably clear and determinate. However the HR perspective is not even easy to define, never mind resolve, which presents us with several key issues that must be addressed, again as a distinct set of steps, if HR strategy is to influence business strategy:

1 HR strategy has to be expressed in terms of how it will, in itself, add tangible value (e.g. complete flexibility to design the optimum organization will generate operational savings of *x* million which, if passed on as price reductions, should increase customer base and revenue by *y*).
2 The line of sight between HR strategy and the new scenario must be clear and explicit (e.g. Germany will lose its billing centre and all of the jobs that go with it to the new global, multi-lingual billing operation).
3 What this means in terms of new structure and processes must be outlined for initial approval (i.e. an organization and flowchart showing how the salesperson and new customer in Germany are linked directly to the billing centre).

Notice how step 1 is always to establish potential value first. Without this who is going to be really interested in what follows? All effective HR strategies need commitment to turn them into reality. Only significant value creation will ensure the level of commitment is right.

Some general lessons for budding HR strategists

Having said all of this, the chances of what I have been advocating actually happening at this mobile phone company, or most other companies for that matter, are currently negligible to non-existent. Why should that be? Most of the answer is contained in the HR maturity scale shown in Chapter 4, but let us look now in more detail.

Most mobile phone operators may be making a great deal of money at the operating level (even if their balance sheets are looking decidedly shaky). There are also many, obvious opportunities still available to them for improving their position, both in terms of cost cutting and ideas for extra revenue. So why on earth would they want to get involved in the difficult area of HR strategy? That is the simplest reason why companies do not do it – most do not really *have* to. Don't forget they are competing with other companies who also do not have competitive HR strategies so they continue to choose the other, easier, strategies available, such as re-designing tariff structures.

Now, despite everything I might say about the potential value that an HR strategy will bring, it is still a great deal easier for each senior manager to stick with what they know best, especially if their targets and bonuses can be achieved without the extra hassle. This is why real HR strategy is more likely to happen in those few organizations where at least one of the following conditions applies:

1 The business has run out of options for easy improvements and fully acknowledges that they can only foresee tough times ahead; unless they start to think differently about the way they manage their people.
2 They have a visionary leader who really does see the long-term importance of developing the human capital side of the business.

Either of these will provide very fertile ground for the development of HR strategy. Then all you need is someone actually to develop it.

Many companies have a VP-HR but they will never have developed the sort of HR strategy we are promoting here. Even if they now wanted to introduce a new, effective HR strategy the first hurdle would be convincing the rest of their board that they have anything new to offer. Second, they may be afraid to admit that what they have been calling HR strategy was not really a strategy at all. Third, they would have to learn that each organization requires an HR strategy designed exactly for its own circumstances, and that entails some really serious thinking. We could also talk now about the capabilities of the HR team in this respect, but this ground has already been covered in my earlier book, *The Bottom Line HR Function*.

Chapter 11

What factors influence the choice of HR strategy?

Probably the biggest criticism that an HR strategist could level at the HR profession is that they talk a great deal about HR strategy but, in effect, are just doing personnel planning. This is well after the big decisions have already been taken around the boardroom table. The next criticism would be that they have produced the same HR 'strategy' as every other HR team.

The whole purpose for producing any strategy is to provide a coherent response to a complex and potentially risky environment. In practical terms, therefore, all HR strategies are bound to be different because no two organizations face identical circumstances. Consequently we need to consider to what extent different types of HR strategies may be influenced and shaped by different internal and external factors. Number one on this list is whether you can start with a clean sheet or have to deal with historical baggage.

Greenfield or brownfield?

So, are you working in a greenfield or brownfield site; an existing business or a new start-up? One of the biggest obstacles to effective HR strategy is the historical and attitudinal baggage that comes with employees' experiences of how things used to be. The whole of this book is really about how to introduce an HR strategy into a brownfield situation. This inevitably means HR strategy is automatically bound up with change management and organizational transformation. One of the big problems with brownfield HR strategies though is that they are replete with compromises and diversions from basic principles. They tend to sway with the winds of change. Sometimes this is inevitable but all too often it is just used as an excuse for why there is no HR strategy.

Greenfield and start-up operations, however, have the luxury of not having to address behaviour patterns that are already well set. They allow the HR strategist to start with a blank canvas – probably the nearest we ever get to pure HR strategy. So what might go on to this pristine canvas? This is actually a good way for any HR strategist to consider what they might do in the absence of so many constraints. HR strategy is the art of the possible, and greenfield situations allow us to view the possibilities by getting the fundamentals right from day one.

Unionization

One decision that has to be in place before the first recruit sets foot on site is whether you prepared to let them join a union.

As someone who has studied and worked in industrial relations for many years, it is not too difficult for me to see why we still have trade unions. What I cannot understand is why every organization that is stuck with a union (let us be honest here, no HR strategist would actually choose to have their workforce represented by a union) does not have a long-term, strategic objective to become 'union-less'. How can any employer hope to get the best value out of their people when employees place more trust in their union to look after their interests than their bosses? This is not intended to be union bashing. Business leaders get the industrial relations they deserve and unions only continue to exist in large, modern organizations because of the failure to devise long-term HR strategies that engender trust among the workforce.

Industrial relations have often been treated like any other profit and loss account item. If the company could afford inflated wage costs it was seen as a lesser evil than having to grasp the nettle of confrontation. Yet one of the most important, strategic HR decisions will be whether to allow, encourage or resist unionization. There are very few standard answers in HR strategy but one of them is that unions have no part to play in long-term, maximum added value HR strategies.

That is fine for the theory. A more realistic and pragmatic view may be that, legally, it may prove impossible to exclude a union and so unions should be allowed; but only with a single union agreement and a constructive relationship built on dialogue rather than confrontation.

This is much closer to the sort of arrangement that companies like Toyota established when they set up their first plant in the UK.

It may appear that a similar, halfway house arrangement is to establish a 'partnership' agreement with the union/s. The cynical view is that this is a compromise that does not suit either side particularly well. No organization *needs* a union to help it run its business. Here is one view on the subject from John Monks, the General Secretary of the UK TUC (Trades Union Congress), who was quoted in *The Sunday Times* on 2 February 2002 as saying:

> I believe that trade unions should aim for partnership-style relationships. It makes for an agenda where people are not just in trenches but finding ways of growing what the company does and what they do themselves . . . I am not anti the private sector. I wish industrial relations in the public sector were as good as the best in the private sector. But I think there are areas of public life where shareholder value should not be the No.1 determining goal.

However helpful the union representatives may be, however impartial or effective they might become as a means for communicating to the workforce, the same ends can be achieved without a union. John Monks is supporting partnership arrangements but is he supporting the creation of value in society? At the moment some union officials may well be making a positive contribution to their organization, but where this is true it has to be an admission that the management are doing an awful job of managing the business effectively.

To have any chance of avoiding a situation where employees want to have union representation, a great deal of effort has to go into managing their expectations about the whole employment relationship. Industrial relations is primarily about psychology and the psychological contract perceived by employees.

Employee expectations and retention

The vast majority of us work, first and foremost, because we have to. We need to earn as good a living as we can within any self-imposed constraints, such as the level of responsibility or working hours we want. There are many, many other considerations that should be factored into the equation, including risks, rewards and job satisfaction. Regardless of the mix of these factors though, what employees expect from an employer and what they have to give in return is the bedrock of the employment relationship. Therefore the ability to manage these expectations positively is a fundamental building block of HR strategy.

For example, if an employee only joins the company to get some initial training or a particular bit of experience then, if they get what they set out to achieve, they should be relatively happy. Offering such people lifetime employment or trying to become their employer of choice is rather irrelevant. What really matters is being able to match an organization's needs with an employee's expectations, as far as possible. While an employee is with your organization you want as much value from them as you can get. I would much rather have a committed employee for six months than an indifferent employee for life. You cannot address this issue however unless you know what your employees' expectations are and they will only share their true expectations with you if they trust you not to use it against them. Honesty is definitely the best policy in HR strategy.

Game theory tells us that, in any relationship, seeking a goal that is mutually beneficial is likely to generate greater total benefits than one in which one side wins and the other loses. The zero sum game is one where for every winner there is an equivalent loser. For example, if I manage to negotiate with a prospective employee to work in my restaurant at £1 hour less than I am actually prepared to pay, then every pound per hour I gain is in fact exactly matched by their loss of a pound per hour. As an employer I may feel that I have won because my costs are lower but in fact all I get is a very basic service from this employee. For a pound more I may get a much more capable recruit, more commitment and better value from a happy employee. They in turn may give a much better service and even convince customers to enjoy another bottle of wine with their meal. Being dishonest with employees is not just morally wrong, it is bad for business. Any decent employer knows that short-changing employees is just a clear sign of poor management and non-existent HR strategy.

There are other reasons though why organizations are not more honest with their workforce, and they are not all necessarily unscrupulous. Business is about risk. Most employees want security not risk and employers do not want to worry their people unduly. So there is a natural tendency, by both parties, to play this side of the contract down.

Some organizations, particularly in Japan, have been known for their policy of lifetime employment. Presumably, the fundamental philosophy on which such employment relationships are based is that the best workforce is a stable workforce. Also, hopefully, a stable workforce is a highly motivated, productive and effective workforce, although perhaps this does not always necessarily follow.

In organizations that value employee retention it is bound to become an integral element of their HR strategy. Yet no organization can actually guarantee lifetime employment, whether they see it as a desirable objective or not. No employer will be able to offer complete protection to their employees from changing markets and the inevitable highs and lows of their own business fortunes. Consequently, they cannot predict employment opportunities with any great certainty. Nevertheless, as long as the pretence of security continues, maybe such organizations do tend to engender greater loyalty among their staff.

It is not too difficult to see how lifetime employment now seems to be an unrealistic proposition. If it is an unattainable goal then perhaps organizations should acknowledge this and start to communicate a message to employees that faces up to this fact. So, instead of offering security of employment, maybe a simple, honest and straightforward message can be conveyed to employees along the following lines:

- There are no guarantees that the business will remain in business unless it continues to perform.
- There is, therefore, an inherent risk in any employment contract because no jobs can be guaranteed for life.
- Moreover, businesses have to change in response to changes in demand and the market. Consequently employees may have to change their roles, skills and even attitudes when necessary.

Now this might not be what employees want to hear. However, if they are more concerned with their own employment prospects it is ironic that those resistant to this honest message are, in effect, undermining their own long-term job security because resistance to change means an increased risk of obsolescence.

Whether the organization takes an honest view of its attitude to retention or not one thing is for certain, it ought, wherever possible, to take a strategic view on the matter. Failure to adopt a strategic perspective means conflicting and contradictory messages will be conveyed and this cannot be in anyone's interests.

Pay and performance

Only when you have established your organizational philosophy on managing employee expectations can you start to formulate a strategic view on pay and performance. If your employees are expecting to share the risk of running the business what is in it for them? Perhaps higher risks should attract better rewards. Or do you take the view that employees are simply employed to do a job and, if they do that satisfactorily, then they should be paid 'the rate for the job'?

Either of these options could be a valid element in an HR plan, as long as your view on rewards dovetails with your views on say selection and performance management. However, how do you get the *best* value out of someone who is *just* paid to a do a job? We may all work alongside many people who do not expect to get too much from their workplace but the HR strategist sees this as hidden potential not as a given or a depressing fact of life.

The third alternative, of course, is to pay the 'going rate' and somehow get the best performance that this allows. Only clever HR strategists can achieve this. By creating all the right conditions for performance, expectations, motivation, capability, structure, process and, of course, culture pay will then be only a minor part of the performance equation. The highest value companies do not have to be the highest paying.

If you do pursue a clear policy of rewarding performance another big question is do you reward individuals or groups? This has been a perennial dilemma for compensation and benefits specialists - how do you separate team and individual rewards? The HR strategist has an answer to this conundrum - their focus on value and where it emanates from. Salespeople may well pat themselves on the back when they see their monthly figures and take all the credit for a job well done. Yet we all know that some 'salespeople' have always been order takers. The brand or reputation of the business has done most of the selling for them. Much of the 'value' in the business may have come from the product designers, the marketeers or the after sales service people. The 'sales' part of the total process is a crucial element but is not necessarily the source of much value.

A good HR strategist's take on pay and performance is that, if anything; rewards should be directed at those who create value. This may just as easily be a call centre operator who comes up with a good idea as the head of research and development. Any reward system should be alive to this. But the HR strategist also knows the power of the concept of value. The output of the business is a product or service. The best salespeople in the world will not sell defective products or lousy services for very long. Value is only created when every part of the value creation process, and everybody involved in this process, works well together. So the HR strategist knows it is very dangerous to reward performance, *per se*, without always checking that the total value process is working and actually producing real value - profitable sales.

However, checking that the process is working is not the end of the story. The HR strategist wants to ensure that the process continues to improve as well.

Continuous improvement

Ask anyone in any large enterprise whether they follow a policy of continuous improvement and you may get a wide range of responses from 'Sorry, I'm not sure I understand the question' to 'Yes, we have been following a kaizen philosophy for years'. When I worked in manufacturing in the 1980s I asked our production director whether we were following a philosophy of zero defects (a very popular concept at the time). He was too polite to say he thought my question idiotic, so he just said 'Of course, we can't afford to send defective parts to our customers.' But of course, he was talking about a zero defects policy, not a philosophy. His operating policy was to minimize defects; even though he had plenty of statistics to prove we were indeed producing defective parts and some were ending up with our customers. What he did not understand was the difference between a philosophy and a way of working, between a strategy and an operating plan.

Continuous improvement, or at least kaizen, is a philosophy. A philosophy is a way of living. Buddhists do not describe Buddhism as a religion, like Catholicism, but as a philosophy. On holiday with some Buddhist friends a few years ago we were all travelling in a large taxi and a fly was hovering around until I swatted it. A couple of days later in an almost identical situation I saw my friend's wife carefully and gently capture a fly before releasing it through the open window. I have enormous respect for people who live their philosophy. I know the difference between those who go to church on a Sunday and those who actively practise their Christian beliefs in everything they do. Many organizations try to improve, but very few understand or follow a true philosophy of continuous improvement.

I am not going to spend time here spelling out what kaizen means in practice. There are plenty of books that already do this better than I could (although a good place to start might be www.kaizen-institute-.com/kzn.htm). Any HR strategist has to know what the philosophy of kaizen really means and then they have to educate their board to the same degree. Only when the board understand the philosophy, *and live and breathe it*, will continuous improvement move the organization away from minimizing defects or complaints and along the never-ending road that is kaizen.

To the discontented eyes of the HR strategist following a kaizen philosophy is a given.

Initiative and innovation

One aim of the HR strategist is actively to encourage and stimulate ideas that lead to value creation. This has to be explicit and reinforced at every opportunity. Organizational cultures that could be described as 'command and control' only expect new ideas to come from the top or certain specific groups of employees (research and development being the most obvious candidates). Many command and control organizations still manage to produce new and innovative products, the pharmaceutical sector being a good case in point, but this is not the same as having an *innovative culture*.

All business leaders know that they may be missing out on the potentially brilliant ideas of their workforce. Even if they, personally, reached the top because of their own control freak mentality, it does not stop them wanting to capitalize on the creativity of their employees. What I have just described here, however, is the control freak's view of innovation: they want to control creativity and innovation, not release it. Such people are very unlikely to capture the value from the latent, commercially exploitable ideas of their human resource.

Of course very few businesses regard themselves as the last bastion of the command and control school of management. They like to see themselves as open and flexible places to work. They run creativity and innovation classes, they employ facilitators, they have all sorts of team meetings in which brainstorming and cross-fertilization are the orders of the day. It may look as if they are much closer to the concept of an innovative, learning organization, but they do not have the strategy in place to make this a reality.

The fundamental problem with trying to create a culture of innovation is that innovation equals risk, and successful companies avoid risk whenever they can. They like their cash cows, not their R&D budget. Ideas are ten a penny. Ideas that generate value are rare. Business history is littered with the failures of ideas much more than it is with success stories. Food producers are always trying to line supermarket shelves with the next greatest brand or product, but they only rarely get it right.

Some would argue that nature, not nurture, provides creative talents. The artist may well say that creativity is innate and spontaneous, and that may be true, but organizations exist for a purpose and only creativity that contributes to that purpose is of any worth in the value sense. Of course, some creativity will happen by chance, and that may well turn into a money-spinner, but you cannot have an HR *strategy* that relies purely on chance. The HR strategist must ensure that the board buys into the total concept of innovation; this will inevitably mean they have less direct control on the business.

Communications

The last item we draw onto our blank canvas, our HR strategy agenda, quite intentionally, is communications. I have always subscribed to the view that it is impossible to over-communicate to your employees. It is very easy to communicate badly but you can never have too much good communication. All of the above elements need communicating clearly and effectively. The crucial importance of communication has to be a foundation stone of any HR strategy, whether on a greenfield or brownfield site.

It is also easy to avoid communicating. For example, how many organizations would be prepared to open their books fully to their employees? They want to be very selective in what they communicate (I am not naive enough to suggest for a minute that organizations should have no restricted information), but they should be prepared to share bad news as well as good. This still adheres to the basic principle that in HR strategy honesty is the best policy.

HR strategy is holistic or it is nothing

Now the world would be a wonderful place if we could all start with a blank sheet, but all of the elements described above can be seen as principles to follow or aim for. You may have noticed though how all of the above sub-headings overlap. Continuous improvement is directly connected to employee expectations and how this is communicated is crucial. HR strategy is inherently about adopting a holistic approach. Companies may have policy statements on some of these issues but they will only form an HR strategy when they all dovetail together, within a coherent management philosophy.

Here is a key lesson about strategy, but HR strategy in particular. Even on a greenfield site, it is impossible to implement every aspect of an HR strategy immediately. However, the different elements must not be introduced as separate initiatives. HR strategy is about continuity. It is a marriage not a series of one-night stands. At the time when the HR strategy is first formulated it must be complete and holistic. All the various elements must form a conceptual whole, even if the implementation is inevitably going to be piecemeal. So, you may have a board member who does not fully understand and follow the principles of kaizen. This should not delay the strategy but the strategist knows that, at some stage, this director will either have to achieve this state or will eventually have to leave the organization.

I do not want to give the impression that it can work the other way around. Ad hoc HR activities and initiatives will never form a complete whole *after the event*. Without an overarching, conceptual, strategic HR framework HR will never operate strategically. We can see, therefore, how the greenfield site has many advantages, not least of which is that the board members could be selected according not only to their track record but their ability to understand HR strategy. They could also be chosen on their basic belief system about how to manage people. Another key influencer of HR strategy

Paternalistic or hard-nosed?

When we covered the HR maturity scale in Chapter 4 one of the perspectives we took was the historical perspective. History is incredibly important in HR. The whole style of organizational management has changed over the past hundred years. Let us look at one example in particular - Cadbury, the confectionery producer.

The original Cadbury family were Quakers. As with my earlier example of my Buddhist friends, they were people who lived their values. When they started the business in 1824 their management style was influenced by their religious beliefs and they came to be regarded as a very progressive and humane employer. We cannot tell with hindsight, however, exactly to what extent they were led by their religious beliefs and when they were more driven by straightforward commercial considerations.

Their main site was in Birmingham, the industrial heartland of England, where the industrial revolution, with its 'dark satanic mills', was in full swing. They developed an area called Bournville into a garden suburb for their workers in 1879. They were the first firm in Birmingham to give half-day holidays; they had pension schemes, medical and educational opportunities and, according to their own literature, they were 'way ahead of anything provided by the state' They recruited people at the age of 14 but had a Day Continuation School (from 1913) where young employees could continue to study for one day a week up until the age of 16. This was progressive people management because it was a standard higher than anyone could expect.

Sexes were segregated, with separate works entrances, work areas and works councils. These were intended to complement union activities, which were also encouraged. On a less politically correct note, by modern standards, married women were not allowed to work there and girls had to leave when they married. All of this was meant to promote the values of good family life and, compared to conditions elsewhere, Cadbury had to be regarded as, dare I say it, the employer of choice.

From a modern day perspective, however, we may well be much more sceptical about this as an example of enlightened management thinking. A more cynical view of the Cadbury approach might be that it was religious fervour and paternalism gone mad. Not only was this command and control at work, it was verging on indoctrination.

While on the subject of confectionery manufacturers, it is worth noting that America's largest confectionery business, Hershey, in 2002 was attracting bids to buy the business and those interested included Cadbury. Hershey also has a long history of philanthropy and of going to great lengths to look after the welfare of its employees. According to a report on the business pages of *The Times* on 19 August 2002 anyone wanting to buy Hershey's would have to take into consideration a 'lucrative benefit scheme . . . for all 14,000 employees . . . that will add about $400 million to the estimated $10 billion cost of acquiring the business'. The report adds that, 'In a bizarre twist, however, it appears that Hershey's has not told its employees that this provision is in place.' It is difficult to see how this benefit could possibly have been seen as part of an overall HR strategy if the employers did not feel it necessary to communicate the benefit to employees.

What is the HR strategist to make of all of this? Maybe we will never be able to provide unequivocal answers to the questions of whether these are examples of HR strategy and, if they are, what impact they have had. However, what we can say is that Cadbury survives as a successful business to this day while many of its competitors have fallen by the wayside. Others are now just part of global conglomerates: Rowntree, another chocolate manufacturer established at about the same time, with similar Quaker values and philanthropic tendencies, is now subsumed into the Nestlé empire. So is it still a paternalistic organization or is it now a much more hard-nosed enterprise? Have the values of nearly two centuries ago survived or is its current HR strategy a totally different solution for a totally different time and climate?

The last time I had any involvement with Cadbury (albeit very superficial), their Chief Executive, John Sunderland, was launching a value management initiative which was a key element in their business strategy to achieve double digit growth and a significant increase in share price. This was definitely in keeping with their long and successful commercial track record but the religious values of the original Cadburys were not much in evidence.

Paternalism, in its purist sense, may still be valued in some organizations and welcomed by the employees but it is unlikely to form the basis of an effective HR strategy. At the other end of the scale is a ruthlessly hard-nosed attitude towards business and people. This, equally, is unlikely to constitute a durable HR strategy.

In fact, neither of these terms is particularly helpful to the HR strategist because they plant an idea in employees' minds that either their employer is interested in them or is only interested in the business. They appear to be mutually exclusive. Whereas the mature HR strategist knows this is a false dichotomy. Let us use different terminology. Caring for employees *and* being business focused are not at opposite ends of a spectrum. There is a perspective that says an amalgam of focused business management and enlightened people management is the only conceptual framework that makes any sense in true, strategic HRM thinking.

Old attitudes are extremely difficult to shift. A fundamental misunderstanding in the minds of many employees that their welfare and the needs of the business may be in conflict, or even diametrically opposed, will not provide a constructive and harmonious platform on which to develop the business. If employees value paternalism maybe there will be some re-education required to show that paternalism should be re-read now as the 'concern of an enlightened employer for their employees'. Simultaneously, this perception should see no conflict with the same employer having to take tough decisions in the interests of the business in a competitive world.

Do different economic models need different HR strategies?

There has been an implicit assumption throughout this book that any organization can create value through HR strategies that value their people. This is dependent on producing high levels of motivation towards a common purpose. In commercial organizations profit, and opportunities for higher rewards through profit sharing, lend an obvious and seductive hand in any attempt to improve or sustain motivation levels. But how much difference, in terms of strategic HR thinking, does it make when the organization works to a different economic model? The public and not-for-profit sectors, charities and voluntary organizations employ huge numbers of people. Could or should they have a similar approach to HR strategy? More interestingly, what could commercial organizations learn from their strategies?

The whole employment model and the psychological contract with employees are very different in the public sector. Public sector employees know their employer cannot go bust. Their customers, the taxpayers, are a captive audience. The demand for their service is regular (bins get emptied once a week, the library is open when they decide). All of this tends to create a very different relationship at work when compared to commercial employees who know they have to win customers and do whatever they can to hang onto them.

Charities are a different model again. My wife used to give up some time every week to work in a charity shop without any payment.

Whether this should be regarded as laudable or not, it presented a different type of managerial issue for the manager of the shop (a paid employee of a hospice charity). Their HR policy was to accept any helpers they could get to staff the shop six days a week. So the manager had to manage a cohort of part-time, volunteer helpers who probably had a wider range of capabilities than any paid workforce, who would have had to go through a more rigorous selection procedure. An added problem is that when people give their time for free, they feel entitled to only have to do the jobs they prefer.

So in this case is the HR policy aligned with the needs of the organization? The purpose of this charity is to provide funds to run a hospice. Actually, let us take another shot at that purpose. The purpose of this charity is to provide care and support for the terminally ill and their families. The objective of the *shop* is to help provide the necessary funds to do this. In this case the objectives match the purpose of the organization perfectly and this particular shop is very successful at providing significant funds.

My wife also has a part-time, *paid* job. It is also for a charity, one that aims to provide a counselling service for individuals. However, this charity makes a charge for its services and is run on more commercial lines: having to break even. The organization also has to be very careful whom they employ. I asked my wife whether she would do this job for no pay. She said no. 'Why not?' I asked. 'Because it is a much more responsible and stressful job,' she replied. At the shop she was not expected to take any responsibility and had some choice in what she did.

I do not want to get into a debate here about the different business strategies of charities or the percentage of their funds being used up on salaries. All I want to ask is would having a better HR strategy help these two charities achieve their objectives or improve their results? Or does the shop, for example, have a subsidiary, implicit objective of providing people with an opportunity to do charitable works? If it does, is this getting in the way of achieving its main purpose?

If the shop employed more professional staff would their takings increase enough not only to pay their wages but also provide even more funds for the hospice? Alternatively, would more training for volunteer staff have the same effect? How about having a more rigorous selection procedure? Would they mind turning some volunteers away if they were deemed unsuitable?

In the counselling service, where limited funds and a lack of resources have resulted in a waiting list, would an HR strategy that included recruiting fund raisers or engaging existing staff in fund raising activity mean that income could be doubled and the waiting list removed?

The strategic HR *proposition* is always going to be about value creation. How can the best value be obtained from the human resource? When not-for-profit organizations lose sight of this fundamental truth potential organizational effectiveness is impaired.

One of Tony Blair's more revealing off-the-cuff remarks was when he admitted that he had the scars on his back from those who were resisting his attempts to modernize public sector bodies in the UK. There is widespread acceptance that too many governmental agencies work in isolation from each other and the aim now is to achieve 'joined up' government where, for example, all organizations involved in child protection would dovetail their operations. So the education authorities, social services, hospitals and the police would all work hand-in-hand in the best interests of children at risk.

As we will see in Chapter 13, bringing about joined up government will be as much to do with attitudes as it will with re-drawing organizational boundaries and re-designing organization charts and processes. For me, this is an area just waiting for someone who understands HR strategy to make real in-roads into these very complex and intractable problems.

One area where joined up government is desperately needed is local government. Having worked with many local government organizations over the past few years the most damning criticism that I would aim at them is their inability to reach clear agreement between all of their key stakeholders (council members, executive team, citizens, central government, employees) on a clear purpose. This is followed closely by a failure to articulate their organizational objectives in a way that encourages departments to work together.

It is obvious that each of the stakeholders has a different perspective. Citizens want their streets swept, their refuse bins emptied and their children educated. They want as much value as they can get for their hard-earned taxes. Central government wants to control the purse strings, so this immediately places heavy emphasis on cost control. These two objectives are not necessarily conflicting but what is the attitude of local government employees? To provide minimum services at minimum cost or to extract maximum value out of a limited budget? These are very different mindsets, very different attitudes. The added value mindset of the HR strategist says they should aim to provide the *best* services at the *minimum* cost.

Meanwhile, council members are elected by citizens who judge them by the services they receive. This throws into the melting pot councillors who bring different priorities to bear, competing for resources to be targeted at their constituents. All of this has to be managed by executives who could be forgiven for wondering who their masters are, central government, councillors, the public or the workforce? Described in this way, albeit rather cynically, a great deal of groundwork would need to be done before an effective HR strategy could be put in place. In fact, the way local government is currently configured, I would argue that it is impossible to formulate a coherent HR strategy.

In a commercial organization, ultimate accountability rests with the board. There are other, key stakeholders, such as shareholders, but at the end of the day it is the board that decides in which direction to take the business. With local government, the ultimate control of finances is held by central government. They impose constraints but take no responsibility for the people who work there. The only options to give HR strategy a chance would be a national HR strategy for the local government sector or genuinely allowing each local authority to operate as an independent organization. Both of these options are probably, currently, too politically sensitive to be pursued. As a direct result, in the absence of effective HR strategy, all taxpayers get less value than they could or should receive.

Chapter 12

Strategic tools and the use of measures

I have already mentioned several times why I believe HR strategy does not generally happen. If this contention is valid then CEOs will have no experience of what an HR strategy looks like. If they had, they would not need convincing that it works. So the first challenge for the HR strategist is to be able to demonstrate that HR strategy will add value in order to get the CEO's complete commitment. So we now need to look at specific tools and techniques that make this possible.

We cannot demonstrate the added value of HR strategy, however, unless we can measure it in some way. Measurement is the key. But only the right sort of measures will do. So what are the right measures? You will only find that out if you know how to ask the right questions.

Organizational performance measurement systems have to change

If we look at the psyche of the average CEO, does he or she want to take over the world or are they just focused on delivering this year's results. Notwithstanding the self-aggrandisement and ego trip that goes with being a successful CEO, anyone running a business aims to do just two things. They want income to be as high as possible and costs to be as low as possible. If the resulting margin is acceptable, they have no problems. This is a very limited mindset and such behaviour is reinforced by shareholders and city analysts who will applaud any performance above expectations or ahead of the market.

The eyes of HR strategists see the world very differently. Of course they will help the business to perform but they see no reason to have any ceiling on expectations. The human resource is a pool overflowing with talent and just waiting to be tapped. So what HR strategists want to gauge is how much value is being drawn off. Unfortunately, organizational performance measurement systems were never designed to do this. They were designed to tell the CEO how the organization is performing against agreed targets.

As life got more competitive though the targets became more stretching. Consequently the questions, about which bits of the organization add value and which do not, had to become more sophisticated and drill further down into the very heart of the organization. This was bound to happen. The expiry of one source of competitive advantage leads to an unquenchable thirst for better ways of working or new product development. The new idea or innovation that adds value today becomes the basic way of operating tomorrow: lean production systems in automotive manufacturing, that were once a radical departure from convention, became the industry norm. Unfortunately, however, the ability of organizations to copy each other's technology means that any hard-won, competitive advantage is very short-lived. Developers of new technology often do not have that technology to themselves for very long.

Historically, the information systems that told the CEO how the business was performing were based on 'internal' figures such as sales and operating costs and 'external' market information and comparative data. However, one fundamental problem with all of these measurement systems was the fact that they reported historically. That may have been fine when the pace of change was slow, but in today's world having a twelve month time lag before you find out that you are not performing could result in your competitors putting you out of business.

So gradually there was a migration away from such conventional, financial management and accounting systems towards the development of full-blown, totally integrated ERP (enterprise resource planning) systems; probably best known by those using Oracle and SAP-type relational database information systems. These systems were meant to answer any question you might ask about organizational performance from any internal perspective; from basic operating costs to inventory control.

This did not address another fundamental problem with traditional, performance measurement systems though: they were seen as a big stick. That is, they were designed by and for managers who belonged to the prevailing 'command and control' school. Measurement tended to cultivate a blame culture where admitting your mistakes was akin to signing your own professional death warrant. Measurement was a stultifying force rather than something that might transform the organization.

So for all of these reasons a new approach was needed, an approach that not only looked backwards but forwards; one that looked at measures in the round and motivated rather than demotivated. Enter the concept of performance measures as a scorecard. Let us take a moment to look at the background to this concept before we go on to look at its relevance to HR.

Continuous improvement could not be sustained through conventional performance target setting and historical, financial management reporting. Setting individual targets often led to conflicting management behaviour, with the VP-Sales aiming to hit sales targets at any cost, while the cost-focused VP-Operations was desperately trying to keep costs down. Meanwhile the VP-Customer Service was picking up the pieces dealing with complaints that were not of their own making. Hardly a recipe for value maximization.

The goal of lean, flexible, seamless, customer-focused organizations is to make sure every part of the organization is pulling together, in the same direction. So, following the fundamental law of organizational life that 'what gets measured gets done' it soon became apparent that if management boards wanted departments to work together they had to put in place a measurement system that encouraged them to do so. Measures had to be mutually reinforcing, not conflicting.

Cutting a very long story short, this led Robert Kaplan and David Norton (1996) to the idea of a 'balanced scorecard', where the organization did not design competing and conflicting internal measures but a range of measures that should work in harmony to produce maximum value. In very simple terms, they suggested that in order to get measures to drive the business strategy the organization had to view performance measurement from four key perspectives, which would be 'balanced' with each other. These four areas of measurement are:

- financial measures
- customer needs and satisfaction
- internal efficiency and effectiveness (usually referred to as internal processes)
- learning and innovation (i.e. are your people learning and innovating?).

The balanced business scorecard was a serious and intelligent attempt to address many organizational issues and, it can work well in the right circumstances. But how well does it actually work?

HR measures must be meaningful

The fundamental problem with all data measurement systems is that they have a tendency to focus on what can be measured rather than on what information is really useful. This is particularly true in people measurement. So, when it comes to asking questions about the value obtained from the human resource, most organizations still only produce 'record keeping ' information such as headcount, grading and the like. While this information is necessary for managing a workforce it says nothing about the connection between the way people are managed and the way the business is performing. At its simplest level, we might want to know what measure will indicate a connection between absenteeism and production delays or quality? Or, perhaps, is there a direct relationship between staff turnover figures and levels of customer satisfaction? An even more interesting, but much more difficult, measure would be one that gauged how many employees were generating ideas that were converted into bottom line, added value.

Measures are only useful if they help us to identify areas of concern and priorities. Furthermore, if the measures themselves do not help us to analyse cause and effect, make some sort of correlation between people effectiveness and organizational effectiveness, then the measures themselves become meaningless and obsolete. There is no point, for example, measuring how many patents your organization produces without knowing which ones were converted into added value. Patents that just sit on a shelf are worthless until their value is realized. Even if you do manage to collect this data you still have to work out how to get your people to produce more of the sort of patents that end up adding value.

In order to address this issue the first and most basic hurdle to get over is how to design management information systems that measure *individual* employee performance. As a trainer I have always subscribed to the view that you can only, ever, train *individuals*. We may choose to train people in teams or other groupings but their reaction to the training is unique to them, individually. What they learn will be different for each one of them. Therefore, how much better they personally perform, as a result of the training, will vary.

This level of individual performance measurement has only tended to be done for the sales force. Presumably this was so because their performance appeared to be so easily and clearly identifiable. Now we need it for all employees because we cannot manage the value of each human resource without measuring it. But as soon as you move away from the sales function such measurement becomes much more problematic.

So we are now saying that any effective HR strategy has to move away from overall, aggregate performance measures to a much more detailed level of individual measurement. This is in keeping with our principle of individually centred HR strategies. This requires a significant shift in conventional performance management thinking.

Measuring individual employee performance

We discussed in Chapter 8 how Jack Welch used something he called the 'vitality curve' (Welch, 2001). All this means is that if you measure employee performance using a rating scale the chances are you are going to produce something like the curve in Figure 12.1. Whoever decides on the performance standards for the organization can then decide where the unacceptable (3 and below) and superior (8 and above) 'goalposts' should be placed. At GE, Jack Welch introduced a policy of 'forced ranking', which meant that there would always be some managers assessed as unacceptable. In effect this meant the goalposts were constantly moved to the right, their performance was always judged relative to the whole management group and each year they removed the bottom 10 per cent. Obviously, when no one can become complacent about his or her own performance it tends to produce a 'vitality' in the organization that may otherwise have been missing. Although I am not sure vitality is an accurate description of the culture this creates.

Figure 12.1 shows a normal frequency distribution. If we measured employee height or shoe sizes the likelihood is that we would produce

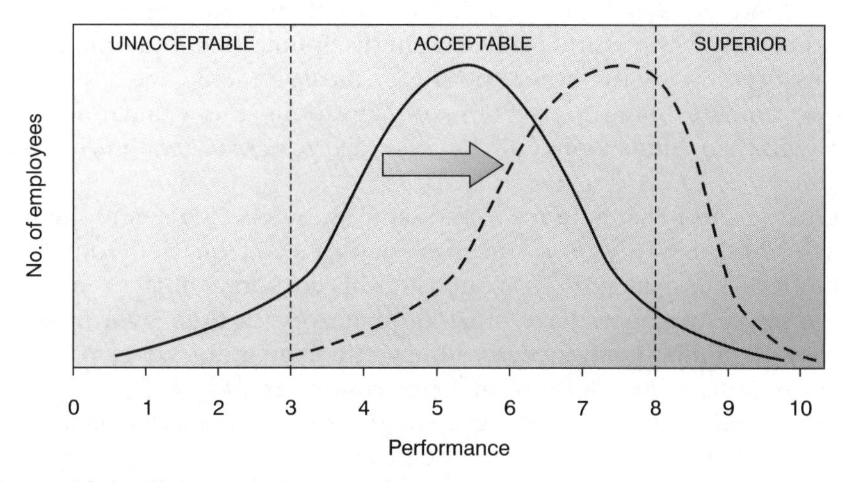

Figure 12.1 Shifting employee performance

a curve like this. At each end of the curve there would be a few with very big feet or very small feet but the majority in the middle would wear average sized shoes. The theory of probability applies equally well to the performance ratings of an entire workforce. We have a few stars, a few who should not be here and the vast majority come to work happy enough to do a decent day's work.

Ideally, the performance measures used on the *x*-axis would be rooted in some hard, measurable business measures such as productivity or quality. In those organizations using forced ranking there may be a range of measures used but with an aggregated score. However, there is always likely to be some element of subjectivity from those doing the assessment.

If you trust your managers to manage effectively then there is nothing inherently wrong with their subjective views. As a management training colleague, Paul Donovan, from the Irish Management Institute once told me, 'managers always trust their own data'. I agree. Managers already perceive the performance of their own team in this way and their managerial behaviour is dictated accordingly. All the performance curve really does is convert their existing perceptions into tangible measures with the sole aim of improving them.

Regardless of what data is used though, subjective or objective, *management information systems will only help us to produce this chart when they are designed to do just that*. Only when we have the information we need, in this format, can we attempt to show both the existing value added by employees and how they might improve that value; illustrated in Figure 12.1 by the movement of the curve from left to right.

The forced ranking approach has its critics. As an article in *Personnel Today* entitled 'Making the grade' points out, 'forced ranking is only as good as the measures and management disciplines that underpin it: used in association with other business measurement and workforce improvement tools . . . it offers organizations the chance to really leverage their human capital' (Keith Rodgers, *Personnel Today*, 2 April 2002).

One business that adheres to the same system is Siebel, and the same article describes how, 'on the first day of each quarter, Tom Siebel (founder, Chairman and CEO) publishes his corporate objectives. By day three senior managers have created objectives for their own divisions. By day 15 all 8000 employees will have their own objectives. Every six months Siebel culls the bottom 5 per cent of employees.'

Maybe GE and Siebel *do* get the best out of their management resource by using what can only be described as tough standards. They are probably brilliant examples of how CEOs can be following an integrated business and 'HR strategy', even if they may not articulate it in that way. Whether they are true HR strategists or not, one thing can be said for certain, organizations that try to copy their forced ranking system, without copying the total strategy, will fall flat on their corporate faces.

Also in *Personnel Today*, on 6 August 2002, there was a short report on Ford's attempts to introduce a forced ranking system. Under the heading 'Ford rethinks cull of its lowest performers' it was reported how the VP-HR for Ford Europe told a Global Talent War Conference 'Boy did it get a bad reaction. It turned a lot of staff against the company just by the manner in which it was done. We've moved away from that now. If you put in a performance management approach, make sure it fits the company culture.' Apparently 'Ford even had to face legal action in the form of "class action" lawsuits taken in the US.' If ever there were proof that HR strategy has to be conceived holistically this is it. Will Ford ever improve their world ranking in Appendix 1 through HR strategy? Not unless they put together a proper HR strategy, that 'fits their company culture'.

Does an HR strategy based on forced ranking make sense?

Many HR practitioners and commentators dislike forced ranking intensely. It seems to militate against a culture where employees are encouraged to grow and develop. It smacks of a return to blame cultures. Yet Jack Welch defends his system in his autobiography, entitled *Jack: What I've learned leading a great company and great people* (2001), by saying that dealing with under-performing managers honestly (he espouses that principle as well) is actually in their own long-term interests. He says hanging onto managers who are likely to struggle is just prolonging the agony; much better to let them go while they have a chance to make it elsewhere. Let us look at this view in a little more detail.

Imagine you have 100 managers and you use a forced ranking system to get rid of the worst five. You then have to replace these managers either from within your own ranks or from outside. Either way, these new managers are untested as managers in that position in your organization. Following the forced ranking philosophy, in six months' time you have to cull another 5 per cent and some of these newly appointed managers fall into this group. In fact, they could even be performing worse than some of their predecessors, whom you ousted six months earlier. Yet, if you replace the latest batch you are susceptible to the same problem in a further six months. If you hang onto them, in the hope that they will improve, then your forced ranking system is actually accepting a lower performance this year than it did last year. So the theory may not be as simple or watertight as it might appear at first sight.

My other concern with forced ranking is illustrated in Figure 12.2. Ambitious people will play the system. If ambition always equalled talent this would not be a problem in itself, but ambition does not equal talent: just look at the ambitions of the thousands of wannabe popstars, movie actors or politicians. I have met many ambitious people without talent who fall into the 'danger zone' in the ambition/talent diagram. Organizations often become blinded by someone's raw ambition and fail to see that there is insufficient talent to support it. Hence they promote these people into positions of responsibility where they can do enormous damage. Enron had a well-publicized talent management strategy but one has to ask whether that talent was translated into organizational performance?

Organizations need a few good leaders, a strong backbone and to make sure they get rid of any dead wood. What they certainly do not want is anyone in the danger zone, and a good HR strategist should have a system to ensure that this is the case.

There is nothing wrong with a performance management system that roots out dead wood or continuously aligns people with organizational needs but forced ranking may leave the organization worse off. Also, it could be that forced ranking is only possible in organizations that are already doing reasonably well. What do you do when the whole

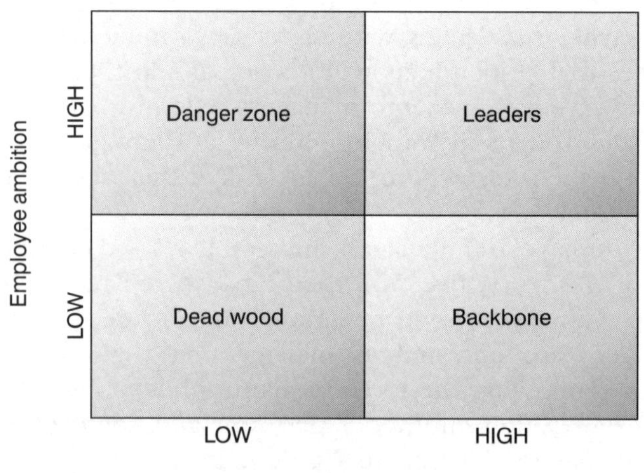

Figure 12.2 Make sure you hang onto the right people

organization is under-performing? Also, managers will try to cheat the system by bringing back, as contractors, employees they have just fired, as many organizations have done after large-scale redundancies.

Another worry concerns the sort of relationship forced ranking encourages between all employees and their employer? What chance is there of getting employees to innovate if the risk of innovation might result in a low score? Is the relationship one of trust and loyalty or more that of the mercenary who joins the army that happens to be currently paying the highest wages?

The performance or vitality curve might improve overall performance, but it is worth asking whether it truly maximizes the full, potential value of all employees.

Individual performance measures as a part of the HR system

We have already raised the issue of HR as function, department or system (see Chapter 7). Perhaps a particularly pertinent point for the HR function here is whether it can play a greater part in adding value by helping to resolve the issue of producing business-related, people information. If we consider how most conventional appraisal schemes, personal development planning processes and competence programmes usually operate we have to admit that really meaningful, individual performance scores are usually missing. This is probably because *measuring individual performance significantly raises personal accountability levels*, an issue that many organizations shy away from.

Producing employee performance measures, therefore, is not just an operational problem but one of culture. This is exactly the sort of organization-wide issue that HR strategy should be addressing. Employee performance measures will be a critical and integral part of any HR *system* that underpins an HR strategy. The strategy has to build a performance culture in its entirety through communicating, acknowledging, recognizing and rewarding performance at every turn or, as with Ford, it will collapse.

HR people who see themselves as 'business partners' must have access to all of the management information available to line managers and have the ability to analyse that information to design effective HR solutions. The 'unacceptables' in Figure 12.1, if you accept that they do not automatically have to be culled, may require training, development, remedial work or even disciplinary action. The issues for the 'superior' staff are totally different – ensuring they are constantly stretched, allowed to develop fully and given increased responsibility at every opportunity.

Experience tells me that the most difficult part of the performance curve to shift is the 'acceptables'. This part of the workforce will probably only improve where a concerted and creative HR strategy has been formulated. In fact, it is for this group that HR strategy really comes into its own. After all, as 'acceptables' there is no obvious reason why these employees should improve at all. HR strategy therefore is primarily a motivational strategy.

Ironically, one obstacle to this approach is the deep-seated belief in the minds of many HR people, and senior executives, that 'a happy workforce is a productive workforce' (see Chapter 12). People who don't know the difference between 'necessary' and 'sufficient' conditions usually subscribe to such notions. This simplistic view of the world leads many organizations to regularly check the views of their employees through attitude surveys, on the assumption that increased happiness will lead to increased performance. Only rarely though do we see such measures directly correlated with actual business performance figures.

A client, a VP-HR in a retail business, recently invited me to join a meeting where the results of the annual employee opinion survey were being presented by the business's survey consultancy. Sitting next to me was the managing director, who was equally eager to hear the results. Fortunately it was mainly good news, even though the survey results indicated only marginal 'improvements'. Employees were generally 'happier' than they were a year ago. After the meeting I confided with the VP-HR that I was never too impressed with such surveys unless there was a clear correlation between employee satisfaction and business results. For example, what about those managers who proved to be quite unpopular with their staff; what if they proved to be doing the best business? With a knowing and very slightly concerned look she told me that she had already looked into this and found that some of the 'worst' managers on the survey were definitely the best at getting the results that mattered.

This seems to run counter to the 'happy employees means good business theory' but does not surprise me for a moment. Effective management was never about being Mr (or Mrs) 'nice guy'. With the best will in the world, virtually no one comes to work to give their soul to the business. Strategic HR management is about getting a decent level of performance out of people who, without any management influence, would be likely to operate below their potential. Employees who score their boss highly may well be doing so simply because he or she does not give them a hard time.

The most interesting aspect of this anecdote though is the reaction of the managing director. During the meeting he tried desperately to articulate how he wanted the employees who worked there to *want* to give their best. This is why he was so keen on monitoring employee opinions. At the same time he acknowledged that, in many stores, it was pretty obvious that performance was well below the average (the performance curve invariably proves to be a true reflection of reality). What he was unable to do was come up with any clear formula for how to get the best of both worlds - happy employees who perform well. He clearly had no understanding of HR strategy (we will look at this case study in more detail in Appendix 5); what he was doing though, whether he realized it or not, was adhering to the latest HR theory.

The employee–customer–profit chain

The, now famous, Sears Roebuck case study (see Rucci *et al.*, 1998) has been used to suggest that there is a direct correlation between employee satisfaction, customer satisfaction and business performance. Even to the extent of specifically linking a '5 unit increase in employee attitude' to a '0.5% increase in revenue growth'. One problem with this case study, regardless of its veracity, is that those who do not fully understand the total picture may latch onto a simplistic point that if they focus on their employees' attitudes it is bound to lead to business performance improvements. I guess even the architects of the Sears Roebuck approach would not support this idea, in isolation.

Perhaps what needs to happen is to re-assess all organizational performance measures to see if they tell us anything about human performance potential. One way to do this is to use a very simple method for categorizing measures according to whether they tell us something about activity, performance or added value.

- An *activity* measure for a salesperson would be the number of calls made per day.
- A *performance* measure would be the number of sales made.
- An *added value* measure would say how much profit was made on these sales.

All these measures are different, even though we would hope that ultimately they would lead to the same results. However, the *only measure that guarantees the right result has been achieved is the added value measure*.

The really powerful reason for only concentrating on added value measures though is that *added value is only achieved if everyone in the process performs well*. High sales figures may not result in profit if the cost of after-sales support is too high, or marketing have spent too much or even if the invoice clerk keeps making errors on invoicing. Attaching added value measures to each person in the chain makes them all accountable for a successful end result on the bottom line, always measured in financial terms. Furthermore, how can you afford to reward any of them if no value is added at the end of the chain?

This simple fact of life has yet to be accepted as part of most performance pay systems. Instead, all too often there is an implicit, albeit specious, assumption that the only value adder is the sales person, or the production manager or whoever. One of the biggest myths generated by adherence to conventional management information systems is that the value emanates from a particular source rather than from the whole system.

Generally, organizations are unable or unwilling to use measures that can be regarded as added value because of the personal accountability issue that we raised earlier. Why, for example, should accounts clerks accept any responsibility for profits from sales? Instead, they resort to activity and performance measures that are easier to collect and less contentious, from the employee's point of view. Obvious performance measures include such things as output per employee, calls per employee in a call centre, sales volumes (in units), customer survey results or average costs. Improvements in all of these *should* be an indication that the organization is performing well but each one, in isolation, is rather meaningless. This was best exemplified by a director of an aero engine business who declared to a conference audience that they had an order book of £4 billion, unfortunately the bad news was that it would cost them at least £4.2 billion to manufacture and deliver them. My guess is that performance measures in that organization gave a lot of employees the false impression they were adding value when, in reality, nobody was.

An HR scorecard

Any organization that says it has an HR strategy needs to be able to measure the effectiveness of that strategy. As HR strategy is usually seen as the preserve of the HR departments we now have to ask how well they measure themselves. To date, most attempts in this area have been the use of benchmarking data. These are usually meaningless measures such as the number of training days per employee or even their own average cost of a new hire. Such measures do not even suggest in which direction the measures are intended to go. Anyone can put a convincing argument either to increase or reduce training days; it all depends on whether the training results in any added value or not. Equally, the 'cost per hire' tells me nothing about the performance of the new employees and, therefore, nothing about the performance of the HR team or the business.

Organizations have an awfully long way to go to design performance measures and management information systems that can do the job that is now required. Once HR people recognize and accept that the only thing that matters in organizational life is added value, and that always shows up on the bottom line, they may start to focus their own measures on something that matters. In the meantime there are some very misguided attempts being made at trying to measure the 'people' side of the business.

One such attempt is the HR scorecard. This is not a proprietary product because there are already several different approaches using the same name but which have virtually nothing in common. All of these approaches strike me as perfect examples of researchers who follow their own logic so assiduously that they fail to realize that their original objective was incorrectly defined.

The lateral thinking expert Edward De Bono sums this tendency up perfectly when he tells the story about NASA (North American Space Agency) engineers trying to solve the problem of developing a space-age ballpoint pen to enable their astronauts to write upside down in a weightless environment. To this end they spent millions of dollars designing a pen powered by a tiny gas canister. Apparently the Russians solved the same problem by giving their astronauts a pencil. The objective was simply to be able to write, not to use any particular type of writing tool.

'The HR Scorecard' described by Ulrich, Becker and Huselid (2001) has produced a similarly, extremely complicated, 'ballpoint pen' solution to what can only be described as a relatively simple problem. But what 'problem' exactly were they trying to resolve? What was their objective? They were attempting to answer 'the question of how best to integrate HR's role into a firm's measurement of business performance'. I am not sure that, in itself, is a valid objective. So what is?

The balanced scorecard needs a new people perspective

I think Kaplan and Norton with their balanced scorecard genuinely, strenuously, tried fully to acknowledge the importance of the 'people dimension' but their learning/innovation perspective seems to me to miss the point. The human element cannot be *separated out* into one perspective because it permeates every perspective. This goes back to the earlier discussion about how you cannot deconstruct strategy. Furthermore, I would go even further in suggesting that their notion of 'balance' is not the same as the concept of a 'holistic' approach to maximizing organizational performance through people. A '*balanced*' diet might mean a healthy diet but the '*whole*' body needs exercise, intellectual stimulus, spiritual well-being and, when necessary, the right medicine if it is to aim at being a perfect picture of health.

I am not saying that Kaplan and Norton are unaware of this. What I am saying is that their scorecard methodology does not actually, effectively resolve the very critical issue that they, themselves, have identified. In their own words they admit that 'one of the most important goals for adopting the scorecard measurement . . . is to promote the growth of individual and organizational capabilities' (Kaplan and Norton, 1996: 144–5). That is easy to say and very difficult to achieve, as the MD in the retailing example above found. The idea that measuring the 'people perspective' will balance with all of their other measures is denying the inherently inseparable, holistic nature of organizations that are, first and foremost, human organisms.

The problems really begin though when organizations that are trying to use the scorecard approach start looking for 'people' measures to slot into the innovation perspective. It is because the measures they have been using in this area have been simplistic and ineffective that a perceived need appeared for another scorecard to plug the gap. Enter the HR scorecard.

Now, behind this simple logic lies another, not very well hidden, agenda – the credibility and worth of the HR department itself, and I mean the department; an overhead cost that is desperately trying to justify its existence. It is no secret that HR is a beleaguered profession and so the HR scorecard is not just about getting HR integrated with the business, it is as much, if not more, to do with *proving* the worth of HR people to the business. That is why Ulrich *et al.* try to answer 'the question of how best to integrate HR's role into a firm's measurement of business performance'.

So, while all these new scorecard ideas have been evolving, many HR teams have been spending a great deal of time and effort trying to measure their worth. Whether by accident or design, this led them to collect enormous amounts of data which then had to be analysed and benchmarked.

Why go to all this trouble? As someone who has spent the past ten years of his professional career as an HR measurement consultant I have to admit that I have never found it difficult quickly to gauge the worth of HR functions, and it has very little to do with measuring or scorecards. I prefer a much simpler method called 'added value'.

Ask anyone working in HR *whether* they add any value and, if so, *how* they add value and *how much* value they add (believe it or not, three separate questions) and you will rarely, if ever, receive a clear-cut answer. They will talk in terms of 'changing culture', 'empowering staff', making their organization 'more flexible', 'developing human capital' but this will never be expressed in added value terms, that is with a £ sign. For me, this is an immediate and clear indication that their 'HR strategy' is not aligned with their business strategy.

If a key objective in a particular organization's current business strategy is to achieve an increase in market share, then 'strategically aligned HR people' should be able to articulate, absolutely clearly, what they are doing to help increase market share. There should be a demonstrable connection, a clear line of sight. 'Changing the culture to become customer focused' does not satisfy any of these criteria and any subsequent HR activity in 'culture change' is very likely to be unfocused and therefore ineffective.

Behind this specific example though is a really fundamental management question. Do complex organizational issues require similarly complex measures if they are to be resolved?

Added value is a simple but very powerful concept – and always has a £ sign

One omission in *The HR Scorecard* (Ulrich *et al.*, 2001) is a definition of added value. If you do not know what 'value' is then how can you *add* it? How could you get more miles per gallon out of your car if you do not understand the relationship between driving habits or engine maintenance and fuel consumption? So let us define what added value is.

Take any manufacturing business as an example. Let us describe its current 'value' as 1 000 000 products a year, produced at an average cost of £10 per product and sold for £15, resulting in a gross profit of £5 000 000. We will assume that customers choose to buy this particular product because they perceive the quality of it to be worth £15. So how can anyone *add* value to this business and how much value might they add?

Well, they could increase productivity by 10 per cent resulting in 1 100 000 products being produced. If all of these extra products were sold at £15 the net added value would be an increase in profit to £6 500 000 (1 100 000 units × £15, minus the original costs of £10 million). This, however, is based on making a very unrealistic assumption that the increased consumption comes from existing capacity with no increase in costs at all. If extra equipment were required and capital expenditure costs increased so much that the new *average* cost had increased by 20 per cent per product (i.e. £12 × 1 100 000 resulting in total costs of £13 200 000) there would actually be a *loss* of net value to the tune of £1 700 000, even though the company would still be making a profit of £3 300 000.

Incidentally, if you think this is a purely theoretical argument just ask Boeing Corporation how much money they lost (and in their case it was a loss) as a result of *increasing* their order book significantly a couple of years ago.

We could do a few more simple, 'added value' calculations on the effect of an increase in price or an improvement in quality that results in an increase in customer demand. However, there are a few unarguable, fundamental truths about added value that need to be pointed out:

- Added value can only be achieved in any organization (and that includes public and not-for-profit sector organizations) by increasing its output, reducing the cost of output or increasing prices. (Note. I would normally also include improving, measurably, the quality of the product or service but only if this, in turn, leads to improvements in quantity, cost or price).
- Added value is holistic both in concept and reality – any change in any of the variables of output, cost, price and quality cannot be viewed in isolation, they are all totally inter-connected and a change in one is likely to impact on another (e.g. efforts to drive down costs may adversely affect quality and result in lower sales – a loss of value).
- Added value always has a £ sign attached. There is no such thing as an 'intangible' when we are discussing added value. Statements that HR is improving 'employee creativity and innovation' are meaningless unless this creativity means more products are sold, either now or at some point in the future. Take a creative business like advertising and ask the question which advertising agency has the highest value? The one with the most 'creative' people or the one with the highest billings and profit?

Who needs an HR ballpoint when you can have an added value pencil?

If those producing scorecards were to re-frame their original objective then maybe a problem well defined would already be a problem half solved. So let us look at the logic of why anyone would want or need an 'HR scorecard'. The only reason that firms measure performance is in order to *manage* performance. They only want to manage performance to maximize it. This, in turn, should lead to maximizing shareholder (or stakeholder) value.

It is now widely accepted, however, that the biggest potential contribution to firm performance is how you manage the potential of your people. So, if you cannot measure the 'people' contribution then you cannot maximize value. But much more importantly, from the employee's perspective, if they cannot measure their own contribution how will they know when they are adding value or not?

Ask any employee in your organization, at any level, whether the work they are currently engaged in is adding any value? After the puzzled expression on their face turns to apprehension make the question much simpler for them. Ask them, specifically, whether they can make any connection between what they are doing and added value, in other words are they helping the organization to:

- produce or sell more of its products/services
- reduce the cost of those products/services
- achieve greater revenue or higher prices for its products/services
- or perhaps improve the quality of its products/services?

I was told by a couple of managers who worked for the cereal producer Kellogg's that they used to have a much simpler way of putting this. Whenever anyone had an idea or wanted to launch an initiative the simple, acid test was 'will it sell more cornflakes?'. Only clear lines of sight qualify.

HR strategy and initiativitis

The latter part of the twentieth century will be remembered for one particular aspect of management thinking in large organizations. This was an addiction to the use of initiatives to try to bring about change and step improvements – usually sold as acronyms. This included TQM, ABC (activity based costing), benchmarking, BPR (business process re-engineering), ISO9000 and a whole range of other similar systems. It is highly dubious whether such initiatives brought any value with them. If they did, then how much value they gained was dependent on their starting point.

Figure 12.3 tries to represent a multitude of concepts on a very simple grid. First, it suggests that what state the company is in, or what level of

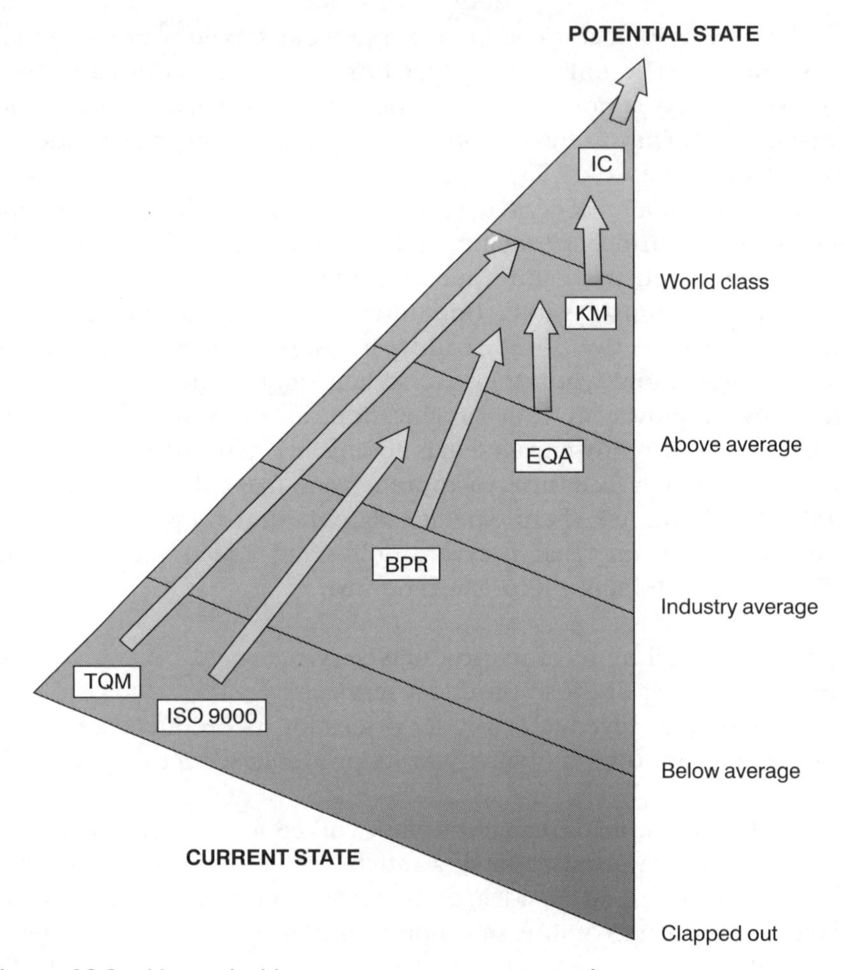

Figure 12.3 How valuable are management initiatives?

performance it is currently achieving, *before* it starts any initiative will dictate what sort of methodologies it can hope to use and how much improvement it will obtain from them. So, for example, there would be little point talking to a 'clapped out', decrepit business about the potential value of knowledge management (KM). Its management would not understand the concept, they would not have developed the right culture and it would have no systems in place to make knowledge management happen. Even if you brought in a modern, enlightened management team, the size of the task ahead of them would be gargantuan.

However, if a clapped out business attempts to become ISO9000 accredited, even if does not achieve accreditation, it has a chance of gaining some benefit from just trying. The requirements of ISO9000 will stipulate that it puts in place quality control systems for the first time. For a business doing so badly this will not be easy but it could take a significant move forward. Producing a quality procedure is much easier than creating a knowledge-sharing culture.

Figure 12.3 also suggests that, as long as the business keeps trying for ISO9000, it might eventually help them to raise their standards above the industry average. But that is as far as it will get them. ISO9000, on its own, can only help them to achieve so much. So this particular initiative, in this particular business, has added value: probably due to a reduction in waste and improvements in quality standards. However, if one of their competitors is already at the industry average level then it too may get some benefits from ISO9000 but there is an absolute limit on how much value they will obtain from it (represented by the same limited extent of the arrow).

Now if we look at the TQM marker it suggests that this can move the organization much further forward, towards world class. It can help even the most clapped out businesses become world class. It would take much longer, of course, but the value would be enormous. Also, TQM is much more of a philosophy than a methodology. Hence it is likely to bring about lasting, fundamental change and improvement.

You will notice that BPR only starts when an organization is already above average. This is because understanding the power of improving processes is unavailable to organizations that do not even understand simple quality systems. Unfortunately BPR, as an initiative on its own, has a short shelf life because only those following a continuous improvement philosophy will realize the longer term, potential benefits of process improvement. Similarly, anyone striving for the EQA (European Quality Award), based on the framework of the European Foundation for Quality Management, would have to have understood and been using TQM for some time to gain anything from it.

Last but not least is the whole idea of intellectual capital (IC). Despite all the talk about this, only world class organizations would have any chance of really getting the best value out of their human/intellectual capital. Organizations that say they 'did' TQM years ago (usually the same ones who have just re-discovered statistical process control under its new label of Six Sigma) would have no chance of using IC at their present stage of maturity.

Obviously the diagram does not do justice to the complexity of the issues here but hopefully it will get you thinking about the difference between 'initiatives' and strategy. The very fact that all of these have been perceived to be *initiatives* rather than a fundamental shift in culture and management thinking is the reason that they are often doomed to failure before they start. Moreover, all of these concepts are inter-related and only the true HR strategist will educate their management about how there needs to be an integrated strategy if the organization is to continue to move forward. They also need to make it clear where the organization is starting from and what potential value can be achieved if the strategy works.

Regardless of the complexity involved in introducing new concepts, ideas and ways of working, one thing can be said with absolute certainty: if you want your organization to generate really high levels of value you will have to design it that way. These things do not just happen by chance.

Chapter 13

Designing the high value organization

HR strategists have to be consummate organization designers

A high value organization is one that grasps every opportunity for added value. In organizations without an effective HR strategy the number of people in the organization with the inclination, never mind the capability, constantly to seek more value will be limited. HR strategy tries to enlist every employee in the search. More than that, though, the HR strategy aims to create the system, the structure and the processes to achieve that end. So, if someone on the shopfloor has a good 'added value idea' it will have every chance of being captured and realized because there is a system designed to do exactly that. There are many reasons though why putting in such a system is extremely difficult.

One reason is simply the confusion over what constitutes an effective system. Many people talk about systems, structures and processes almost in the same breath and do not always make clear distinctions between them. Some organizations refer to themselves as matrix organizations where reporting structures and processes tend to be relatively fluid, the intention being to combine the best elements of control and cooperation, but often they appear to be a 'matrix' only on paper. As such they are unlikely to produce any more value than some of their more rigid, hierarchical competitors. Organization design to an HR strategist is about creating value, not a 'nice place to work'.

Many matrix organizations seem to have missed the point. All organizations need some form of command and control, how else do you keep everyone pulling in the same direction? It may be naive to think otherwise. However, we do not have to have our behaviour dictated to us every day by the organization chart. If I report to manager A but I have to work closely with manager B then for 95 per cent of my time I should feel unfettered. I want to do my best for manager B without having to refer back to manager A. There will be occasions though when I will need to check with my own manager (for example, I cannot work on a new project for manager B unless someone else in my team takes over some of my work), but they should be few and far between. Flexible, adaptable organizations may look like conventional hierarchies but should *act* like cooperative communities. This is more to do with the right culture than it is with how you draw the organization chart.

System, process and structure

The added value HR system

We all frequently use the words 'system' and 'systematic' when we talk about how our organizations operate. We also looked at 'whole system thinking' in Chapter 4. How many of us though actually stop and consider the power of the word *system*? Do you know what a system is and how would you go about trying to design one? Dictionary definitions do not help much here and the word itself is over-used. Where is the commonality, for example, between a payment system, a computer operating system and a road system?

My own working definition is that

> *An organizational system is a means for making sure that what you plan to happen actually happens.*

Payment systems make sure clients pay on time. Computer operating systems make sure the computer operates. A road system makes sure you can transport goods or people from A to B. All of these systems have checks built into them. Part of the payment system includes generating a reminder for late payers; a diagnostic tells you whether the software has loaded properly; a series of signs makes sure you end up where you need to be. That is why the whole concept of a system is so powerful.

It is especially powerful when allied to the concept of HR strategy. The reason we need an HR system is to make sure we get all the value we want from the human resource. But what does it actually look like? I can show you the bits of paper that constitute the payment system,

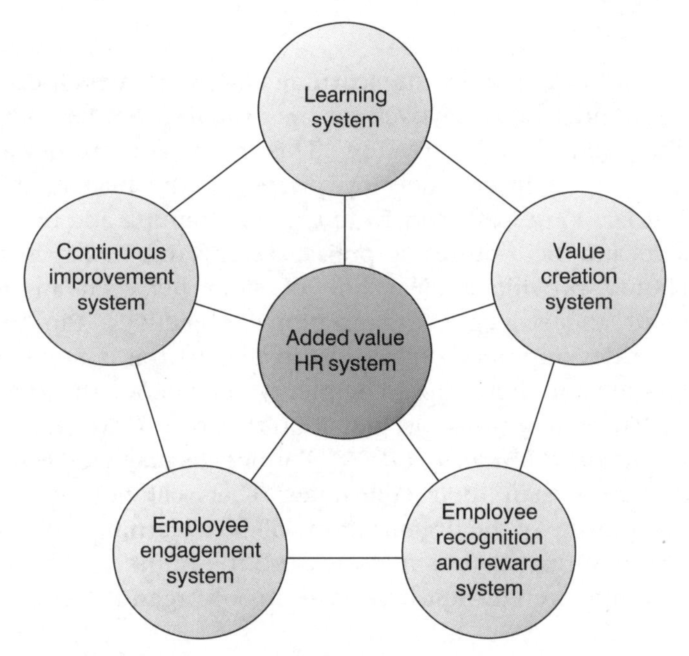

Figure 13.1 The added value HR system

I can draw a map of a road system and I could even produce the code from a computer operating system. So my first attempt at producing an HR system is to draw it as in Figure 13.1. Each of the 'satellites' represents a system in its own right but they must be part of a whole system that is installed as part of the HR strategy. So what does each of the satellite bubbles mean in practice?

Employee engagement system

An explicit system to engage and motivate staff is probably the lynchpin of the whole system. Simple questions can be used to check that the system is in place and working. High staff turnover and absence rates are a contra-indicator. How much time employees are spending on new ideas or improvements to the way they work is a positive indicator. There are plenty of instruments around to gauge employee engagement and any findings from such measures have to be addressed.

Continuous improvement system

Although there are many variations available on the same theme, evidence of the use of Plan, Do, Check, Act (PDCA), kaizen or similar quality systems should be readily apparent.

Learning system

No one should be spending time learning anything unless it can be seen to have a potential value payback for the organization. Learning should equal value and wealth creation. This is meant to be a system systematically to train and develop people to the best of their value potential. It is a long way away from existing training and development departments and the toothless appraisal systems that most organizations use. It should provide a clear line of sight between all individual development and strategic, organizational objectives. But the words training and development do not do justice to this system. This is a learning system and there should be plenty of evidence that double-loop learning is happening (for more detail on that read Chris Argyris's book *On Organizational Learning* (1999). Employees may well learn how to do things better than their colleagues. This will not be a problem because the culture of the organization will be a learning, not-seeking-to-blame culture. Organizations that measure the number of training days per year are not even at first base in terms of organizational learning.

Value creation system

Ideas are ten a penny. Good, value added ideas are less common but present many opportunities nevertheless. The value creation system should help new ideas to be properly assessed and then integrated into the business operation so that their value is realized.

Employee recognition and reward system

Those who create the value should be recognized and rewarded accordingly otherwise there will be no reinforcement of what they have learned. If there is no reinforcement there will be no continuous improvement. This is also meant to be a talent recognition system. You may think your present personal review and succession planning systems already fulfil this element. That is unlikely unless you employ people with specific responsibility for talent spotting. All successful sports teams have trusted talent spotters or scouts. You cannot leave this crucial job to line managers who do not have the necessary specialist expertise. Moreover, talent spotting is not just a system for identifying future managers. It is a system that aims to spot talents other than managerial potential.

It should be noted that there is no particular sequence in this system; every element has to be in place. Strategic systems are intended to be dynamic. Starting to recognize who is adding value should identify where that value is emanating from and unearth some hidden talents. The simple key to all of this though is that everyone should be aware that a system is in place. Any manager should be capable of answering the question 'Where is the talent in your team?' If they are unable to answer this either there is no system in place or the system is not working. Equally, if employees feel that they have untapped talent or potential then they should know how to have that self-belief checked out within the system. The first question the system will ask them is how they believe their untapped talents will add value. That will always be the gateway to the whole system.

However good your systems are, though, they will only work well when the right processes are in place. So what is a process? Fortunately it is a bit easier to offer a working definition of a 'process' than it is for a system:

A process is a series of steps that turns inputs into outputs

In other words, all of the time, energy and money that goes into the system must produce value. Processes define the value chain. Also, in terms of measurement, measuring inputs is pointless unless you also measure the outputs of the process. Get the process wrong and value will not be produced at the end. So for each element of the HR system we need specific processes. This means we need:

- a selection and recruitment process (to get the right capability and talent)
- a role definition process (to put them in the right jobs)
- a recognition, reward and retention process (yes, probably three processes but totally interdependent, to get resources to the people who add the most value)
- a capability development process (including career and succession planning).

If you asked any VP-HR whether they had these processes in place they would all say yes. To a certain extent they would be right. Take the selection and recruitment process. They could easily point to job descriptions, person specifications, vacancy notification procedures and a whole series of selection and interviewing techniques. These are all inputs into the process. What would be less obvious are the outputs from this process. The only output we are interested in is the value added by each new recruit. Only added value performance measures (see Chapter 12) will tell the organization that they have recruited the right people. But these measures are not just in the first year. How many of your employees are asked whether they have produced any added value ideas every year? How many have plateaued and are in danger of becoming dead wood once the enthusiasm of their early career wears off?

Hopefully this illustrates the difference between a recruitment procedure and a proper process that is part of a well-defined system. If you do find that you have a lot of dead wood then that is a sure-fire indicator that you do not have a continuous improvement process in place – something that most organizations lack. So your employees do not generate ideas because they have not been motivated to do so. By the way, no HR strategist who is thinking correctly would have an HR system that tries to *force* people to come up with ideas. Organizations that try to force these things to happen set up a suggestion box; the HR strategist creates a suggestion system, with everything that entails.

This simple example demonstrates quite clearly how organizations get HR departments and HR functions, not HR *systems*. As such, they are never going to become high value organizations. We could go through each of the processes in the same way but the key message is the same – that the intended output from all of the processes is added value.

Now where does the structure fit into this picture?

Organization structure

Structure and process should fit like a hand in a glove but they rarely do. This is an area where the HR strategist is presented, simultaneously, with one of their most difficult tasks and yet one that offers so much opportunity for added value. For example, the product development process should involve everyone who has a contribution to make. This means someone, say, from sales, marketing, production and distribution. Yet the way organizations are structured immediately militates against this. Each function has its own boss and maybe none of them owns, or has any direct responsibility for, the product development process. The CEO may get very frustrated when they see in-fighting and lack of cooperation but then they should acknowledge that this is a direct consequence of the way they designed their organization.

There is only one person who can play the honest broker in this situation and that is the HR strategist. Some try to produce matrix organizations where different reporting lines and shared bosses are meant to alleviate most of the worst effects of functional silos. Only the best HR strategists know, though, that internal cooperation is much more a cultural issue than it is a simple matter of drawing boxes on an organogram.

The HR strategist's guide to organization design

We could go into great detail here about the intricacies of organization structures but, for the purposes of this book, particularly in keeping with its 'how to' nature, there are some simple principles, lessons and guidelines that all HR strategists should follow. Those shown below are just a distillation of the lessons I have personally learned over the years by watching the way organizations operate, through a healthily sceptical pair of eyes. Of course, there are many organizational pressures that mean we do not always stick to such principles. However, such pressures should be resisted because sound principles, if followed correctly, will always lead to added value.

Here, for what they are worth, are my own guidelines, in no particular order:

- All organizations need a hierarchy of some sort. Some are more democratic than others but they are hierarchies nevertheless. Therefore no apologies need to be made for them. After all, the only alternative to a series of reporting lines is no reporting lines, otherwise known as anarchy.
- Don't be seduced by terms such as the 'virtual organization'. It is a meaningless phrase. 'Virtual' organizations may refer to geographically dispersed organizations or those where electronic communication is the only link between different parts of the organization. These factors may present some operational difficulties but they are still real organizations in every sense of the word. Everyone may not be under the same roof but they should be designed to create as much value as possible, just like any other organizational configuration.
- An organization chart should reflect reality. It should never be an attempt to give credibility to managers who cannot earn it for themselves. Regardless of who the organization chart says is in control, staff will generally deal with those whom they regard as being in control. The de facto organization structure rules so why not get the chart to match it?
- Do not try to 'con' your employees into thinking they are more important by drawing your organizational pyramid upside down. It is about as convincing as a magician's three-card trick.
- Do not employ prima donnas or those too precious to accept open criticism.
- Never give anyone power or authority in excess of their own capability; a very obvious rule and yet one that most organizations break on a regular basis.

- Ambition and talent are not always equal. Of course, the highly ambitious will be convinced in their own minds that they have the talent they need and many senior managers will confuse the two when succession planning. Those with naked ambition can make disastrous commercial decisions if they are not talented. It is great when someone possesses both in huge quantities, but such people are extremely rare.
- In a similar vein, personal effectiveness does not amount to organizational effectiveness. For example, you may employ a 'brilliant' product designer but that does not mean you will achieve an acceptable profit margin on the goods they design. Brilliant engineers have often cost their organizations dearly even though their engineering excellence is unquestionable.
- Every time a new post is suggested, by whomsoever, the key question to ask is how will this role add value? If the person suggesting the new post finds it difficult to provide a clear and unequivocal answer they have not put enough thought into their decision. Management layers only add value if they achieve a better performance from those who report to them.
- Most managers can only cope with about six to eight direct reports. Certainly never go over ten because none of these people will be managed as effectively as they could be. Clever bosses cope by leaving the good ones to manage themselves. In such cases that boss adds no value to the people concerned.
- Of course, the number of direct reports should be even smaller when each position is highly technical. Technical people who have a greater understanding of the technology than their boss tend to create a very dangerous situation and a very awkward relationship between manager and subordinate.
- The management team should reach agreement on which are the *key* positions. They should be identified as such on an organization chart and have successors identified. The risk of losing key people should be closely and regularly monitored. You should go to the ends of the earth to keep them because they will take so much of your potential value with them should they leave.
- Anyone suggesting a matrix organization had better get the culture right first. Never give anyone two bosses no matter what the justification may be. This leads to all sorts of political games and playing one boss's priorities off against another's.
- Organization charts that change too often are a symptom of bad organization design. Some organizations change their structures so often that the latest chart is never up to date. Every time the organization structure changes it automatically means everyone

directly affected has a new role. No one can change their role that often, or that quickly, and still be completely effective. HR strategists should counsel against all changes unless they are absolutely necessary and have been thought through thoroughly.

- There is no reason why the principle of empowerment should be constrained by an organization's desire to adhere to a principle of systematic control. Even empowered employees will ultimately be accountable to someone. Empowerment is actually more to do with system than it is culture. Anyone can have a great idea but they should not be empowered to try it out without putting it through a system to check that it works. Innovation outside the system is as likely to sap value as it is to add value.
- Avoid simplistic technical/production/marketing/finance divisions. Why not put some technical people in marketing as a balance, or vice versa? Production people will have to produce what sales can sell, but only at a given cost. It is better to get this dialogue working before the final production design is agreed.
- Never appoint anyone in a managerial position purely on technical merit – another classic managerial fault. There is a very high probability that they will not be a brilliant technician as well as a manager and, when they realize that, they will hide their managerial inadequacies behind their technical expertise.
- Never appoint someone just because they are 'the best of the bunch'. If you cannot get the right person in the right role then maybe you need to re-think the role.

Employee retention and organization design

Machiavelli told us that employing mercenaries was not a particularly good idea either. Effective organization design is really dependent on achieving a high level of employee stability. Consequently, employee retention will usually be a key element in any HR strategy. The art of HR strategy is to make every employee feel that they are valued, in every sense of the word. They should be respected as an individual who can make a unique contribution towards a very clear, common purpose. It would be incredibly difficult to do this when the average length of service is measured in weeks or months rather than years.

Employee retention is one of those subjects that waxes and wanes. At a macro level there are occasional scare stories such as the 'demographic timebomb' that everyone in HR circles talked about in the late 1980s, when a big drop in the number of school leavers was anticipated. Fortunately this particular bomb never exploded. In fact, the subsequent downsizing débâcle of the 1990s meant there was very little interest in retention. Now, low unemployment levels, particularly in certain parts of the UK and USA, have drawn attention to the subject again.

At the micro level, in specific markets and individual organizations, retention considerations have to reconcile long-term manpower planning with short-term operational requirements, which can be difficult. Every now and then a boom in a particular sector results in a short-term supply shortage, as we have seen with the exponential growth in e-commerce. At such times retention actually becomes a live, critical issue and it gets pushed back up the corporate agenda.

In low-skilled and what might be termed 'commodity' labour markets, globalization has resulted in multinational corporations being prepared to open and shut plants according to cold calculations of labour costs and efficiencies. In such instances they show apparently little regard for the other, less tangible, benefits often associated with employee retention. Other organizations may take the view that they want to maintain high retention rates but they are not be prepared to do so at any price. Consequently, trade-offs will have to be made and establishing the value of those trade-offs is a key task for an HR strategist.

As always with HR strategy, the basic proposition on retention should be a value proposition, not an ethical one.

Employee retention is a value proposition

Most businesses will obviously try to minimize the extra recruitment and training costs and disruption caused by high staff turnover. Regardless of how high these costs may be, the true HR strategist sees every HR proposition as a *value* proposition, not a cost consideration. The eyes of the HR strategist see the opportunity costs of losing experienced, committed employees in terms of:

- lower productivity
- less operational efficiency
- deteriorating customer satisfaction
- increased exposure to risk
- lack of innovation
- failure to achieve premium prices for a premium product or service.

All of this adds up to enormous lost potential value so it is easy to make the business case for producing an employee retention strategy. However, no organization can predict the future so they had better choose a retention strategy that can cope with uncertainty and change. Not having a retention strategy leaves you vulnerable to the vicissitudes of the labour market. Reacting to such changes, rather than planning for them, has to be the lower value option.

Admittedly, staff retention policies will, to a great extent, be dictated by the relevant labour market conditions. So, in a fast food business, where employee turnover is notoriously high, it might be very difficult for any player to adopt an HR strategy that aims to promote a significantly higher level of employee retention. It is no accident that McDonald's has a system of gold stars for its serving staff. They need something to keep them motivated for the short time that most of them are likely to be with the company. Interestingly, a relatively recent addition to the fast food burger market in the USA, 'In-N-Out Burger', strives to achieve a much lower staff turnover than its 'hire and fire' rivals and is seeing some benefits in margin and customer satisfaction as a result. Nevertheless, the main benefit of developing an employee retention strategy is to engender the level of commitment required for employees to want to make a greater contribution.

Some organizations have made strenuous efforts to fulfil most of their changing resourcing needs from their existing pool of employees. For example, the UK-based supermarket retailer Tesco has 185 000 staff in the UK and 240 000 worldwide and according to *The Sunday Times* on 7 April 2002 they developed a clear policy of promoting from within because six of the ten board directors, all four regional MDs, 27 retail directors and nine store board directors are all home-grown. Furthermore, in 2001 800 of their workers were promoted into management positions.

Some years ago the big retail banks used to follow a similar policy. They were loath to bring in outsiders unless it was absolutely necessary. Whether this approach was the result of an insular culture or a clearly thought out HR strategy is unclear but the question that has to be asked is whether their employee retention strategy was effective?

It was probably all right while they needed traditional banking skills but as the need for marketing and selling skills increased, in line with growing competitiveness in the world of banking, they could not always expect to find the necessary skills and experience among their own banking staff. Their manpower planning obviously had to change in response to a rapidly changing market but did this signal a change in HR strategy? Did they want different types of people, with different attitudes to customers (who now had more choice) or just different skills?

Similarly, we could cite many examples from the public sector but the police are an interesting case in point. They have had to address some fundamental, organizational issues as a direct result of having to change their *modus operandi* to meet the changing needs of society. This, in turn, has compelled them to take a fresh look at their HR strategy and policies. Do the police officers of yesterday, for instance, have the required attitude, skills and knowledge to perform the role demanded by society today? Are they as sensitive as they need to be to the extra constraints imposed on them by a more politically correct and liberal society? If not, what implications does this have for the present profile of the average police force? Will it require a positive and determined attempt to re-adjust this profile through a fundamental change in selection and retention policies?

Regardless of whether a strategy is in place or not, actual levels of retention are inextricably bound up with the way an organization is structured. A company's attitude to staff retention, whether explicit or implicit, automatically starts to become part of the way it operates. If it does not really commit itself to retention then it pays less attention to the need to get the employment relationship right and inevitably gets its just deserts.

Structural staff turnover and retention

Staff turnover and retention is something that is actually built into the fabric of the organization – sometimes consciously but more likely by default. Some of the most obvious examples of the former are to be found in those Japanese organizations where lifetime employment and the culture of the 'salaryman' conspire to ensure maximum employee retention. In the face of more open markets and increasing globalization this type of HR strategy is becoming increasingly difficult to maintain. As recently as 2000 a very large Japanese company I happened to be working with was retaining staff who, in any other type of organizational culture, would have been made redundant a long time ago.

No doubt this policy was still being pursued because they genuinely expected further growth in their business. It might also be because they were extremely reluctant to ditch a strategy that had served them well for many years. This is in spite of the fact that the excess staff costs were seriously denting the company's current financial performance. Why would they continue to pursue this course though? Because they genuinely thought it was in their long-term interests or were they afraid fundamentally to change the psychological contract with their entire workforce?

Also, what effect does this have on the role of the manager? If everyone knows the organization has a policy of not wanting to shed staff it tends to undermine everything a manager has to do. In the Japanese company mentioned above I was told that the people who were openly spending their days reading the paper were waiting for their next job to appear. Regardless of the reasoning behind the company's policy, it will send many subliminal messages to managers.

In one particular restaurant chain, where staff turnover rates were as high as 100 per cent per annum, managers came to accept this as the norm. So strenuous efforts were made by senior management to keep a focus on the high costs associated with this turnover. They constantly exhorted managers to try to reduce this figure but restaurant managers, who were always more concerned with day-to-day operational decisions, felt that nothing much could be done about a problem that they had become inured to. In other words, they regarded it as part and parcel of the way the business was structured and operated.

Each organization has to develop its own HR strategy and, as part of that strategy, its philosophy, attitude and policies on employee retention. One industry that has developed a very poor image in terms of staff retention has been the call centre sector. They have come to be regarded as the 'dark satanic mills of the twenty-first century' except that maybe the technology and the general ambience have less in common with this image than its management attitudes to employee welfare.

Call centres are generally geared up to handle calls as efficiently as possible. Productivity is the name of the game and the skill levels required from staff are usually quite low. This is a recipe for pressurized working conditions with minimal levels of job satisfaction for employees. These centres are often characterized by a transient workforce comprised of casual workers, students and others who are between 'proper' jobs or earning money for their next backpacking trek. In such circumstances there is usually very little pretence that serious efforts are being made to ensure greater employee retention.

Where no coherent strategy has been thought through, high staff turnover often becomes a vicious circle. I was asked to come up with ideas for one call centre on how to deal with a level of staff turnover that was spiralling out of control. Operational managers were always crying out for replacement staff to operate the phones, particularly on the most unpopular shifts. This undermined any efforts they made to maintain discipline, for fear of losing their hard-won staff. This led to a loss of confidence in their ability to manage staff effectively and they therefore failed to hit tough productivity targets. To make matters worse, the same managers, when interviewing new candidates, tended to paint a very rosy picture of what life was like in the company, in a vain attempt to attract more staff. This set up false expectations in the minds of new recruits that inevitably led to disillusionment after a few weeks of experiencing the reality.

This is a good example of how many factors come into play in the staff retention equation and illustrates why staff turnover, which always appears to be a simple problem on the surface, is invariably much more complex, problematic and intractable in practice.

Although it was going to be painful, in the short term, my simple advice to the head of HR was to pluck up the courage to develop a more honest 'sales pitch' to new applicants, in an attempt to break this vicious cycle. However, to know whether he was doing the right thing he first had to decide what level of retention he was aiming for.

Deciding on a desired retention level

If you were asked what annual percentage of staff turnover your organization wanted what would your first stab at an answer be? Zero? Probably not, because you would immediately feel that there are some employees you would quite happily lose. I am also not sure that zero would ever be desirable or possible. Whether you like Jack Welch's vitality curve or not, I think we would all have to accept that, with no fresh ideas or new blood coming in, it would be more likely to breed a culture of complacency and lead to organizational atrophy.

However, at the other extreme, a 100 per cent replacement rate is equally undesirable. You would not have to produce any figures to support this argument; it would be self-evident that it would lead to serious organizational difficulties and unnecessarily high costs.

So between these two extremes there has to be an optimal level of employee retention for your organization. A restaurant chain may be very happy with a 75 per cent staff turnover rate. However, a target of 5 per cent might be a much more appropriate figure for a nuclear power plant. Choosing the right level for you is never going to be an exact science but the HR strategist will definitely want to agree a target.

The aim is to have the level of staff turnover that you planned to have. An HR strategist will already have calculated how much salary, selection effort and training will then have to take place to run the organization effectively at that level of turnover. Organizations that want to develop high value knowledge workers cannot do so if their people keep changing. If staff turnover or stability is not close to what you want it to be it means something is fundamentally wrong with your HR strategy. If the turnover problem cannot be resolved, then the strategy has to change.

This is just an introduction into the whole complex area of organization design from a strategic HR perspective. Nevertheless the more HR strategists start to influence organization design the more we start to see organizations change in form and culture from what we know today. So let us take a brief look at the wider ramifications and longer-term implications of what HR strategy might achieve in the future.

Chapter 14

The future for HR strategy?

If you were looking for the simplest and shortest statement of the thesis presented in this book it would have to be that even if HR strategy cannot make up for a poor business strategy, it will add enormous value when it is done properly. However, it can only be done properly by effective HR strategists, and these are in short supply. When more HR strategists come onto the scene we will see some serious efforts being put into developing high value HR strategies. So let us look at a few factors that will decide whether HR strategy has a bright and illustrious future or whether it will fall into the same bottomless pit occupied by legions of other management fads.

HR strategy represents a new paradigm

HR strategy is really a whole new paradigm. This paradigm is about how organizations will learn to improve in the future. A report by the UK's Campaign for Learning entitled the 'Future of Corporate Learning' (freely available from www.dti.gov.uk/support/corporate/pdf/learning1.pdf) sees the future as being about corporate universities and e-learning - or at least that is what the twelve case study organizations were doing.

If you are thinking of following suit it suggests that one of the key 'issues to consider' is 'How does the structure you have in mind directly add value to your business strategy?' So how well do the organizations cited answer this question? If you think it is worth copying Motorola's corporate university, for example, make sure you realize that they soon discovered one of their first priorities was to provide much of their workforce with the basic education they should have received at school. If that has made you think again, then how about their policy of five days' training per annum for all employees. Is that an example of best practice, enlightened thinking - or quite the opposite?

As a trainer of some years' standing I have learned that everyone's training needs are different and unique to them. Fixing a target number of hours or days per employee makes a nonsense of the whole concept of individual centred learning and smacks more of the traditional sheep dip approach. More importantly, the only measures that interest me are output measures - what impact did the learning have on the business?. The 'impact' measures of e-learning in this report showed that Motorola delivered '77 000 days of training', BT generated 'lots of enquiries', BA managed to 'rationalize the number of courses offered' and M&G saw '4200 user sessions and 113 000 page views from 500 people in just eight months'.

It is this sort of unfocused, broad brush, scattergun learning paradigm that we need to move away from. We should also be very careful who we choose to learn from and make sure that whatever we learn really adds value. So where are we going to learn about added value HR strategies?

Strategic HR taught in business schools

If we are going to produce better HR strategists where are they going to be taught? At the moment I cannot recommend anywhere for a really excellent education in HR strategy. How could I if my assertion that HR strategy is so rare is true? That does not mean, of course, that there is a shortage of 'HR strategy' programmes in many universities and leading business schools. As we saw in Chapter 12 though, if you do not buy the current theories on the employee-customer-profit chain; or the present, facile attempts to measure human capital; you have to ask yourself what are you likely to learn on such programmes?

More worrying still is that the people who really need to understand what HR strategy is and what it has to offer, our future CEOs, may be learning management theories today (e.g. balanced scorecards and competencies) on MBA programmes that will actually prevent them from employing effective HR strategies. They probably do not even see HR strategy as a priority when they may believe that marketing or financial strategy will provide them with greater commercial leverage. There is nothing wrong with this of course if such strategies help them achieve their objectives, but what about those organizations where HR strategy is the crucial, missing element needed to transform the organization (e.g. the public sector in the UK)?

Maybe my recommendation is that we should eschew the normal business school approach of researching existing HR practices. They are of no help when there are very few great HR strategies to go and research. After all, even if there were, looking at how one organization did it is missing the point. HR strategy development always presents a unique combination of circumstances. Telling me how somebody else did it is not the same as telling me how to do it in my organization. Copying it does not mean it will have the same effect for me. Imagine what would happen if you took Wal Mart's approach and tried to use it at the John Lewis Partnership.

Business schools may serve a better purpose by telling future executives that HR strategy is a new, untapped source of competitive advantage; that they should try to do some simple things first like treat people as people and not as 'headcount', or even as one perspective on a balanced scorecard. The practicalities of HR strategy are fraught but the principles are actually very simple.

One principle that may continue to cause confusion in the future though is the matter of 'ethics'.

Ethical HR strategy

I have held a sneaking suspicion for many years that many writers and commentators in the HR world have been hiding their real agenda. This agenda is the creation of a better society through educating employers that treating their workforce well is a win–win situation. Actually, believe it or not, I subscribe to the same notion. Where I differ from the conventional thinking on this subject is that treating people 'well' (whatever that means) will only ever be a necessary condition for a high value organization, it will never be a sufficient condition.

One reason this view holds so much sway currently in HR circles is that it is perceived by many to be a very ethical view. Focusing on employee needs is seen to be the right thing to do. The other reason is that it seems to have become the desired view through the writings of the most prominent thinkers. At the top of this list has to be the American academic Dave Ulrich, who developed the idea of HR professionals as 'employee champions'. At the time of writing he is taking a sabbatical of several years to carry out missionary works for his church. At his last public speaking event at the American Society for HRM annual conference in Philadelphia, he was reported in *Personnel Today* on 2 July 2002 as having 'credited the HR profession with exerting a caring and ethical influence. "In the long run", he said, "such warmth . . . produces results."'

I find it hard to be convinced that businesses, generally, are run by leaders who are guided primarily by ethical considerations. The Quakers who formed their chocolate manufacturing businesses in the nineteenth century were always the exception rather than the rule and did not leave an indelible mark on the world of commerce. The challenge for HR strategists is not to convince business leaders that their strategy will make the business more ethical but to convince them that it will make them more valuable. It is for society to decide what it regards as ethically acceptable and to deal with organizations that transgress.

I am sure we all would welcome a closer adherence to higher ethical standards. Personally, in well over twenty years in HR I have only ever had to seriously question my conscience on a few occasions. I see no real conflict between trying to generate value and having the highest regard for the feelings and well-being of those who have to work in the organizations I advise.

The real, practical problems for HR strategists who have an explicit, ethical agenda is that they will confuse the strategy rather than enhance it. If CEOs and senior managers feel that they have to work within two different and distinct parameters, value and ethics, they have not been given a clear strategy to follow. This is bound to undermine the effectiveness of their decision making.

The political dimension

Although space allows only the briefest of mentions here we should also consider the wider political dimension. After the collapse of the doctrines of both communism and unfettered capitalism the 'third way' has arisen as a seemingly attractive, political alternative. Although the details of how this will work are still being challenged the third way does suggest that history is telling us something about the best way we need to organize ourselves socially.

For the HR strategist this poses some very interesting 'what if' scenarios. For example, if HR strategists start to get it right then we will see organizations that have developed employees who have knowledge and expertise that they have never possessed before. They will also have been encouraging such employees to bring as much of that knowledge to bear on their business fortunes. Greater contributions from employees will then tend to generate more decision sharing. The workplace will inevitably become more democratic (probably never totally, but who knows) simply because that will be the best way to achieve greater value. Organizations themselves may start to be the 'third way' in microcosm, just as large corporations have become microcosms of the capitalist system.

Interestingly, political theorists of yesteryear may have always seen this as the future of cooperativism; where the whole was definitely meant to be greater than the sum of the parts and cooperation was the guiding principle rather than command and control. Successful cooperative organizations do exist but it never became a serious rival to the bigger, profit-driven commercial entities. Was this because the incentives for innovation were always lacking in the cooperative model?

I do not know what the future holds, politically, for the development of HR strategy but I know it is going to be fascinating to see how things evolve. And it will be an evolution because things that evolve *naturally* tend to last.

HR strategy *'au naturel'*

In the face of the advent of such portentous developments as GM crops, test tube babies and cloning many of us are inclined to react with an 'it's not natural' response. We do not like E numbers or artificial flavourings in our food because we feel that unnatural additives are more likely to do us harm than good. When 'selling' new ideas to employees, they are much more predisposed to welcome anything they regard as 'natural' rather than unnatural. Successful HR strategies in the future will be those that have heeded this fundamental principle.

'Unnatural' initiatives, those that do not blend easily with people's everyday behaviour and preferences, impose an obstacle to change that organizations can do without. For this reason I frown on schemes such as 360° feedback systems because they are imposed. If the culture is such that people are naturally encouraged to be open and honest with each other you do not need an imposed system. It is one of human resource management's great Catch-22s that where there is a need to impose such a system (i.e. in organizations that perpetuate blame cultures and place internal politics above honest dealing) then the new system itself is an admission of defeat (i.e. we cannot create an environment where our people want to speak to each other naturally) and is doomed to failure from the start.

It is easy to discern the sort of factors that militate against getting the best value out of employees. These include blame cultures, politics and rigid command structures. Most of us may find these traits distasteful and frustrating but in the sort of organizations we have built this behaviour is actually quite natural and to be expected. If playing politics gets you to the top then those who want to get to the top will naturally play politics. The trick for the HR strategist is to make natural behaviour become bound up with the best interests of both the organization and the individual, rather than either/or.

This might seem to be very difficult, because the natural behaviour of many people does not automatically lend itself to the generation of improvements. When you think about it, it is quite natural, for example, for some people not to want:

- too much accountability or responsibility
- to take a risk
- to have to accept blame for their mistakes
- to receive bad feedback on their performance.

Future HR strategies will have to work tirelessly to remove these barriers without throwing the baby out with the bathwater. Removing a blame culture should not result in its being replaced by a careless or apathetic culture. Getting that balance right, however, is difficult. Resorting to new rules ('no one will be blamed in the following circumstances . . .') merely builds in new rigidities. The HR strategy will have to encourage things to happen naturally. Generic HR initiatives are totally antithetical to the HR strategist. 'Generic' means standard, not woven into the fabric. Such initiatives have little ownership or commitment behind them; they are not moulded and adapted by the people involved. HR strategy works best when it plays to people's natural inclinations and strengths, not when it is imposing a pre-determined solution to an ill-defined problem.

For this reason my greatest hope of all is that HR strategy will actually start to mean 'strategy' in every sense of the word and rid organizations of the quick-fix, off-the-shelf, universal answers to what are so obviously highly complex organizational issues. Then we will truly start to see how much the real value of people is worth both in organizations and society at large.

Appendices

Appendix 1

How much is a good HR strategy worth?

Study the details in Table A1.1.

Table A1.1 The top six automotive companies in the world by market capitalization ($ billion)

Company	*Market capitalization*[1]	*Global 500 ranking 2002*[2]	*Global market share 2001 (top 3 manufacturers)*[3]
Toyota	106.36	28	10.20% (target for 2010 15%)
Daimler/Chrysler	46.02	81	
Honda	41.40	97	
General Motors	33.87	126	14.80%
Nissan	33.01	131	
Ford	28.63	156	12.40%
			Comparative data
GE	372.08	1	
Microsoft	326.63	2	
IBM	179.21	12	
Verizon	125.26	19	

[1] and [2] from *FT Global 500* – the world's largest companies, 9 September 2002
[3] from *Automotive News Data Center*, www.autonews.com, 11 September 2002

How can Toyota, with the smallest market share amongst the top three, have a market capitalization of over three times that of General Motors and nearly four times that of Ford? How worried would you be as a CEO of either GM or Ford if you knew Toyota wanted a market share of 15 per cent?

Toyota is the only manufacturer that has a crystal clear, totally integrated business and HR strategy. Imagine what difference such a strategy could make to your organization.

Appendix 2

Are you engaged by your organization?

Regardless of your present position in your organization, read the questions below and see whether they provide you with some insights into the way your employer tries to engage you as a means of hoping to get the best out of you.

1 *New or recent employees only:* Can you remember what your first impressions of the organization were? When did you first consider working for them? If it was through an advertisement, was it impressive? Had much thought had gone into it? Did the organization have a clear image that it wanted to portray? Did it already have a good reputation as a place to work? Did you see this as an organization that was really going places and might help to further your career? Or was it just a job? What about when you received some company literature or were interviewed? Did you feel that everyone you dealt with knew what they were doing? Did they respond to you as though they really wanted you to join? Did they give you a level of confidence that this was a good place to work?
2 Have you ever seen or heard from your Chief Executive? Has he or she ever made direct contact with you, personally, either by e-mail or through the post? Do you trust them? Do they show any interest in you? Do you know what plans they have for the business? Do you feel they care about you as an individual? How would they react if you made direct contact with them?
3 If you know what strategy or plans they have, do you agree that is the way the organization should be going? Do you have personal

experience of any ways in which the existing business plans are more likely to result in failure rather than success? Are you getting negative or positive feedback from customers that is not being listened to by senior management?

4 If you want to disagree with the direction in which the business is heading do you have any means for letting the CEO know your feelings and concerns? Do your opinions count? What about new ideas? Is there a system or established avenue to explore any good ideas you may have? Is it difficult to get anyone to take them seriously or give them the time and consideration they deserve?
5 What about your own career and personal development? Are you growing in your present position? What additional achievements or experiences will you be able to add to your CV after being in this position for another year? If you believed further studies would help you contribute more would the organization welcome this and support you in your endeavours? Have you got much more to offer but can find no opportunity fully to utilize your talents?
6 How would you describe your relationship with your employer? Is it of mutual benefit? What level of trust is there? Is there a balance between your interests and theirs? If you were to have a serious illness or domestic problem how understanding would your boss be? How much help would you get?
7 How would you describe the culture of the organization? Does it have its own distinct culture? Is it very political? Do you work for a hard-nosed, paternalistic or enlightened employer? Is it fun to work there or is everyone deadly serious most of the time? Do you get blamed when things go wrong or is there a constructive search for what can be learned? Can you say honestly and openly how you feel?

These questions should give you a real understanding of just how all-embracing and profound the concept of 'employee engagement' is. There are many facets to it.

The questions may well elicit a range of responses from you such as 'I can't expect the Chief Executive to show interest in every employee' to 'These questions are just making me feel more disgruntled'. Regardless of your reaction, the big question is to what extent has your organization engaged you? Do you really feel involved in the running of the business? Are you very highly motivated?

Every negative response to one of the questions above adds up, until it is like the death by a thousand cuts of your level of motivation and potential. A negative response to any one question is not, in itself, disastrous, but try to spot the next time you feel like criticizing your leadership or feel frustrated by the limitations placed on your abilities.

Then think whether this undermines your willingness to make as great a contribution as you could.

If you are a senior manager the main lesson here is what can you expect from employees whose motivation is severely dented by a lack of attention in the area of employee engagement? Also, if you are not sure about the answers to these questions, or the range of possible answers is inconsistent, then this is a clear indicator of a business without a clearly articulated HR strategy.

If all of the above issues are to be addressed properly then a coherent HR strategy should be in place. An effective HR strategy will lead to clear decisions about the required level of employee engagement and it will be measured and monitored on a regular basis.

Appendix 3

Do you have an HR strategy or just a series of policies?

The vast majority of organizations I have worked with over the past ten years confuse HR policies with strategy. Anyone can produce HR policies but very few organizations develop their policies from a holistic and coherent HR strategy. It is very important to know the difference and these questions should help to provide a clear indication of whether you have an HR strategy or merely a set of policies.

1. Is strategic HR thinking represented at main board level? If not, the board cannot have adopted an HR strategy.
2. Does someone with in-depth, senior level experience of HR represent the HR perspective at board level? What experience do they have of formulating and implementing HR strategy? What evidence could they produce that it worked?
3. Is there already a clear business strategy in place? If this was produced in the absence of strategic HR thinking then any possible HR strategy is already one step behind.
4. Do you openly communicate the organization's performance on a regular basis to all employees? If not, why not? What is there to hide? What does this tell you about attitudes to employees (and employee attitudes to the way the board runs the business?)
5. If there is an HR strategy is it a written document? Does it spell out why you have the policies you have?
6. Are there any guiding principles adopted by the organization? Are they clear and communicated to all employees?
7. Is your organization in need of transformation? If this is not a live issue why do you need an HR strategy?

8. What specific measures link your HR strategy to your business strategy?
9. Do you have a union? If so, does your HR strategy anticipate that the union will continue to represent employees ad infinitum?
10. How are all of your employment policies integrated? Does your reward policy fit perfectly with your policy on performance management? To what extent does your reward policy reward those who are eager to develop themselves? Do you accept that some training and development will bring no benefit to the business?

Appendix 4

A strategic dialogue between the HR strategist and the CEO

One of the key skills of the HR strategist is to have a strategic, HR dialogue with the CEO. My own experience tells me that CEOs, generally, do not know the difference between a personnel policy and an HR strategy. The following dialogue is based on an amalgam of many such conversations I have had over the years. Hopefully it highlights how HR strategists have to ensure that CEOs see HR strategy as a distinct addition to their options for creating competitive advantage and adding value. The dialogue may be simplistic, even cheesy, but the lesson should be clear.

For the purposes of this exercise we will use the CEO of an imaginary financial services business.

HRS: *How far ahead can you see into the future for the business at the moment?*

CEO: Well, I have my own views, of course, about what the future might hold for us but I do not try to work to a specific timeframe.

HRS: *I know none of us can predict the future with any certainty but you must have a mental picture, say, of what we will look like in five or maybe even ten years' time?*

CEO: Why are you so keen to pin me down on the timeframe? Things can change so quickly these days.

HRS: *Oh, lots of reasons. But the main one is that I am trying to find out what sort of people we will need in the future. If we are planning to change the way we operate they may not be the sort of people we recruited and selected in the past. We may have very different roles to fill; depending on the direction in which we are heading. If we are really only looking two to three years ahead and, if the organization is not expected to change much in that time, then maybe we can continue as we are. But if you see any significant change looming in, say, 5 years' time then maybe we ought to start planning for those changes now.*

CEO: What sort of changes are you thinking of?

HRS: At the moment, mentally, I have a blank sheet in front of me. I don't want to second guess where you and the board are. But if you want me to be more specific let us just look at the role of branch managers. We have an awfully large pool of them already and many of our younger graduates see that as an obvious career path. But will we still need branch managers in five years when the industry seems to be moving to smaller, specialized business units, never mind the amount of business that will be transacted online?

CEO: OK, I see what you mean. The board have never discussed that particular scenario yet. If you want my own view though I guess we will see a declining trend in the number of general business branches and the managers we require in the next few years. I am confident though that we will manage the situation effectively. We have always managed to realign our people with the demands of the business. I don't foresee any great problems there.

HRS: I'm sure you're right but I was only using that as a simple example of a bigger issue I would like to explore with you. In fact, how many branch managers we might need in the future is only a minor concern for me. Like you, I think we will usually manage to get the people we need. I was hoping we could talk more about how we use those people to move well ahead of our competition. I am not just talking about putting names in boxes.

CEO: I'm not sure what you mean. We already hold the number one position in several of our markets and I think our results over the last few years have shown that we have consistently stayed ahead of the competition. That must mean we are doing something right with our people, doesn't it?

HRS: Yes, I think it does, but maybe I am not making myself clear enough. Let me have another go.

CEO: Go ahead.

HRS: What are the top three indicators in your mind that tell you how well we are doing?

CEO: Return on capital, operating profits and, over a longer period, share price of course.

HRS: *If everything goes as well as you hope over the next five years how much change would you expect in all of these?*

CEO: Things are going to get harder not easier so, barring any unforeseen calamities, I hope we can achieve the 5 per cent improvement per year that we already have planned, in each of these.

HRS: *Why not plan for 10 per cent?*

CEO: That's funny – everyone on the board agrees we are being ambitious aiming for 5 per cent in the present market conditions.

HRS: *Well, based on the way we are configured at the moment, and bearing in mind we are already ahead of the competition then perhaps 5 per cent would be an admirable improvement. But would you be interested in looking at a slightly different strategy based on 10 per cent? For example, those branch managers we talked about.*

CEO: What about them?

HRS: *Well, I have some figures here that show if we brought the bottom 20 per cent performers up to the average performing manager it would increase operating profits by 8 per cent. Plus, if we also put more effort into to developing the top 10 per cent of performing managers I am confident we could expect at least another 5 per cent but we would have to allow them a bit more freedom.*

CEO: Let me have a look at the figures.

HRS: Here they are. But before we look in too much detail at the figures I would like to suggest that this would have to be put together as a complete strategy. One that simultaneously manages the low performers, the high performers and has an impact on the ones in the middle; who maybe are getting a bit complacent about being targeted on 5 per cent this year. I guarantee this idea will not work unless it is planned thoroughly. Oh, and I may want to stop the management development programme we have been running for the last two years. It is not focused on any of the key indicators you identified yourself.

CEO: When can you have the plan on my desk?

HRS: *It's not a plan – it's a strategy. I have been working on it for some time. It will take quite a bit more time to put together properly. I just wanted to sound you out on the basic idea first before I spent too long on it.*

CEO: I am interested – so make time.

Appendix 5

Some strategic HR insights using a case study

This short case study is based on a real business. Some details have been changed, partly to disguise the business concerned and partly to provide a neat case study rather than one with too much complexity. The aim here is to show very briefly what having an HR strategist's insight might mean. It should also help to provide a clear contrast between operational HR and strategic HR.

A quick overview of the business and its business strategy

They are a specialist retailer but they also manufacture a small proportion of their own products. It is a publicly quoted company now but it had a long, family tradition and, although it has transformed itself as a business, some of the traditional attitudes appear to be hard to shake off.

The majority of their products are bought in from overseas manufacturers. It is a market where margins are usually very tight but this particular company holds a large market share as a quality provider. It is therefore able to achieve higher margins than many of its competitors. Also, one of its major competitors went out of business three years ago and it is still gaining sales as a direct result of this.

There are currently 800 stores and no plans significantly to change this number. About 200 of these are operated by franchisees. Any growth in sales and profit is intended to come from the existing level and scale of operation. Other product offerings are being considered (e.g.

developing more into the sports goods market) but none of these will signify a major departure from their core business. The main thrust of the current business 'strategy' is to develop a significant increase in profit through generating more sales. These sales are to come from converting new shoppers into customers and existing customers into higher volumes and value of sales.

The performance of the business, in terms of retail sales and profit, is already running ahead of forecasts. In 2000 the projected profit target for 2004 was £52 million. This was already easily exceeded in 2001 when profits reached £58 million. This appears to be a well-managed business.

The main strategic question is not how to maintain current performance levels but how to move the business forward from an already successful baseline. However, whether this really constitutes a clear, long-term business *strategy* is open to debate.

Is there an HR strategy?

The organization chart suggests that two separate HR functions are operating within the business. There is a significant retail HR operation, reporting to the Retail Operations Director, and a head office and Manufacturing HR function reporting direct to the CEO. The HR function had been run along very conventional lines but had gradually been moving to a higher level of professionalism and greater impact through the development of HR specialists in resourcing, training, rewards and employee relations. Due to the wide geographical spread and multi-site nature of the retail business the creation of an HR business partner role was meant to provide a direct point of contact for regional managers and a coordinating role with the rest of the HR team.

As the business strategy is focused mainly on operational objectives the efforts of the HR team are following suit at the moment. In a business that is operationally driven the HR function tends to have to be reactive, dealing with recruitment or disciplinary problems, for example, as and when they arise.

It is easy to see how business is improving but that is not the same as saying it is developing a high performance culture. To develop such a culture every part of the organization has to be moving in the same direction. One organizational issue here is that the rump of what used to be a much larger manufacturing operation is seen as virtually a separate business entity to the retailing operation.

There is an existing HR strategy document that sets out the key goals for each section of the HR team and is of great benefit in offering a clear guide to all members of the team. However, there are several important respects in which it could be developed into a much more powerful strategic document. There could be a greater emphasis on measures and measurement (e.g. how is career progression currently measured?). The HR team could be asked to contribute directly to business goals and targets (e.g. HR Partners could be asked to specify how much they will 'improve performance . . . of regional, area and store teams'). All such measures could be expressed in £s (e.g. recruitment objectives could be expressed in sales performance of new recruits, the use of coaching could be correlated with real shop performance). Finally, the 'strategy' is *following* the operational plan and not *informing* it. There is no suggestion of questioning or changing the organization chart or broadening job roles.

Key strategic HR issues

One key HR issue arising out of the business strategy is that if sales have to improve through the existing operational set-up then this business will have to ensure that the talents and capabilities of people who work for the company are maximized. Maximizing the value from people is not something that can be done in an entirely reactive or short-term fashion, so a more strategic approach would be imperative.

As with all HR strategies, many of the objectives are inter-dependent. So, getting maximum performance is directly related to attracting and retaining the right talent. This in turn is dependent on being able to offer satisfactory career progression. This is dependent on the organization of the shops and the management structures put in place.

Moreover, increasing commercial pressures on managers will inevitably mean that some managers, who are currently performing at a satisfactory level, will not necessarily survive as the demands of the job continually increase. The managers of the future are as likely to be effective coaches as they are cost and sales controllers. This will require a different breed with a different range of skills. The HR team are addressing these issues but their impact is restricted by the extent to which they are allowed to think and act strategically.

Appendix 6

A statement of employer and employee commitment

This is an example of the sort of clear statement an employer should be able to make to any new recruit. It may look like many similar statements made in employment letters or handbooks but this is meant to be part of a strategy, not just a paper formality. The recipient of this letter could check how serious their HR strategy is by ringing the CEO immediately.

Of course, we could produce a very different statement for an employer with a different business and HR strategy. A fast food business may only offer great experience for an expectedly short period of employment. A public sector organization may refer more to its civil responsibilities and be less prepared to have an overtly payment-by-results culture.

The main point here is simple. The HR strategist should ensure that the commitment on offer matches that which is expected. A clear and unequivocal commitment statement should then represent this. They should already have in place an HR system that makes both a reality.

We would like to offer you a very warm welcome to ABC Incorporated and hope that you will see this letter as a clear statement of the commitment we are prepared to offer you as one of our employees. However, in return for our commitment to you we expect a corresponding commitment from you.

We believe that ABC is a great company and are proud of the fact that our customers continue to choose us. We hope this will continue and put every effort into trying to make that happen.

However, with the best will in the world, we cannot guarantee that it will. We face relentless competition in a tough market and we will have constantly to look for ways not only to hold onto our existing customers but also to attract new customers in the face of such fierce competition. We hope you will help us in this challenge. We cannot afford to become complacent or stand still for one moment

From the moment you responded to the advertisement for your position you may not have realized it but we knew exactly the type of people we were trying to attract. You have successfully completed a selection process that tells us we have found the right match. You have been selected for your knowledge, experience, brainpower, creativity, innovative thinking and other capabilities that match our needs. We want people who like continuous challenge. We also need people who are prepared to challenge our way of doing things. That means we recruit people who think for themselves and behave in a way that brings about constant change.

If we fail, you fail. If you fail, we fail. We are totally interdependent.

Our belief is that the happiest and most effective employees are those who are allowed to make their maximum contribution in a well-organized and focused business. We will endeavour to create an environment in which we can both excel but you have to tell us if we become ineffective or lose focus. If you cannot express your opinions openly and freely then you should contact me immediately.

We are a results-based organization. No one is interested in how many hours you work or the quality of your presentations. Only results count. We do not tolerate under-performance or complacency but those who get results are well rewarded.

If you believe your own opportunities for personal development are lacking tell us. We will actively support any developmental actions that are mutually beneficial. We do not subscribe to education without an anticipated organizational benefit.

We cannot make our own commitment and the commitment we expect any clearer. If we have made the right decision, you have made the right decision.

Welcome on board.

John Smith, CEO

Appendix 7

Spot the strategic HR decision

Which of these case studies represents a truly strategic HR decision?

Case study A

A call centre decides to set up a satellite operation in another country where higher unemployment means they will make savings on salaries. They will also take advantage of government grants for companies moving into unemployment blackspots. The only disadvantage is that staff recruited locally in the foreign location are likely to require more training and closer management. A strategy has been put together to ensure that the new call centre will be operational on time and working within agreed costs and customer complaint targets. All managers and staff will be subject to these targets through the performance management scheme.

Case study B

A local government organization has been asked by central government to invite competitive tenders for outsourcing its refuse collection service. This is an attempt to deliver services at a lower cost. A strategic decision has been taken by the management board to instruct the in-house refuse department to prepare a bid to try to win the contract and keep the work within the authority. They are asking them to look at ways of cutting costs so that their tender is highly competitive. This may include renegotiating the working rule agreement with the union and including a no-strike clause.

Case study C

A financial services company is facing increasing competition, which is eroding its margins. In order to maintain its current cost/income ratio of 85 per cent it has constantly to look at ways to lower its cost base. It regards the expertise of its existing managers as crucial for the future success of the company but feels that this emphasis on costs is a new departure for them. Their managers do not have a 'cost control' mentality and are finding it difficult to maintain levels of service whilst at the same time trying to act cost-consciously. A strategic decision has been taken that these managers are going to have to change the way they manage. They have been given performance targets that balance service levels with cost controls and only those managers who manage both will be able to remain as managers. In the meantime the selection criteria for new managers have been completely revised.

An answer

My view is that only case study C represents a truly strategic HR decision. It contains the key elements of:

- An absolutely clear and direct link between the HR strategy and a strategic business need and it can be measured.
- There is a conscious attempt to manage the workforce in a different way rather than 'buy-in' a new workforce.
- It aims to bring about a genuine transformation in the existing human resource.
- It will gain a competitive advantage if its HR strategy is successful.
- It takes a long term perspective.

Appendix 8

Strategic HR at MAFF?

'HR team rallies behind scene in farming crisis'

I have made many references in the main body of the book to the notion that real HR strategy is rare and is very far removed from what HR people refer to as 'strategy'. The best example I can give to illustrate the crucial difference between strategic HR and operational HR was contained in a front page story in *Personnel Today* on 27 March 2001 (which can be read online at www.personneltoday.com). This was at the height of the foot and mouth epidemic that had gripped the UK. The headline declared 'HR team rallies behind scene in farming crisis' and it told of the HR team at the Ministry of Agriculture, Fisheries and Food (MAFF) who were desperately trying to help resolve a crisis that was costing the UK farming industry and the government billions of pounds. So what exactly were they doing?

The story refers to them having to recruit 273 vets and 700 temporary veterinary investigators, both from within the UK and from as far afield as the US, Australia and Switzerland. They were also 'looking at a special remuneration scheme in recognition of the disturbance caused to individuals' and, according to the reporter, the '170-strong personnel team are monitoring staff to ensure they do not contravene European working hours regulations or compromise health and safety through fatigue'.

The first question the HR strategist would ask is what is the value of the work of the HR team at MAFF? The answer is obvious. This work is highly important and highly valuable, in one sense. Every day that they fail to have enough veterinary investigators to control the foot and mouth outbreak is an extra day of cost through the slaughtering of livestock. Each day's delay could add millions of pounds to the overall costs.

But what would be the cost of contravening the European working hours regulations? In the circumstances there might be one or two tribunal claims that arise but in the scheme of things this would not be disastrous.

Regardless of the value of these activities though, they could be described as both reactive and purely operational. The team is reacting to the crisis and dealing with issues on a day by day, operational basis. The HR strategist would argue that the value of the HR team would rise exponentially if it had been more strategic in the first place. Here are some strategic HR activities that may have reduced the impact of the foot and mouth outbreak significantly, or even prevented it altogether. The value of such preventative strategies could be counted in billions of pounds.

Strategy and risk management

The HR director could have had a risk management role and asked whether MAFF had a disaster plan and the personnel identified to deal with any emergency. In the specific case of foot and mouth disease there are key questions that could have been established following on from the previous outbreak of foot and mouth in 1967 – to what extent do livestock have to be culled and how should the carcasses be disposed of? In the actual crisis in 2001 there was still debate on these subjects as the crisis deepened.

Culture at MAFF

This leads to an interesting question about the culture that existed within MAFF. Why were such disaster plans not in place and why could there not have been agreement on courses of action in the thirty-four intervening years? If there is a cultural problem of a lack of attention to such risks, then the HR strategist would need to address this issue straight away.

Learning organization

Although still a cultural question, HR strategy is always about a strategy for learning. What confidence can the British (or even foreign governments) have that MAFF has learned any lasting lessons from the crisis? Have they learned enough to prevent it happening again, or at least to mitigate any potential costs and disruption?

Performance management

Performance management is more of an operational issue, but there are strategic considerations. The initial outbreak of the disease was traced to a farm in Northumberland, in the north of England. This farm had been inspected by MAFF and was in such a poor state of management and hygiene that it was threatened with closure. But the closure never happened in time to prevent the outbreak. So why did the MAFF inspectors not act quickly on their fears? Why did no one realize how close they were sailing to the wind by allowing this farm to remain in operation?

Hopefully it is painfully obvious from the considerations above that an HR strategist could make a huge difference at MAFF. The existing HR team may be excellent at picking up the pieces after disaster has struck, but the value of such work is negligible when compared to what strategic HR could have achieved.

Postscript

In *Personnel Today* on 19 March 2002, almost a year after the original story, the Corporate Services Director in charge of HR at the recently formed Defra (Department for Environment, Food and Rural Affairs – which has taken over MAFF's role) was reported to be 'developing the department's formal HR strategy'. As part of this process 'Defra managers are being put through leadership programmes, which aim to improve their people management.' An earlier news story (12 March 2002) on the same department referred to a new performance bonus scheme which would allow 'directors and heads of departments . . . about 0.02 per cent of the total salary budget to give away for the new bonuses'.

On 4 September 2002 a further headline in *Personnel Today* – 'Defra faces industrial action over failure to close pay gap' – appeared over a story remarking that 'Former Ministry of Agriculture, Fisheries and Food (Maff) are voting on industrial action today over the failure of the Department of Environment, Food and Rural Affairs (Defra) to close pay disparities of up to £2,000.'

Does this look like an HR strategy that will transform the way people at Defra work?

Bibliography

Argyris, C. (1999) *On Organizational Learning.* Oxford: Blackwell

Buckingham, M. and Coffman, C. (2001) *First, Break All the Rules.* London: Simon and Schuster

Hammer, Michael, and Champy, James (2001) *Reengineering the Corporation*. London: Nicholas Brealy

Kaplan, R. and Norton, D. (1996) *The Balanced Scorecard - Translating Strategy into Action.* Boston: Harvard Business School Press

Kearns, P. (2000) *Maximising your ROI in Training*. London: Financial Times/Prentice Hall

Kearns, P. (2000) *Measuring and managing employee performance*. London: Financial Times/Prentice Hall

Kearns, P. (2002) *The Bottom Line HR Function.* Birmingham: Spiro Press

Lewy, C. and Du Mee, L. (1998) 'The ten commandments of balanced scorecard implementation', *Management Control and Accounting*, April

Machiavelli, N. (1995) *The Prince* (trans. George Bull). London: Penguin

Ohmae, K. (1982) *The Mind of the Strategist.* New York: McGraw-Hill

Porter, M.E. (1998). *Competitive Strategy: Techniques for Analyzing Industries and Competitors.* New York: Simon & Schuster

Rucci, A.J., Kim, S.P. and Quinn, R.T. (1998) 'The employee customer profit chain at Sears', *Harvard Business Review,* January-February

Semler, R. (2001) *Maverick*. New York: Random House

Senge, P. (1993). *The Fifth Discipline.* New York: Random House
Treacy, M.E. and Wiersema, F.D. (1993) 'Customer intimacy and other value disciplines', *Harvard Business Review*, January
Ulrich, D., Becker, D. and Huselid, M. (2001) *The HR Scorecard.* Boston: Harvard Business School Press
Von Clausewitz, C. (1832) *On War* (orig. German), Berlin: Dümmlers Verlag; trans. Colonel J.J. Graham, London: N. Trübner, 1873
Welch, J. (2001) *Jack: What I've learned leading a great company and great people.* London: Headline

Index